More praise for *Virtuous Meetings*

"*Virtuous Meetings* is a must-read book for anyone who wants to learn the fundamentals of how to work with large groups to ensure that the outcome of a gathering is clear, concrete, and actionable, and that it represents the collective views of the participants. All of us at AmericaSpeaks were proud and delighted to work with Covision's talented team to integrate their technology platform into our 21st Century Town Meetings."

—Carolyn J. Lukensmeyer, PhD,
founder of AmericaSpeaks;
executive director of the National Institute for Civil Discourse

"When we started DTA and Whole-Scale Change consulting in the 1980s and 1990s, our thinking quickly outran the technology to do it fully. We did magic with post-it notes and flip charts, but Danskin and Lind are the jet engine of system change. Technology is either a constraint (when you don't have the right stuff) or an accelerator (when you have it right). Covision has it right."

—Albert B. Blixt,
senior partner,
Dannemiller Tyson Associates

VIRTUOUS MEETINGS

Technology + Design for High Engagement in **Large Groups**

KARL DANSKIN
LENNY LIND

JB JOSSEY-BASS™

A Wiley Brand

Published by Jossey-Bass

A Wiley Brand

One Montgomery Street, Suite 1200, San Francisco, CA 94104-4594—www.josseybass.com

Jossey-Bass books and products are available through most bookstores. To contact Jossey-Bass directly call our Customer Care Department within the U.S. at 800-956-7739, outside the U.S. at 317-572-3986, or fax 317-572-4002.

Wiley publishes in a variety of print and electronic formats and by print-on-demand. Some material included with standard print versions of this book may not be included in e-books or in print-on-demand. If this book refers to media such as a CD or DVD that is not included in the version you purchased, you may download this material at http://booksupport.wiley.com. For more information about Wiley products, visit www.wiley.com.

Library of Congress Cataloging-in-Publication Data

Danskin, Karl, 1957–

 Virtuous meetings: technology + design for high engagement in large groups/Karl Danskin, Lenny Lind. — First edition.

  1 online resource.

 Includes index.

 Description based on print version record and CIP data provided by publisher; resource not viewed.

 ISBN 978-1-118-57338-9 (pdf) — ISBN 978-1-118-57345-7 (epub) — ISBN 978-1-118-53866-1 (hardback) 1. Business meetings. 2. Telematics. 3. Decision making. 4. Information technology—Management. 5. Organizational behavior. I. Lind, Lenny. II. Title.

 HF5734.5

 658.4'56—dc23

2014009978

Printed in the United States of America

FIRST EDITION

PB Printing   10 9 8 7 6 5 4 3 2 1

CONTENTS

We dedicate this book to those who aspire to bring the voice of the participant into large meetings, and who focus their wisdom and effort on finding the ways that people in large groups can work together productively in meetings.

THE EVOLUTION OF AN IDEA

The year is 1991 and the first Apple Macintosh laptops have just been released. Lenny Lind and Jim Ewing, an OD consultant and former satellite programmer, are in a hotel meeting room late one night, networking twelve of these new laptops together with telephone cables so that a senior executive team can have a "groupware" facilitated offsite meeting in the morning. Jim clicks a button on one laptop and eleven screens around the room all change all at once. The atmosphere is that electric combination of anticipation and anxiety (mostly the latter) that always accompanies a thing that's never been done before . . .

Lenny, a successful commercial photographer in San Francisco in the late 1970s, switched from shooting still images to shooting video and in 1985 founded Covision as a video production company . . . with a twist.

In his work photographing meetings—in particular the first Apple Leadership Experience in early 1985—he discovered the field of organization development and the astounding experience of a meeting that was *facilitated*. In this meeting the purpose was made clear, each segment was designed to that purpose, and the design considered how participants could interact most effectively, with a facilitator either in front of the room or in the wings helping the owners of the meeting provide *the most engaging meeting process* to achieve the stated purpose and goals. It was a "Eureka!" moment for Lenny. When it came time to make videos for organizations, he positioned Covision to make them for developmental purposes and not for sales and marketing as was the norm. These videos would provide feedback from customers, share knowledge across an organization, promote certain values, or serve as a means for leaders to articulate their visions.

In 1990 Covision was hired to produce a video for IBM to promote a new concept in software called "groupware," a tool for electronically facilitating meetings. Lenny had to learn TeamFocus® in order to produce the video. But even as a novice, he could see it was too complicated for normal people to use in important meetings (he'd been in hundreds of them already). So he convened a group of experts to look at it and give their advice on how to make the introductory video most effective. One member of that group, who was one of the experts Lenny had met at the Apple Leadership Experience, was Jim Ewing. Jim was trained as an electrical engineer and wrote programs for satellites early in his career. He had shifted to organization development and coaching, and had secured a long-term consulting contract (on culture change) with British Petroleum in Scotland. He realized quickly that he needed something like TeamFocus in the challenging meetings he was facilitating for BP. Something *like* that software, but much easier to use. So he began to write his own, more user-friendly software—one that had an intuitive interface. Over emails and a few meals, Lenny made a deal with Jim that Covision would test his new software in live meetings.

The die was cast. Lenny was now thinking intensely about the meeting experience from the participant's perspective and seeing the leader's role expanding at the same time. But he wasn't alone. The Catalyst Consulting Team in Santa Cruz, California, also knew Jim Ewing and by agreement had worked much of his thinking and models into their own consulting practice. Sean Gerrity and Bill Underwood, two of Catalyst's founders, designed their Vision & Strategy process to rely on the new software, called "Council." Together, they worked with scores of small executive teams in strategy meetings—a veritable *Who's Who* in Silicon Valley in the early 1990s, including Cisco Systems, Sun Microsystems, Hewlett Packard, and Apple Computer.

The small groups used the software on networked laptops to let everyone record their thoughts at once, anonymously, and then sat back as a group and read through everyone's ideas. Each member could get his or her starting position out at once—as if they had all talked simultaneously—and all of the statements were anonymous so everyone felt increasingly safer about being honest. With Lenny and Jim's innovation and Catalyst's facilitation, client groups were enabled to move into and through complex strategy scenarios quickly, honestly, and with everyone's perspective. The uptake on this method was strong.

At the same time that Lenny and Jim were innovating "Council," Karl and Todd Erickson had been renting the video-editing suite at Covision to work on training videos for a video library they were creating for Mantak Chia, a Taoist teacher. Karl and Todd had collaborated for several years on large site-specific theater pieces around San Francisco. Todd had also freelanced with Lenny as a video cameraman and editor. In 1992, we came together from these widely different backgrounds and a unique and dynamic group was formed.

Karl had been directing and producing large outdoor theater events as the artistic director of two theater companies he founded in San Francisco. He was looking for a way to integrate the excitement and energy of live theater with a holistic view of the world cultivated through a deep study of Taoism and other Chinese arts. Participant-centered meetings became a laboratory for him—a way to focus on the value of each person within a larger system and to design meetings that were opportunities for all of the participants to contribute to the success of the whole.

Todd had recently received his master's degree in interdisciplinary art from San Francisco State University. His master's thesis had been a universitywide project that used early bulletin board technology to enable cross-campus, interdisciplinary dialogues focused on finding innovative solutions to complex problems. He pursued the development of participant-centered meetings out of his belief that the challenges we face—in organizations, communities, and across the globe—are complex and require tapping into the collective intelligence of all stakeholders in order to create sustainable change.

Although we didn't know it then, as we merged our sensibilities, we were embracing the project that would focus our lives for the next two decades.

We pushed hard in those days, all of us with a hunch that we were onto something big. The same could be said of the clients. Those early adopters didn't just use us because it was a cool new technology (although to be honest, some did); they were doing business in fast and furious times, trying to develop the strategies that would enable them to get up on the first internet waves and ride them into history.

But these first meetings were also limited in size. In the early days, each participant was given a laptop because it seemed like the obvious way to do it. At the same time, there was a limit to how many laptops could be networked together, as well as a limit to how much data could be entered. Despite these limitations, we realized that the innovation was not simply technological, but that the *convergence* happening via the technology was changing the way the people were participating in the room. The human element itself was shifting, and the leaders of these maverick internet companies were excited by the results they achieved. Once we realized what the *human* potential for this type of meeting could be, we became obsessed with overcoming the limits of the technology so we could bring it to larger groups. Lenny knew from his background in large corporate communication events that the large meetings had the potential for transformational change in organizations. The focus of the Covision journey shifted from *Can we actually do this?* to *Can we scale up this process in the room and create a situation where everyone is able to contribute to something that the whole group recognizes as its own creation?*

In 1996, Josh Kaufman joined Covision with a master's degree in psychology and an extensive background in computer science. He wanted to find a balance between his psychology background and his fascination with the application of computer technology. Covision was the perfect fit, blending technology and group process to change how people worked together. And Josh liked the small entrepreneurial environment at Covision and was excited to bring his business management experience to grow the company. Josh joined and the core team was complete. With him on the team the technological scaling of virtuous meetings started to gain momentum.

Josh brought knowledge of programming, server administration, and computer networking—and as a result we began to understand both the technical feats and limitations of what we could do. Jim converted the Council software to run on IP (Internet Protocol) as it quickly became the standard. Lenny kept developing the capacity of the software to add value in real meetings with Silicon Valley's key players. Gradually, the number of participants increased and clients were asking for more laptops than we could network. So Covision began supporting meetings in which two or three executives shared a laptop. Instead of each one quietly entering his or her own thoughts about the topic of discussion, we asked all of the small groups to have short conversations and enter the fruits of their thinking into the software.

While Covision never set out to discover participant-centered meeting design, this is exactly what began to emerge. In an unexpected and serendipitous intersection of a more human-centered approach to innovation, a series of fortuitous collaborations, and the rapid and inexorable development of computer and communications technology, Covision began to redefine what was possible in a large important meeting. The idea of "large group dialogue" was now a reality.

To do all of these early meetings, we were driving around Silicon Valley in our cars, the trunks and backseats loaded with computers and wires. Every laptop had to be hard-wired to others using miles of telephone cord. And there were boxes of power supplies, extension cords, power strips, and all kinds of gizmos. The early experiments required a great deal of hardware schlepping.

But the experiments weren't primarily about the hardware; they were about the group process. You had to have a car full of equipment to be able to pull off the technical feat, but the real prize was getting to see how the group process worked.

Once we decided to have more than one person share an input device, we opened up a new world of meeting process and design. Now suddenly there were two types of participant experience—the whole large group and the small group—back and forth. And there were no guidelines for how to structure the small group conversations, how to synthesize their input in real time, how to make that available to the group, or what the presenter could or should do with it. Every meeting was a learning event, feeling like a giant wave, and our focus was on getting down the face of it gracefully and living to tell the stories. But each year the waves grew larger.

From the first meetings of twelve to fifteen participants, to the meetings of a hundred, then three hundred, and later, thousands, there was no manual. We were inventing and refining the processes that worked best. At each of the thousands of mission-critical meetings for large organizations that we supported, we paid attention to what questions the group was asked, how long they talked and in what size groups, how their input was processed, and how the presenter or leader responded to what the group had produced. We carefully watched and absorbed it all in order to continue to learn how to make the large group experience that much better for *everyone* in the room.

When wireless networking became available, we quickly adopted it and became even more simplified in our technical setup. When the Internet took off, we were again swept along by technological developments and rewrote our software so that it was browser-based and capable of being accessed from anywhere over the Internet. Once the small group discussions were networked together over the Internet, the participant-centered experience we had designed became an even easier and more natural means of conducting real-time meetings in multiple locations.

As the group sizes grew, the rules of engagement we had learned in small leadership team meetings in Silicon Valley were not enough. We had to develop new methods for synthesizing ever-larger amounts of input, soon relying on specially selected and briefed groups from the client organization that looked through the group's comments in real time and picked out the key "themes." We presented these themes back to the group as an "executive summary" of their thinking in eight to ten items on the big video screens. By having the group prioritize that list of themes, it was possible to see which ideas were the most important at the time and then use the same process to take a "deep dive" (deeper discussion and processing) on one or two of those topics. In this way, we began working with processes *where the participants themselves were determining what they were going to talk about.* The meeting leaders were now connected as never before with the real ideas and feelings of those they were leading. The focus of the group work was on the organization's immediate needs and critical areas of concern.

We were still working heavily in the organizational realm. We supported leadership teams at many Fortune 500 companies. At each meeting we continued to hone our understanding of the large group and small group dynamic. It was during the breaks at a large senior leadership meeting for a division of Bank of America in Miami that Lenny and Karl first articulated and wrote down the specifics of the Virtuous Engagement Cycle—an organizing framework at the core of virtuous large-group meeting design, and an integral part of this book.

In the last several years our work has taken us more to Europe and Asia. We left the laptops behind for tablets. We are now able to use the wireless infrastructure in meeting venues and do large meetings online. What is most critical to us is *how to use the technology to make participants active contributors, so that the top leaders in organizations aren't relegated to being passive audiences in large group meetings.* The wave is cresting again for participant-centered design, and we hope that the following chapters will give readers not only the tools but also the mind-set to understand and appreciate the advantages of bringing the participants' voices and contributions into the large group context.

Karl Danskin and Lenny Lind
Covision

ACKNOWLEDGMENTS

We would like to thank our teammates at Covision, Josh Kaufman, Todd Erickson, Laura Gramling, and Tracy Cone, who are our daily partners in designing and delivering virtuous meetings and who are the ones that make it possible. Especially Josh and Todd, who have been equal partners in developing all that we have written about in this book.

We give heartfelt thanks to all of those who worked so hard for so many years to explore and develop the field of virtuous meetings, particularly all of our friends and colleagues in the AmericaSpeaks network and its leader, Carolyn Lukensmeyer. Everyone at America-Speaks dedicated themselves to developing a style of meeting that would return citizens' voices to a meaningful role in our democracy.

But equally, we would like to thank those who took the first germ of the idea and brought it into being: Jim Ewing for partnering with Lenny to create the first versions of the software; Sean Gerrity and Bill Underwood for taking it into the first high-level meetings.

We would like to extend a deep thanks to Nathinee Chen, our development editor, for energetically and creatively guiding us through the actual writing of the book.

After our long search for an inspiring title for this book and David Sibbet's wrestling with our concepts, he exclaimed one day, "This is like a virtuous cycle!" We would like to thank David for his years of friendship and mutual learning, and for turning some of our key concepts into the graphics that you will find in the coming pages. David also read the first draft of the manuscript and offered comments that reshaped the book.

We are indebted to Kobus Smit for his graphic design skills and great eye in helping us create the cover we wanted.

We would like to thank Barbara Bunker for reviewing multiple drafts of our book, lending her vast expertise and wisdom on sections detailing the large group processes she helped to define and bring to prominence, and providing us with insightful direction that helped us shape the final manuscript. We would also like to thank Ingrid Bens for serving as a reviewer of an early draft of the manuscript.

We would like to thank all of our clients who took the chance to do a different kind of meeting, and who carried the torch for the participants in their meetings. In particular, heartfelt thanks to Mike Horne, board member of the Organization Development Network, for his input and strong support of this book and of virtuous meetings.

Finally, we would like to thank our partners:

Karl: To my partner, Melinda, who took me at face value when I said, "Hey, I'm going to take a hike. You want to come along?" Not realizing that I would be on the trail for two years, and that it mostly went uphill. I am deeply grateful that she kept the homestead flourishing during the prolonged periods of my absence.

Lenny: To my wife, Stephanie, a similar sentiment. Sometime a long while back, "I need to work on the book" became stale as a reason for absence. I thank her with all my heart for supporting this effort as she has—with grace and good cheer.

This book could not have been written without the deep support of both of our partners.

INTRODUCTION

Most people are awaiting Virtual Reality; I'm awaiting virtuous reality.
—ELI KHAMAROV, "LIVES OF THE COGNOSCENTI"[1]

This is a book about *virtuous* meetings. Not about virtual meetings or technology. In the chapters that follow, we won't be talking about replacing face time with being plugged in, or about replacing human interaction with technological connectivity. We won't be advocating for substituting the conversations that people have with each other for any version of linking up, logging on, or dialing in. Virtuous meetings are about using technology to enable the conversation in the room. They're about understanding how technology can actually bring our ideas to life in the minds of those we want to reach and those we thought it was impossible to reach.

The notion of large group virtuous meetings is really very simple: giving participants back their voice and enabling them to generate ideas, solutions, and understandings that move the whole group, no matter how large, forward together.

The elements of it are simple: an in-room network of tablets or laptops, six to ten participants seated at round tables, and time structured into the agenda for some small group conversations at those tables. It would seem that the only difficult part is to set up a reliable in-room network. As long as you can get that in place, any seasoned meeting designer should be able to create convergence in a large meeting.

The disparity between how intuitive it seems, and how surprising and almost counterintuitive the design considerations sometimes are, is what prompted us to write this book. The consultants at Covision have been working in this design arena for many years now, since the early 1990s. What we have seen is that more often than not, people designing what wants to be a virtuous large group meeting, utilizing technological connectivity and striving for a participant-centered approach, will misunderstand their choices. As a result, they will make choices that feel intuitively right—based on their experience with front-of-the-room-centered meeting design—but that actually compromise their opportunity to achieve convergent outcomes. It is only because we have seen so many wise, experienced designers make less than optimal choices that we began to realize that there was something that needed to be captured about why this works, how it works, and how to design well with it.

It seems the world breaks down into two types of large meeting designers: those who can imagine achieving a convergent outcome with a large group, and those who can't. Those who can't are convinced that the only achievable outcome with a large group is imparting information and providing opportunities for individuals to learn new skills and network with each other. Although they may say the purpose of the meeting is "alignment of the group," what that really means is that the participants all hear the same message and hopefully (miraculously) agree with it and take it as their own. This book is not for those meeting designers.

The other type of large meeting designers can imagine that a large group could achieve convergent outcomes. In fact, they see the value and necessity of it. But their design repertoire is conditioned by years of designing large meetings without access to the connectivity that recent technology has enabled. This book attempts to lay out the landscape of this new approach so that those who are unfamiliar can understand the important elements and choice points when designing with this new connectivity.

We hope that this book will enable large meeting owners and large meeting designers around the world to embrace a new way of working in which participants spend time in active conversations and contribute to generative outcomes that they consider to be of real value. Our hope is that the totality of our experience over the last twenty-odd years will serve others so that the learning curve will be shorter and the outcomes more instantly virtuous than would be the case otherwise.

This book is for the type of large meeting designer who can already imagine a virtuous meeting and see the necessity and value of it, without even knowing what it is or how to do it. Much of what we present as the concepts, principles, and keys to holding virtuous meetings are there to enable *what you have already conceptualized yourself* when you have thought about where the large group meeting could take your client, your organization, or your community. The following chapters attempt to lay out the details of this new approach and crystallize what so many of us as large group meeting designers have been seeking: a new and connective process that uses a basic, small-group, highly engaged (and highly human) approach.

THE ROAD MAP TO THIS BOOK

Part One: Choosing Virtuous Meetings defines the virtuous meeting and its alternatives. It also defines the two key elements of the virtuous meeting: a participant-centered design and technological connectivity. It describes how these keys work in unison—their codependence and simultaneous functioning. It will describe how a virtuous meeting is one in which each participant's thoughts are captured and translated into a team sense of alignment, paving the way to focused and efficient action.

Part Two: Anchoring Virtuous Meetings defines two powerful keys for designing virtuous meetings: the use of small groups within large groups and specially designed engagement cycles. The former explores the dynamic that is created for the participants when they move quickly and repeatedly back and forth between small group discussion and large group focus on the stage. The latter introduces a process model for a Virtuous Engagement Cycle in which four stages are rapidly completed in repeatable loops. That cycle is enabled by technological connectivity, yielding a meta-conversation between table groups and the front of the room and generating even more ideas and greater human connectivity.

Part Three: Designing Virtuous Meetings explores how to design meetings with the intent of creating more active contributors. Although it is becoming easier to bring the hardware and software for connectivity into the meeting, it is still difficult to know how to use them efficiently and effectively to accomplish the most far-reaching meeting purposes. With a good understanding of the process options and their effects, you can design a large group meeting that has the energy and productivity of a small team offsite.

Part Four: Facilitating Virtuous Meetings looks more specifically at the role of facilitation—which is critical to these meetings. Sometimes it resides in one professional facilitator; other times the responsibility is spread across multiple leaders, presenters, and process specialists. When participants become active contributors, the process must become similar to that of a much smaller meeting, in which everyone is in one circle and can speak up. The facilitation has to manage the clarity of process in a large room together with the safety and trust issues at play—much more so than in a front-of-the-room-centered large meeting. The facilitation can be indirect through coaching and instructing an executive who is the one actually explaining the process to the participants from the stage. In facilitating a virtuous meeting, some basic human values about how we exercise virtuousness toward others come into play.

Part Five: Scaling Virtuous Meetings explores the frontiers of working across multiple sites with participant-centered processes and technological connectivity. It takes the idea of small group interconnectedness global. It scales up the idea of "good for the organization" to what is possible for communities and countries working together. Networked meetings are unique in that the processes they rely on are built to be scaled easily and to work perfectly in multiple sites simultaneously. "The room" now can be any number of rooms, or even distributed individuals, anywhere on the planet. And participants can be included in the meeting in many different ways, at different points in the meeting. Ultimately, these capabilities are leading to more effective meetings that save a lot of resources by not requiring everyone to be in the same room and for the same amount of time.

Throughout this book you will find longer Case Stories that detail an experience with a virtuous meeting concept in depth, and shorter vignettes that we call View from Inside a Meeting. Quick Summaries at the end of each chapter summarize the core concepts and principles. We hope these features will assist you in designing meetings that engage participants to achieve the most ambitious outcomes for their organizations.

Let's begin the journey, which starts, as most journeys do, with an idea . . .

VIRTUOUS MEETINGS

PART ONE

CHOOSING VIRTUOUS MEETINGS

REALIZING VIRTUE IN LARGE GROUP MEETINGS

The concept of being virtuous is as old as the oldest civilizations, from ancient Egypt, where the goddess Ma'at instilled principles of truth and order, to Lao Tzu's enduring Chinese classic from the fourth century B.C. *The Tao and Virtue,* to ancient Greece and Plato's Cardinal Virtues. As our ideas about morality, order, and justice have evolved, the notion of doing right and caring for others has remained as the implicit "goal" of many of these efforts. Essentially, being virtuous is doing good—toward someone, some group, or some thing. Part of the meaning of virtuous in "virtuous meetings" is about the intention to do good, for the participants, for the leaders, and for the larger endeavor of the organization.

Another meaning has to do with cycles. From a holistic perspective, when certain activities occur and recur in cyclical order, they either create accumulating positive results or accumulating negative results. When each successive repetition of the cycle increases the desired outcome, then it is referred to as a "virtuous cycle." Virtuous large group meetings are designed as a series of cycles, and the trust and engagement of the participants increases with the completion of each cycle. Virtuous meetings are virtuous both in their intention and in the format or configuration with which they are run.

During the last thirty years, virtuous cycles have been identified in a wide variety of fields: management, medicine, education, IT, diplomacy, psychology, and macroeconomics, to mention just a few. The identification of virtuous cycles arose as a response to the widely held notion of vicious cycles. "Vicious cycle" is practically a household term.

3

Most people know, for example, the idea that "homelessness is a vicious cycle." When we look at a cycle, it is easy to see if the results lead to a downward spiral, and if the cycle keeps reinforcing that downward trend. But it is becoming more widely appreciated to look for the cycles that are spinning upward, in which positive results from each stage of the cycle lead to increasing positivity as the progression continues. This is where we see the enduring value of virtuous meetings.

But can a *meeting* be virtuous? We believe that it can. Meetings are about people wanting to connect with other people, and there is no greater virtue than this desire to connect, create, and share. Virtuous meetings are about people. The best intention at the heart of every meeting is to connect people—across functional groups, departments, states, vast differences in mind-set, countries, and time zones. The real virtue in a large group is being able to let people talk to each other and share their insights, feelings, and ideas.

In the Virtuous Meeting Cycle (Figure 1.1), everything begins with full engagement. When all of the participants' voices can be heard, then there is the possibility to build a shared understanding within the whole group. When participants use shared understanding, as a group, to generate plans and solutions, they have a sense of

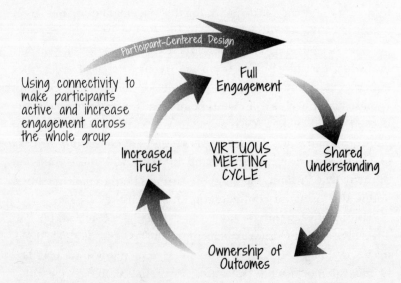

Figure 1.1 The Virtuous Meeting Cycle

ownership of them. As the participants, and the leaders, see the value of the outcomes of their interactions, their trust in each other, in the process, and in the intention increases. With an increase in trust, the engagement can become even fuller and more robust. And in this way each revolution continues upward . . .

In the past, it has been assumed that success in the competitive world requires control of information and a single point of view in execution. But to survive and thrive in the future environment, organizations will have to find ways to harness and leverage the experience, knowledge, and creativity of their people.

In the past, resistance to designing highly interactive meetings using high-speed connectivity has been based on unfamiliarity and unreliability of the infrastructure and a fear of losing control. This has given way to an urgent need to utilize new methodologies and thus accelerate and widen communication—a factor now seen as essential for survival.

Three trends have converged to create the "wave" of demand that we are now seeing for high-speed connectivity in meetings:

1. The technology enabling these methodologies, and the infrastructure to support it, keeps improving every year and has become increasingly ubiquitous.
2. Members of organizations have a proclivity for using the infrastructure; they already use it to offer their insights, experiences, and evaluations in their daily life, and they want and expect to have those opportunities in their work life.
3. The environment in which organizations operate has become increasingly complex and the rate of change in the environment has greatly accelerated—diminishing the value of top-down planning and increasing the need for cross-functional, interdisciplinary collaboration.

THE VIRTUE OF COLLABORATION

Before turning our attention to new ways of designing and conducting large meetings, let's entertain a more virtuous vision for the future of today's organizations. What kinds of experiences and outcomes should we aim to create in large meetings?

Organizations operating in today's environment are under great stress to be competitive. But maintaining a competitive edge no longer means being able to simply "ramp up" production to meet an increasing demand in the market. Rather, being competitive requires being innovative, integrated, and nimble. Amy Edmondson, Novartis Professor of Leadership and Management at the Harvard Business School, in her book *Teaming: How Organizations Learn, Innovate, and Compete in the Knowledge Economy,* frames the nature of what organizations are facing:

> In today's complex and volatile business environment, cor-
> porations and organizations win or lose by creating wholes
> that are greater than the sum of their parts. Intense compe-
> tition, rampant unpredictability, and a constant need for
> innovation are giving rise to even greater interdependence
> and thus demand even greater levels of collaboration and
> communication than ever before.[1]

Her research shows that a legacy dependence on command-and-control processes has become ineffective in an environment where certainty and predictability have given way to uncertainty and rapid change. She demonstrates the counterintuitive lesson of our times— learning has become a more critical objective than execution. Surviving and thriving is more dependent on how you work together, and learn and innovate together, than on finding any "right" formula and "cascading it out" to everyone in the organization. Collaboration and communication need to take place everywhere throughout the organization.

> "The value of your organization is not the individuals, but the way the individuals work together. Companies are competing with each other on the basis of collaboration."
>
> —Professor Lynda Gratton, renowned author and professor of management practice at the London Business School.[2]

One example that illustrates this principle of collaboration comes from our work with a particular client who is in the enviable position of having an industry-leading pipeline of new products coming out in the next few years. And while this is a great problem to have, it is still a very real problem. They are realizing that in order to successfully bring this volume of products to market, they will need to reinvent their development process. And they see that this can't be done solely from the top down, or with a single new process design. What it will take is fostering innovation at every level in the organization. Everyone in the organization needs to be stimulated to find innovative new solutions to how the work gets done.

That's a fairly steep hill to climb, but it is not unusual today. In addition to resources and direction, many organizations are identifying other elements that are essential to their success within their environment. These needs include flexibility, speed, flattened decision making, innovation, and ownership.

Another recent client, a large manufacturing organization, put out five attributes—goals they had to reach as a culture. The goals were to become more Innovative, Agile, Reliable, Efficient, and Inspired. One of the things that all of these aspirations have in common is that they aren't just aspirations for greatness; they are aspirations for survival and competitiveness. In other words, they are not nice-to-haves, but essentials. Edmondson points out that in an environment where "knowledge is a moving target," being able to learn new skills has become a competitive imperative.[3] Not only is the knowledge a moving target, it also resides in many different individuals. Edmondson is arguing that the act of "teaming" is essential and that it is not just one individual who has to learn the new skills, but groups or teams of individuals. The need for self-awareness by these teams is very high. They have to be able to form quickly out of the broader group, do their work, disperse quickly, and reform again. The whole group, or organization, has to become more self-aware. As Lynda Gratton puts it, "What's important is not what is inside each mind, but what is in the space between the minds."[4]

Furthermore, while all the aspirations have to be embraced and endorsed from the top, they are dependent on the attitudes, beliefs, and behaviors of each person in the organization. You can't *tell* someone to be innovative or inspired. It's a nurturing role, rather than a managing role.

Leaders can provide an environment for these competencies to take hold, but they can't execute the transformation. The whole organization has to do the heavy lifting. Every member of the organization, including each participant at your meeting, is critical. Even more critical is how they *work together* to build the future.

THE VIRTUE OF ACTIVE CONTRIBUTION

A virtuous meeting is, in simplest terms, a meeting in which the participants are active contributors to the direction and the outcomes of the meeting. Rather than being passive members of an audience, participants are engaged in frequent small group discussions, which are captured, synthesized, and shared with the whole group, and then responded to by the leaders. The organization gets the full value out of every person in the meeting, and the meeting is stimulating and engaging for the participants.

What It Means to Be an Active Contributor

First, let's define what we mean when we say *active contributor*. If the participants are *active,* they are processing what they hear and explaining it to others. They are brainstorming and evaluating. They are presenting their own ideas, and listening to others present theirs. They are actively thinking about the presentations they've heard from the stage and how those presentations fit into the context of their own work and role—and sharing those thoughts with their peers.

The vehicle for an active participant role is the small table group conversation. When there are only three to eight participants in the group, they naturally all become active. In a small group, it's possible for each person to get his or her perspective out on the table, to examine the differences and the similarities between the positions, and to start to brainstorm new solutions that accommodate everyone's point of view and experience.

Active—actually participating in give and take conversation over a period of time (not just asking someone in front of the room a question).

If the participants are *contributing*, the content of their active conversations is informing the group. In practice, the key ideas or reactions or questions that the participants are having in their small, active conversations are getting communicated to a specially tasked team that reads through all of the input. The fruits of the collective small group interactions are synthesized and then presented back to the whole group. Thus, the leadership and all of the participants have a real-time window into what everyone is thinking and how they are feeling.

Contributing—when the content of a participant's active conversations is somehow informing the group.

One way to think of these small group conversations is that they are "micro-breakouts." They are much smaller than usual breakouts and last anywhere from five to twenty minutes, and they occur frequently during the day. Because they take place right at the tables in the plenary, it doesn't take the participants any time to get into them or to get back from them. The groups are small enough that everyone gets to be active in the conversation the whole time. The "reporting out" happens through a synthesis process, and it can be presented back to the group quickly.

What Active Contribution Looks Like

View from Inside a Meeting

Visualize fifty tables with six participants at each table in a large meeting of top leaders of a global organization. The room is

(continued)

(*continued*)

buzzing; every table has a lively dialogue, with participants taking turns jumping into the discussion. The topic they're wrestling with is critical to the future of the organization. There are tablet computers at each table, and folks are tapping the screens quickly while the discussion is raging. Someone on stage begins calling the group's attention back to the front, and the buzzing slowly subsides. The person on stage, a senior vice president, says, "That *felt* great! What energy! Thank you. I can't wait to see what you've come up with. Can we see the themes now?" A moment later a list of seven statements, or *themes*, is shown on the big screens for all to see. She takes a moment to look over the list, while the whole room does the same. You can hear a pin drop. In another moment she begins addressing the themes, which have been distilled quickly from the hundreds of comments participants entered into the tablet computers. As each of the seven themes is read, the group recognizes a truth about their current situation. And the VP takes a little time with each one, focusing her own spotlight on it, and telling the group what it means to her and to the organization. It's as if a mirror has been raised to the group, and they get a deeper view of who they are and what their collective situation is—a view that is normally not available.

In its simplest form, someone will give a presentation about the topic from the front of the room. Then as soon as the presentation is over, participants will be given one or two specific questions about the topic to discuss. The participants will turn to the other people at their table and get involved in discussing the answer to the question(s). As they talk, one of the participants at the table will record the responses that they come up with into a laptop or tablet.

All of those responses, or small group thoughts, are captured in a structured database. Somewhere in the room a specially tasked group of between two to eight people from the organization (depending on the size and purpose of the meeting) read through the groups' input in real time and synthesize what's coming in from all of the different table group conversations. While the rest of the participants are talking, this group is "listening" to everybody. This synthesis is like an executive summary and usually is captured in eight to ten bullet points.

This synthesis is shown to the larger group so that they can see what the whole group was saying in answer to the question(s). Then the person (or panel) in the front of the room has the opportunity to address the ideas and concerns of the group directly in the moment. After the meeting all of the small group input can be revisited and reviewed, so that the more varied and detailed aspects of the groups' input can also be addressed.

THE KEYS TO CREATING A VIRTUOUS MEETING

Creating the environment, spirit, and process for a virtuous meeting requires two keys and one overarching goal.

The Goal: Convergence

A crucial point to remember is this: In large, important meetings, you are making the participant an active contributor not just for the sake of the participant, but also for the sake of the organization or, in the case of multi-stakeholder meetings, for the stakeholders as a whole. The goal of the meeting should be *convergence:* integrating the thinking, experience, and passion of a broad range of people to create a mutual way forward. Convergence is the outcome that makes a virtuous meeting virtuous by creating a whole (in solutions, strategies, implementation) that is greater than the sum of the parts:

- You create conversations that would not otherwise have existed
- You make information available that wasn't before
- You incorporate the myriad perspectives and realities within the group

- You make contributions productive and focused on the needs of the group
- You build a new level of trust within the group
- You give leaders better visibility to the realities within the group
- You make the group smarter: foster learning and awareness versus assumptions and stereotypes
- You keep the meeting experience engaging, energizing, and focused

Convergence—integrating the thinking, experience, and passion of a broad range of people to create a mutual way forward.

The Keys

The chapters that follow will examine two keys to achieving convergence in large group meetings:

1. A participant-centered approach to design and facilitation
2. High-speed connectivity that makes the content of many small conversations visible to the large group

A virtuous meeting in which convergence occurs is one in which each participant's thoughts are captured and translated into a team sense of alignment, and then catalyzed into collaborative, focused, and efficient action. The meeting becomes more of a design thinking experience for both the participants and the conveners. Rather than passive consumer participants and active leaders/presenters, the two groups work together to design solutions that work for the whole. Thus, participants who are "end users" of the strategy are invited to give input and ideas to influence the designing of the strategy.

The barrier to convergence in normal large group meetings is that no one knows what anyone else is thinking. And even more important, because there is no opportunity to digest and process what they are taking in, many are unsure what they themselves are thinking.

Opening the doorway to convergence requires two keys. First, participants must process the topic and come up with their own ideas and feelings. This can only be done efficiently in small groups. This is the heart of the participant-centered approach. Second, participants and conveners need to know what the major trends are from all those conversations. This can only be done efficiently with networked technology and a well-designed synthesizing process.

You have to have both the small group conversations and the tools and processes to "digest" those conversations in order to be able to use large group meetings to create and converge. Without both parts of the process, large group meetings fail to be productive and become by default informational, and the only opportunities for the real conversations are "on the side" or at the breaks.

HOW LARGE MEETINGS HAVEN'T CHANGED

How much have large meetings changed in the last thirty years? On the one hand, you could say they've changed a lot: thirty years ago there wasn't PowerPoint; wireless microphones were a revelation; registration was done by hand; and participants were looking for telephone booths, not Wi-Fi access. But the most critical elements about the meetings have remained unchanged:

- The reason for holding the meeting
- The roles involved
- Who is invited to participate
- The time frame
- The format

The fundamental format of meetings hasn't changed very much at all. They are front-of-the-room-centered meetings: a group of people is assembled and a few people speak while most of the group sits and listens.

Most large organizational meetings (for example, the ones that include extended leadership teams from across the organization)

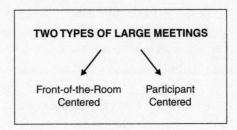

Figure 1.2 Two Types of Large Meetings

take place over one or two days in a large ballroom at a hotel or other venue. Most of the meeting time is taken up with presentations from the stage, backed by PowerPoint images. At the end of each presentation there may be a few minutes of open Q&A with microphone runners stationed around the room. The presenters include senior executives, motivational speakers or experts, and sometimes panels of executives or other experts. Often the group will go into breakouts for an hour or so and then come back into the ballroom and deliver report-outs, sometimes accompanied by hand-drawn flipcharts.

Meetings like this take place every day, all over the world. This front-of-the-room-centered format is a legacy. It is a holdover from a period when it was the best solution to an historical predicament: organizational leaders realized it was important to have a large group gathered face to face, but the size of the group made it impossible to have everyone speak up and talk with each other. Since the individuals couldn't talk to each other, or to the group, they were treated as an audience. Everything was communicated in one direction, from the stage to the audience.

Over the last thirty years, there has been significant work on particular designs for making large meetings more productive and inclusive. We will look at the roots of this new type of design, participant-centered design, when we discuss large group methods in Chapter Two. But outside of the use of these specific large group methods, the format of large meetings has remained static (Figure 1.2). There is a default norm for large meeting design that centers on presentations, panels, Q&A, and breakouts.

This front-of-the-room-centered norm is so pervasive that it has become unconscious. People in organizations who have to put

	Front-of-the-Room Centered	Participant Centered
Goal	Informational	Convergence
Participant Experience	Large group experience (plenary)	Large group (plenary) and small group discussion (table group)
Participant Role	Passive audience member	Interweaving of audience member and active contributor roles
Activity	Listening	Listening, discussing, processing, contributing
Outcome	Heard presenters' messages	Alignment, Ownership

Figure 1.3 The Way We Meet versus the Way We Want to Meet

together a large meeting don't think, "Let's do the norm!" They just do it. Most of the time they don't think about it at all, but just do what they've always done. For these people, the notion of a presentation from the stage followed by a brief Q&A is really more than a "norm": it is their only conceivable option. *Virtuous Meetings* will propel us forward, showing us that we have access to the virtues and ideals that we have been wishing we could embrace all along. We'll first look at the fundamental differences between the way we want to meet (virtuous meeting) and the way we have been conditioned to meet (front-of-the-room-centered meeting) (Figure 1.3).

Today, a front-of-the-room-centered design is still considered by many to be the best way to organize a large group gathering. This book focuses on a better approach to these important meetings—an approach that integrates the thinking, experience, and passion of all of the participants in order to create a shared way forward.

When Convergence Is Unattainable

You can't have a meeting if no one is there. But in many meetings, the world over, the participants are not *there*. They may be in the room, sitting in their chairs, and perhaps even looking directly at the person speaking at the front of the room who is leading the meeting. But where they really are is back at their desks, working on a project that the meeting interrupted, or back at home, or on the beach. . . . They are not *in* the meeting because, frankly, the meeting barely includes them. Despite the amazing progress we have made in organization development around teaming, collaboration, and shared leadership, we are still conducting large meetings "from the front of the room," with little or no participant engagement. We are missing the virtues of coming together, not just to create rituals of belonging, but also to create processes for how we will work, evolve, and progress.

There sometimes comes a moment in the afternoon when you are sitting at a meeting and you realize that you cannot stay awake. You are in the middle of a group of people, perhaps many of whom you know, so you can't *really* fall asleep. But try as you might, there's nothing you can do to stop it: the fateful moment comes when your head drops and you catch it and use all your might to lift it back up and try to focus on the PowerPoint slide up in the front of the room.

Let's look at something completely different that may be similar: traffic congestion. The estimate for the cost of traffic congestion is $87 billion a year.[5] That's the cost of having people sitting in their cars, out on the highway, waiting to go somewhere. That's an incredible sum of money in lost productivity—$87 billion in the United States alone.

And what is the cost in productivity for meeting participants— sometimes the highest paid people in an organization—to be sitting in a dark room somewhere fighting to stay awake? The cost to that organization is enormous. Not only is all of the cost for staging, traveling, and feeding everyone lost when the participants lose interest, but also the cost to the organization of having those leaders out of work is critical. And those costs pale in comparison to the cost of the lost opportunity: the opportunity to catalyze critical members of the organization into embracing a more collaborative and pro- ductive way of working together on a large scale.

Many large organizations are stalled. They aren't growing and innovating enough to realize a robust and expanding future. Many governance processes are stalled, and inevitable, slow worldwide catastrophes are not being addressed because the many stakeholders can't find a way to generate inclusive solutions. Everyone is present, but it is as if they are all in some transcendent traffic jam, unable to move even though they know they need to.

Large group meetings are a reflection and a symptom of that giant traffic jam. Large organizational meetings, even at the highest levels in the organization, don't reinforce collaboration, speed, and open innovation. Large multiple-stakeholder meetings, even though their purpose is to create inclusive solutions, don't provide a means for the stakeholders to work in a truly generative mode, together, in real time.

A New Design Choice

An intuitive assumption for most people is that the difference between a small meeting and a large meeting is that one is participant centered and the other is front-of-the-room centered. In other words, whether to design a participant-centered meeting or a front-of-the-room-centered meeting isn't a choice that designers have. Rather, it is dictated by the size of the group. Without the new high-speed connectivity, this is largely true—particularly the larger the meeting gets. The option, or choice, to have a *large, participant-centered* meeting is made possible by this new connectivity.

What Do We Mean by "Large"?

Before we go further, we want to address a question we are frequently asked: When exactly does a meeting become "large"? Here's what we've learned: Once there are too many people for everyone to have a chance to contribute to the discussion, and once there are too many people for the more introverted members of the group to feel comfortable speaking up, then a meeting has become large. A large meeting, conducted in a traditional way, is characterized by many of the participants not participating in any active way. Instead, they are merely passive listeners for most of the meeting.

Even a ninety-minute breakout with forty or fifty participants is generally too large for a lot of the participants to be active. Half of the people may get to contribute to a discussion, but half of the people will remain inactive and silent. "Large" isn't defined by a specific number of participants. Rather, large is defined as the point at which the size of the group discourages or prevents active contribution for many of the participants.

To illustrate the relative nature of defining a large meeting, consider how time is a factor. How long the meeting lasts can affect how large it feels. If you have fifty participants for three days, most all of them will get to contribute over the course of the three days, and the meeting will not seem particularly large. But if those same fifty people are only going to meet for three hours one afternoon, then many of them probably will play a mostly silent, passive role, and it will have the feel of a large meeting for them.

> **Large** (meetings)—the point at which the size of the group discourages or prevents active contribution for many of the participants.

SEEKING ALIGNMENT

Why do organizations have large meetings?

One reason is to bring people together face to face. In most large organizational meetings, the participants gather together in person only once or twice a year. That is the only opportunity to viscerally feel a part of this group, and for this group to have a sense of identity. Actually being physically present together is the best chance the group has to feel like a working team—to set aside their own individual viewpoint and realize that there is a collective viewpoint that is the sum of all of many real individuals present in a room: individuals you can see and touch, with whom you can shake hands and have conversations.

The other reason is that these meetings serve as *communications events*. They are the vehicles for disseminating the view from thirty thousand feet. They are opportunities for the leadership to throw a sharp focus on the things that need to happen throughout an organization during the coming year.

Because it is handled as a communication event—regardless of whether it's the annual leadership conference, a strategy summit, or even a merger integration meeting—everyone knows it will be about the participants receiving the leadership's point of view. They know it will be about everyone receiving that same point of view *in the same way*, and taking it away with them to focus their actions. The desire is for alignment and the process to produce it is to have everyone hear the same presentation, from the same person, at the same time. In the end, this type of process does produce an *aligned message*, but not an *aligned group*.

Alignment and Communication

Communication is most effective when it is interactive: when everyone involved has an active role. This is obvious on a one-to-one level, but it tends to get overlooked or dismissed as impossible in designing large meetings.

For example, if a manager is intent on changing an employee's way of looking at something, she will be much more effective by presenting her view and then soliciting the other person's thoughts in response to it. Then the manager can weigh those responses and try to provide more context, data, or insight to address whatever part of the picture the employee is struggling with. Maybe there are things that the employee tells the manager that cause the manager to change certain details of her view as well.

This same process will also work if she sits down with three of her direct reports at once. Going into the conversation, she doesn't really know what they are thinking, how they are feeling, or what they will say. She may have her hunches and her assumptions, but she has to have a dialogue with them in order to effect any change in how they are looking at things. Not only does she want to share with them the direction she thinks they all need to go, but she also wants to hear from each of them and respond to what they are saying.

When we do this with thirty people, the interactive communication becomes complex, and the manager or executive must have good facilitation skills. Even then, with a group of thirty, it takes some time.

When we do this with three hundred people, most managers and executives believe the task is impossible, and they feel forced to turn away from interactive communication. When three hundred people are in the room, everyone—participants and leaders alike—believes that the participants have to play a passive role. We all believe that the only ones who can be in an active communications role are those standing in front of the room holding a microphone. By default, everyone else's role is reduced to listening.

Virtuous meetings, at their core, are about the difference between an active role and a passive role for the participants. Are participants in the meeting going to be active contributors or merely passive listeners? The answer to this question is the fundamental point of leverage for any organization or multi-stakeholder group that wants to extract the maximum value out of a large meeting.

THE HABIT OF CREATING PASSIVE AUDIENCES

What do we mean by a passive role? Very simply, the participants are inactive. They can listen, but they can't talk. They have no opportunity to contribute. They don't know what anybody else is thinking about what is being said. They may not even have a clear sense of what they think or feel about what is being said, because they have no opportunity to digest what they're hearing. They are just listening and taking things in, as much as they can.

By contrast, an active role means the participants are *contributing*. They are listening at times, but they are also processing what they hear and explaining it to others. They are brainstorming and evaluating. They are arguing for their own ideas and listening to others' ideas. They are actively thinking about how the presentations fit into the context of their own work and role and sharing those thoughts with their peers. By means of this active role, the leadership and all the participants have a real-time window into what the participants are thinking and how they are feeling.

The Confusion about "Passive-Audience" Style Design

What does the passive role look like in a meeting? Listening to presentations is the most obvious (in)activity that comes to mind: 175 participants sitting in a darkened ballroom listening to a Power-Point presentation on the stage. However, that is only the starkest example of the passive role. Perhaps because it is so stark, other examples seem "active" by comparison. That's the basis for a lot of confusion in large group meeting design. Many (in)activities that designers use to create an "active" role for the participant are just as passive as listening to a presentation from the stage.

Activities That Create a Passive Experience

Let's look at some classic examples of activities and processes that are considered alternatives to straight presentations and evaluate them from the active/passive perspective. We need to keep in mind that the active role means that participants are talking, thinking, debating, and contributing to the knowledge and awareness of the group.

Q&A. Although this often appears as "Group Interaction" on an agenda, it casts almost all of the participants in a passive listening role. Except for the person who has actually asked the question, everyone is just sitting passively and listening—first to the question, then to the response. Even the person who asks the question hasn't been very active. That person hasn't been involved in any give and take about the topic, but has merely posed a single question that is on his or her mind and then sat down to passively listen to the answer.

Whole group discussion. Sometimes in an agenda-design meeting someone will suggest, "After his presentation we'll do some Q&A and then let's open it up for a group discussion. We'll already have mic runners in place from the Q&A section." Whole group discussion works well within small-to medium-sized groups. A group of fifty, if they are meeting for a couple of days, can start to have fairly meaningful group discussions if they are well facilitated. But if you have a group of 150 or 300, then it is essentially a symbolic statement about honoring the voices in the room. Such a symbolic statement is extremely valuable and communicates a lot to the participants. But this should not be confused with offering them an active role in which they are contributing to the meeting.

This could be seen as a delicate differentiation, but in fact it is not. It's quite plain and clear. For the vast majority of participants in the meeting, whole group discussion means sitting passively and listening to a few different people put out their point of view. Most of the participants don't get to say anything. We often hear senior executives say, "If these people are our leaders, they'd better be willing to speak up!" This points to a fundamental misunderstanding: if they all wanted to speak up, there certainly wouldn't be enough time for all of them to do so. The only reason that whole group discussion can be entertained as a viable agenda activity in a large meeting is because so many people aren't comfortable speaking up. Speaking up becomes a symbolic activity with a few of the extroverts, or people confident in their position in the hierarchy, who speak up to symbolize the voice of the rest of the participants in the room.

Panel discussions. The participants are in the same passive listening role as with any presentation from the stage. Adding Q&A doesn't change that role, as mentioned above.

Breakouts. If there are more than about fifteen participants in a breakout, a lot of them will spend the breakout passively listening, while a handful of people do most of the talking. This situation can be improved if there is good facilitation and more time allotted. Once you get up to twenty-five or thirty participants or more, even good facilitators are unlikely to keep all of the participants active and contributing to the conversation. So breakouts can work as a way to give participants an active contributing role in the meeting if they are kept small enough to allow everyone to participate. However, with large meetings that means a lot of breakout groups.

The consequence of all these breakouts is that you have many separate experiences to reassemble for the larger group. If you have many small breakout groups go out and have discussions, how do you converge those discussions into something of value for the group and the organization? Generally, the device that is chosen is the dreaded "series of report-outs." Representatives from each group get up in front of the room, one after another, and give a synopsis of what their group discussed. There are variations of that format, of course. You can have representatives just stand up at their table and report out. You can have the representatives add only new thoughts to what has been said already. You can have representatives use a flipchart created in the breakout as a visual aid. You can have a gallery walk of all of the flipcharts. But in the end, the result of having breakouts is usually some lengthy period of the agenda when all of the participants are sitting passively and listening to a whole series of reports of what went on in the other breakouts.

Vicious Cycle of Participants as Passive Audience

A vicious cycle occurs when outcomes created by an activity or condition lead away from a positive end. The negative outcomes created make it increasingly difficult to change or improve the original activity or condition. In this way, vicious cycles become a downward spiral (Figure 1.4).

Treating the participants at a large meeting as a passive audience creates a situation where no one can tell what the participants are thinking. Since no one knows what anyone else is thinking, and there is no venue for discussion, no one has a means to resolve doubts or overcome reservations. Participants remain distant from what is being presented and can't generate a sense of ownership. The lack of ownership makes the leaders of the group feel that they need to step in and take control, which reinforces the decision to treat the participants as a passive audience.

Today there is an alternative. Communication connectivity enables everyone to air their ideas and to hear the main messages from everyone else. Because this alternative exists, it becomes imperative to revisit our deeply ingrained habit of treating participants as a passive audience. We have to ask ourselves:

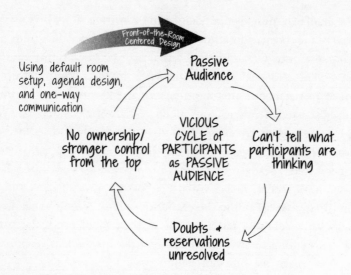

Front-of-the-Room
Centered Design

Using default room
setup, agenda design,
and one-way
communication

Passive
Audience

No ownership/
stronger control
from the top

VICIOUS
CYCLE of
PARTICIPANTS
as PASSIVE
AUDIENCE

Can't tell what
participants are
thinking

Doubts &
reservations
unresolved

Figure 1.4 Vicious Cycle of Participants as Passive Audience

Does it serve the participants?

Does it serve the leadership?

Does it serve the organization?

First, let's talk about the participants. If you are gathering with two hundred other people from a hierarchical organization, most of whom you don't know very well, you may find comfort in a format where you simply sit and listen. At breaks and evening events you can socialize with people you know but don't see often, meet some new folks, and have quiet, earnest chats with people there whom you know and trust.

So on the one hand this passive role of the legacy meeting serves your needs. It is a safe format for the most part. On the other hand, it is flat. It's neither stimulating nor challenging. You get some summary figures and a general sense of what's at stake, but for the most part you don't learn very much.

There are no "Aha!" moments, little new perspective, and little time to really think about the content of what is presented. Mostly you file it away to revisit after the meeting. The politics and the egos are mildly interesting and important to keep track of, but the overall experience ends up being routine and uninspiring.

In addition, nobody learns anything from *you*. Your perspective on what has been said, thoughts about the business, and ideas about the future of your organization aren't shared with anyone. Some conversations at the breaks and evening events may be stimulating, but they quickly fade from your mind, and they never make it to the awareness of the group.

For the leaders it is no better. The meeting is the opportunity to make sure that everyone hears the same message in the same way. The meeting is the opportunity to try to shape the thinking and the activity of all of the participants who have been invited—focusing them, ideally, in the direction that will have the clearest strategic effectiveness. At stake in all of these "audience members" is the survival and the success of the organization. These are all the people who have to get the work done.

Before the meeting there are countless emails and meetings to decide the content of the presentations and get the slides built. Decisions are made about who will present what. The energy goes up as the meeting nears, and with one week to go, preparations are at a fever pitch.

Then the meeting happens: the presentations are made, there are a few questions from the group, and you try to answer them as fully and precisely as you can. At the end of the day, there is a dinner and networking activity.

In reality, you have no idea what all the participants were thinking: what they heard, what they thought about it, if they understood it, if they agreed with it, or if they are willing to apply themselves with their minds and hearts to achieving it. You know what you said, but you have no idea what was heard and what effect, if any, it had on these people. You probably won't ever know. You may not even see all of them again until the meeting next year.

Ultimately, it is the organization that suffers. Suboptimal meetings, and meeting formats, are not just hurting the participants and the leaders. The participants may be bored and uninspired (and think that's just how these things are), and the leaders may be flying blind in their effort to inspire and focus their "audience" (and see no way around it), but the real loser is the organization itself. If the organization is unable to access the vast resource of its people's knowledge, experience, and creativity, it cannot perform to its potential. The meeting itself weakens those virtues and ideals that drove the original desire to meet. The whole group, as a team, misses out on the chance to build the creativity, flexibility, and unity of the organization.

THE VIRTUOUS MEETING *ITSELF* IS THE MESSAGE

The *design* of the meeting is a communication too—a very obvious and visceral communication. No one sits and ponders it or figures it out. The participants simply experience it, and they understand what you are telling them.

How you design and conduct your meeting says as much about your organization as any of the words that get spoken from the stage. The meeting *is* the message. The question is: What are you telling them? What kinds of things could you tell them? How would it make a difference?

With your design you could tell them they are important. Or you could tell them that they're not. You could tell them that you are interested in what they are thinking. Or that you are not. You could tell them you want to coach them, or you could tell them you want to micro-manage them. You could empower them, or you could disempower them. You could tell them they are a large, focused, interdependent team, or you could tell them they are all individual players.

But the important point is that you are telling them these things through the way you design and conduct the meeting. Whatever you say when you get up on stage, if the format of the meeting doesn't make the same communication, your content message will be badly undercut. You can say all of the right words, but if the meeting format shows the participants that their opinions are only secondary, they won't be very inspired to take risks, innovate, or martial their efforts for the benefit of the whole.

If I'm sitting in a huge ballroom and I'm treated like the audience to some entertainment—talked at, bored, forced to sit still and watch the stage for hours—I'm not likely to believe you when you say, "The people of this organization are its greatest asset. It's all of you that constitute our competitive edge, and I'm confident that you will bring the innovation and inspiration we need to . . ." As I listen to your words, I realize there is a disconnect somewhere. And I have my doubts about what will actually come of all of our efforts.

But if you can get me talking and thinking so I start to have some flashes of insight, *and* you make me feel part of an extended group and help me feel that everyone here is my peer and has my back, then I might start to feel bolder and more stimulated to take up a challenge. Then I'll start to believe your words, and I'll begin to think that you believe and respect mine. And I honestly don't know how high and how far we can all go together.

The most important point is that *every meeting design* is a loud, clear, and unequivocal communication. There is no neutral design, no design that doesn't communicate something. This is a difficult but crucial point to grasp: whatever design you create, whatever role and experience you give the participants in the meeting, you are making a clear and unmistakable communication. It is as powerful as all the content that gets presented from the stage, and it is more quickly understood and assimilated by the participants.

The virtuous meeting is about being conscious of that communication. More important, it is about designing meetings that empower and inspire people and that make groups feel like teams, giving all the courage to take risks and the resources to reach farther.

℃ CHAPTER ONE · QUICK SUMMARY

- Collaboration and inclusion are key virtues that organizations will need to fully embrace in the future.
- Large meetings have traditionally been conducted as front-of-the-room-centered meetings—where participants are in the role of passive audience members.
- Many people believe that as meeting size increases, interactive communication becomes impossible.

- There is a vicious cycle in traditional large meeting designs that enforces a passive role on the participants.
- An alternative to this tradition is the virtuous meeting, where the participants are in an active, contributing role.
- The goal of the virtuous meeting is convergence.
- Convergence can be achieved via participant-centered design and high-speed connectivity, together.
- The form of a virtuous meeting itself is a message about how much you value the participants and what you think is possible for them and for the organization.

CHAPTER TWO

THE FIRST KEY:
THE PARTICIPANT-CENTERED APPROACH

T he participant-centered approach is based on a certain design concept. The focus is on what the participants are experiencing. Significant energy goes into devising what the participants will talk about; significant time is devoted in the meeting to having the participants be in an active, contributing role.

Although this approach is still relatively rare, this is not a brand-new design concept. In the last thirty years, we have seen a small but burgeoning movement of meeting methods that are based on what we would call participant-centered design. The success of these methods has proven that participant-centered design is valuable and transformative.

WHERE IT ALL STARTED

Beginning in the 1980s, a few different organizational consultants began to develop specific methods for structuring and running large meetings. To a great extent, large group methods for meetings arose as a response to the recognition that it was important to somehow involve the whole system in making organizational change or in planning the future. Including representatives from throughout the system made it more likely that the solution or direction would be realistic and achievable. By giving everyone ownership, it ensured a faster and more complete implementation. Because the early designers knew they needed to get many stakeholders together, they devised means for working with ever-larger groups in meetings. Although they didn't give it a name, the people who created these methods were the first to apply a participant-centered perspective to large meeting designs. They started from a position of focusing on what the participants were doing in the meeting—what they were experiencing and contributing.

These methods rejected the role of passive audience for the participants. They sought to make the participants active. They believed that through the involvement of the whole system, the subtle strands of a common vision would begin to appear. These strands, as they coalesced, would create a synergistic movement toward solution, or toward a shared understanding from which the individual could act as part of the whole.

Of course, this wouldn't come about from everyone listening to a presentation, or from polling on a preset list of solutions. Conversation was required: creative dialogue that involved every person. But it didn't come about solely from the individual conversations either. It came about from participants also having access to the *synthesis* of all of the conversations.

Participant-centered perspective—is in contrast to front-of-the-room-centered perspective, and focuses on what the participants are doing, experiencing, and contributing to the meeting.

Participant-centered design—proceeds from that perspective and, in contrast to front-of-the-room-centered design, develops opportunities for the participants to be active contributors to the outcomes of the meeting.

Several methods were developed, such as Future Search (developed in the 1970s as a task-focused planning meeting for large groups)[1] and Whole-Scale Change (developed in 1981 by Dannemiller Tyson Associates at the Ford Motor Company).[2] For the most part these practitioners were not focused on large meetings per se, but rather large meetings as part of a larger organizational intervention for driving change or planning the future. In the 1990s several more methods emerged. The Conference Model (developed by The Axelrod Group for systemwide change through a series of integrated conferences),[3] Open Space (Harrison Owens's groundbreaking approach),[4] and others.

Covision began doing the virtuous meeting approach in the early 1990s, and by the mid-1990s we had learned how to take it to scale. At that time AmericaSpeaks was developing what would become the 21st Century Town Hall method, and they were able to integrate our approach into their larger vision to create an effective way to bring the public's voice into critical civic decision making.[5] It was an enormous experiment, conducted continuously since 1995, which showed the world that the public's voice could play not just a role, but the most meaningful and important role, in creating public policy. The 21st Century Town Hall is a true virtuous meeting, in the way we talk about them throughout this book. AmericaSpeaks meetings are still the best examples of this process in action. Working primarily in the civic and nonprofit sectors, they designed the largest and most ambitious virtuous meetings that have been undertaken so far. They are a laboratory of international significance.

The different large group methods are plainly distinct from each other, yet they could all be considered participant centered. Taken together they have comprised the cutting edge of thinking about how to work with large groups. In their book *Handbook of Large Group Methods: Creating Systemic Change in Organizations and Communities*, Barbara Bunker and Billie Alban identify four common characteristics of large group methods based on their extensive work in this field:[6]

Bunker and Alban's Core Characteristics of Large Group Methods

- Inclusion of stakeholders
- Engagement of multiple perspectives through interactive activities
- Opportunity to influence
- Search for common ground

Each of the large group methods has a different specific methodology for achieving its ends, but despite the different components and sequences of activities of the methods, their meetings all exhibit these core characteristics.

Achieving Bunker and Alban's core characteristics is at the very heart of virtuous meetings. When we support one of the large group methods to make their meeting more of what we call a virtuous meeting, the advantage is that we accelerate their already participant-centered process or broaden the achievement of one of the core characteristics. For instance, we make the search for common ground happen more fully in real time, broaden the access to stakeholders so that more can be included, or enable more perspectives to be engaged.

In most cases, when we help someone design a large virtuous meeting, they are not using one of the formal large group methods, and yet the design still achieves the core characteristics. In many cases this approach is designed into a large meeting that is held regularly but that has always been a one-way communication to the participants. By designing-in the capability to follow presentations with table discussions, synthesizing, and response, rather than the usual Q&A from the floor, the core characteristics noted by Bunker and Alban are achieved.

In addition to the four characteristics shared with all of the large group methods, another key characteristic of virtuous meetings is the ability for everyone to have a sense of what everyone else is thinking—not just in their small table group, but in the larger group as well. Not only are the participants active, they are also contributing, and their contributions are visible to the whole group.

PARTICIPANTS GETTING THEIR VOICE BACK

The impetus behind the large group method movement was to bring the whole system—the entire network of stakeholders and their means for working together and communicating—into the room. The reason for bringing stakeholders together was not to give them some precrafted communication, but rather to let all parts of the system communicate with each other, in order to find a way forward that was most efficient, effective, and leveraged for the whole system.

Because the goal was to facilitate communication between the different parts of the system, the pioneers of large group methods turned the participants away from looking at the podium in the front of the room and had them sit and talk with each other. This was a fundamental breakthrough in holding large meetings. The value of the participant was embraced. The focus shifted away from being solely on the front of the room and the presenter. Instead the focus was turned on the group as a whole and what they could communicate to each other and create together.

When this point of view arose in the 1980s and 1990s, it was quite radical. The whole framework for having a meeting was turned on its head. Instead of asking, "What will the participants receive from the presenters?" the meeting designer asked, "What can the organization receive from the participants?" The expertise of the participants was recognized, and methods were developed to take advantage of that expertise—to get both participants' input and their commitment to the task or outcome.

It was further recognized that the way for expertise to reveal itself was through discussion. Emphasis was placed on how to get the participants talking to each other about the relevant topics in their small groups. Some methods specifically had the same group staying together all day, while others had participants changing their small groups in order to get exposed to many different points of view. Some methods had very small groups (only four people) while others had larger groups (ten people with a facilitator). Still others had groups of every different size depending on the interests of the individual members of the group. But most of them embraced the small group as the way to enable the participants' expertise to manifest itself.

Making Everyone's Ideas Visible

Convergence in a participant-centered meeting requires conversation and creative dialogue. But conversation itself is not enough.

Participants also have to have access to the *synthesis* of all of the conversations. Convergence is possible because:

There are participant discussions in which everyone is a contributor.

There are presentations back to the group of what they have said—
the synthesis of all of those conversations.

This was understood by many of the pioneers of large group methods. They had the vision to set up the room in round tables, in order to move away from the dominance of the presenter and toward the value of the conversations the participants could have with each other. They developed various ways of trying to synthesize the fruits of those conversations into something that was visible to the whole group and that the whole group could work with.

In many cases, flipcharts or Post-it Notes were distributed to each small group, and the group used these to record the ideas gathered in their conversations. In other cases, one group member was entrusted with summing up these collective ideas and sharing her spontaneous insights about the conversation with the larger group.

The process for making these ideas and insights visible to the whole group varied as well: individual groups could use the flip-charts for report-outs; the flipcharts could be posted for a "gallery walk"; the main points from the flipcharts could be extracted and combined overnight to create a whole group list to show to the group in the morning. If sticky notes were used, they could be posted on a wall, and participants could read through them and arrange them into thematic areas, and then the group could walk along the wall and see what the groupings were. Designated reporters from each table could stand up in random order and give a synopsis of what the conversation had been at that table.

By these means, the whole of the system was made visible to its various "parts" (the participants in the large group meeting). Again, this was a breakthrough at the time, in terms of meeting design, and the developers of these methods were ingenious in figuring out ways of achieving this visibility. Necessity became the mother of invention, because the whole value of having the system together at once was to generate insights, plans, and solutions based on the synergistic expertise of all of the participants. The virtuous meeting concept owes much to these forefathers and foremothers of large group meeting design.

Advantages of the New Connectivity

Although low-tech means have been used for many years to make the results of small conversations visible to the larger group, the efficiency of those means breaks down as the group gets larger. As people choose to do bigger meetings, with more content areas covered in less time, and sometimes in multiple simultaneous locations, the need for a new connectivity enabled by technology steadily increases.

The Need for Efficient Connectivity Increases as . . .

- The group gets larger
- The variety of topics engaged constrains the time available for each
- Anonymity becomes more crucial as groundwork for trust building
- The participants convene in multiple locations

One compelling example demonstrating the combination of the participant-centered approach and technological connectivity is the 21st Century Town Hall. This method is frequently used to engage very large groups, usually for only one day, with the goal of emerging from the meeting with a clear unified voice. Accomplishing this seemingly impossible outcome requires the ultimate efficiency in making the small group work visible to the whole. Carolyn Lukensmeyer, who created this model, has said, "Using information technology to summarize what each table has discussed and decided, and then using the Theme Team to summarize the work of all the tables while the participants are engaged in the next task, enables the focus and work to move forward without losing any energy and no chance of boredom with the reporting out process."[7] She compared it with trends in OD work over the last twenty years, where there has been a combination of small group and plenary work: "The advantage [of the technological connectivity] lies in the fact that—no matter how good you are at moving back and forth from people taking notes and recording—there becomes a scale issue, at a certain size you just can't do it anymore."[8] In summary, she highlighted three advantages of using connectivity: "the appropriate use of participant's energy and commitment, the enhanced time factor, and the ability to significantly increase the scale of participation."[9]

These can be paired with Bunker and Alban's core characteristics to get a full picture of the value of virtuous meetings:

The Advantages of the Participant-Centered Approach + High-Speed Connectivity

- Engagement of multiple perspectives through interactive activities
- Opportunity to influence
- Search for common ground
- Inclusion of stakeholders
- Most efficient use of time
- Greatest opportunities for scaling
- Most appropriate use of participants' energy and commitment
- Ability for everyone to have a sense of what the group as a whole is thinking

---

In the next chapter, we'll look at the nature of the technology for connectivity that enables these advantages.

C CHAPTER TWO · QUICK SUMMARY

- Over the last thirty years, large group methods have been developed in order to involve the "whole system" in making organizational change or in planning the future together.
- Participant-centered design evolved from large group methods. Although they didn't call it such, certain practitioners started the ball rolling by focusing on the participant's role in the specific methods they developed.
- The participant-centered approach is a key aspect of the virtuous meeting. This approach enables the virtuous meeting to achieve the same core characteristics that Bunker and Alban identified by studying large group methods.
- Virtuous meetings embrace a new connectivity, which is technologically enabled, to gain the highest efficiency in making the results of all the small conversations visible to the larger group.

CHAPTER THREE

THE SECOND KEY:
HIGH-SPEED CONNECTIVITY

A dvancements in technology have often led to major shifts in how we communicate and relate to one another. Think of the printing press, the radio, the telephone, broadcast television, the fax machine, and then the conference call, personal computer, and video conferencing. Each of these has ushered in new eras of communication and collaboration, creating exponential shifts in how we are able to publish and receive information.

Technology = Capability

Today, with the proliferation of the Internet, smartphones, and social media, increasing numbers of us are always connected, always online, always communicating. It is easy to get swept up in this widespread connectivity, the wave of the Internet seemingly washing over everything. Not only has this expanded our capabilities, but it has also increased everyone's familiarity with technology whether they know it or not. And yet as we've seen, how we engage in a large group meeting is largely unchanged since the days when meeting technology meant a microphone and a slide projector. Large meetings are still commonly a large room, a stage with a presenter, and an audience.

However, technology *is* a source of tremendous possibility for transforming old paradigms. Let's take a look at an example of widespread connectivity changing the way we think about how group opinion is formed and gathered: "Tweets," those short, personal messages sent over smartphones have flooded the world.

Who could have guessed that Twitter would *change the world?* Within five years of its birth (2006–2011), Twitter became an enabling force in the "Arab Spring" of independence movements that swept the Arab world.[1] However you feel about those outcomes, it is hard to miss how they were shaped by large numbers of people who seized a technology that was new on the scene and literally ran with it. By mid-2011, there were two hundred million tweets per day, worldwide. By mid-2013, four hundred million per day.[2]

As each new technology washes over us, it is loaded with implications that are barely visible at the start. Even before the revelation of Twitter's impact on world politics and financial markets, people were exclaiming how it could spice up a meeting, especially with younger audiences, by opening a channel for gathering quick, hopefully meaningful, comments and projecting them onto big screens. In reality, most of these experiments turned out to be disruptive, resulting in a loss of focus and sidelining of the main topic. There was little forethought about how Twitter would actually work in the room or what the process before and after its use would be. And there was little thinking about design.

Technologies that actually do enable more effective, virtuous meetings started quietly in the 1980s, evolved slowly through the 1990s to the present, and have not had anywhere near the impact of the Internet. But the technology supported and then accelerated communication in large meetings that could not have occurred in any other way.

THE SLOOWWW GROWTH OF CONNECTIVITY IN MEETINGS

The mental picture of a meeting is wildly different across a kaleidoscope of cultures, but most are similar in their underlying structure. No matter if you add speakers or more discussions, traditional meetings share the same elements—the person or people in front leading, directing, or presenting, and the audience listening. This underlying process is deeply ingrained within the psyches of individuals and organizations alike around the globe. The image of *meeting* is as solidly built into people's perceptions as those of *school,* *store,* or *place of worship.*

So despite the waves of technology crashing around us for decades, the evolution of process design (how we actually conduct our meetings) has barely changed. The underlying structure of meetings has remained as strong as a seawall against the tide. To be sure, the effect of the Internet on the meeting *industry* has been significant. It has led to easy online access to vast meeting site information, online registration software, overall meeting management software, travel websites, online transportation purchasing, and more. But the effect of the Internet on a meeting's *process,* and the ability to actually change or improve what unfolds inside the general sessions of large, important meetings, has been negligible.

Against this backdrop of slow growth, experiments in meeting process design, including the introduction of various technologies, have explored the impact of interconnectivity in meetings. As we saw in Chapter Two, some intrepid explorers have defined effective processes that have made meetings more engaging for participants and far more productive. In the 1990s, Covision first brought portable networks of laptop computers into large meetings. These experiments were driven by the possibility of making quantum leaps in whole group communication. Twenty years and thousands of meetings later, supported by technologies that have connected all participants and speakers, we have refined the recipe for producing the highest engagement and the best overall results in these meetings.

Achieving convergence in a large meeting is unusual—so much so that most leaders don't even think about it or believe it is possible. As a result, it is no surprise that today's large meetings still consist largely of presentations. But the times are changing. There is a greater need and interest in achieving better outcomes from the investment required to produce a large meeting. Meeting designers and leaders alike are beginning to see how simple processes that converge many points of view can generate much more productive outcomes. You need more than raising hands or flipcharts to facilitate and accelerate this process. You need technology, well applied. To that end, we will now take a few steps here into "techno-speak" but have made every effort to keep it as close to English as possible.

WHAT THE TECHNOLOGY ALLOWS

The technology tools that support participant-centered meetings allow for:

- Any number of small table groups to input their ideas simultaneously
- Input to be collected in a way that makes it possible for a specially tasked team to distill it in a very short time
- Statements of distilled input to be formatted easily for quick presentation back to the group on the large video screens; the same with poll results

The participants' experience with any type of meeting software needs to be straightforward, intuitive, and require few if any instructions. If more than a few seconds are necessary to learn it, it shouldn't be used in large groups. Leaders shouldn't allow it if there is great potential for it getting in the way. If technology is used in a large meeting for capturing the questions, concerns, and ideas of every participant in the room, it must adhere to the principles that underlie this approach—it must be fast, reliable, and easily configured.

There are a variety of capabilities that interactive technologies enable in meetings that couldn't be done without them:

The Seven Capabilities of High-Speed Connectivity

1. Increases the number of people who can give feedback at once
2. Makes giving the feedback instant and available for synthesis
3. Captures the feedback in the participants' own words
4. Allows participants to include as much detail as is needed
5. Accumulates the feedback instantly in a form that is easy to distill
6. Allows the feedback to be anonymous
7. Enables shifting from whole group format to small group and back again in minutes, not hours

The tools that provide these capabilities are computer devices, that are networked together and running software designed to allow multiple, anonymous, text entries and polls. The input devices are distributed one to each small group. That means that every person isn't recording his or her own thoughts and reactions. Rather, first there is a discussion and then one of the group members records the best insights and ideas. The computers capture the fruits of group discussion. You can think about the location of the computers as a metaphor for their status and role within the group—they are not in the middle of the group process, which is a free-flowing organic conversation, but rather they stand to the side of the group and function as a channel for that group's thoughts to move out to the larger group via the synthesis/convergence process. They are, essentially, a connected flipchart. These tools enable all participants to be involved in simultaneous small group discussions, and make it possible for everyone to be assured that soon they'll hear results from all the groups.

View from Inside a Meeting

Picture a group of three hundred participants breaking into fifty table groups, six per table. The ten-minute discussion segment has just begun; at one table three people are trying to talk at once. None are focused on the computer or tablet . . . but rather on the discussion in front of them. They are focused on working together, drawing on their different experiences and knowledge, in order to generate an answer to the question that was posed. And these questions, which were designed before the meeting, are now real and urgent. They are about generating solutions to problems the whole group needs to address. The guy who grabbed the laptop computer at one table is asking one of the members if he understood her point correctly. The laptop simply provides a way for all of them to capture and transmit their ideas . . . so they can be rolled up. Looking around, you can see that every table is engaged in the discussion. Ideas are flying . . . and participants have never felt this level of energy before in a meeting.

Let's look more closely at each capability that the technology enables in virtuous meetings:

1. *Increases the number of people who can give feedback at once.* This capability is highly scalable. Since every table group can "speak at once" through the input on their tablets or laptops, the number of tables can be ten or a hundred or a thousand and the experience inside the table conversations will be the same.

2. *Makes giving the feedback instant.* No time is spent retrieving the input from the table groups. Whoever is synthesizing the input has immediate access to it as soon as the recorder at each table hits the Send button. No matter how large the room is (or in how many different geographic locations the group is distributed), all of the input is available immediately for synthesis.

3. *Captures the feedback in the participants' own words.* The fruits of the table group discussion are not simply choices from a preset list (multiple choice questions), they are the actual thoughts of the group expressed in their own words. This means that the ideas are uniquely their own, and there is a valuable level of nuance in how they are expressed. Also, it means there is sometimes an emotional tone to the input that is important to the discussion. Feelings as well as ideas are captured.

4. *Allows participants to include as much detail as is needed.* In this kind of software there is no set limit to how much text can be entered. Not only are the inputs from the groups recorded in their own words, they can also be whatever length is needed to capture the detail of what the group has discussed. Meeting designers can focus the questions more specifically to control the amount of detail that groups input on average. But there is no limit imposed by the technology.

5. *Accumulates the feedback instantly in a form that is easy to distill.* All of the ideas are immediately viewable as an organized database rather than more commonly on dozens of flipcharts or hundreds of sticky notes. The software is specifically designed to facilitate quick analysis among a team of synthesizers in real time. This real-time synthesis is what allows the participants to have a view of the ideation of the whole group, which allows them in turn to achieve a sense of shared understanding at the whole group level.

6. *Allows the feedback to be anonymous.* This aspect of the process is particularly useful in organizational meetings where there is a hierarchy among the participants or where some topics are difficult to discuss openly. Anonymity allows the ideas to come out to the whole group, so that they can be understood and considered, without those ideas being attached to certain groups or individuals. This allows large groups to address topics that were often avoided because there was no safe way to approach them. But these very topics may contain the greatest possibility for change and improvement.

7. *Allows shifting from whole group format to small group and back again in minutes, not hours.* Perhaps most important of all, this format-shifting capability is at the heart of participant-centered design in large meetings. We will explore it in depth in Part Two.

The advent of software for groups and meetings, labeled early on as *groupware,* came in the late 1980s. At that time, the software was designed to do everything imaginable—perhaps too much. It was complicated and required users to learn how to use it. After much experimentation, it became obvious that simplicity and "no learning curve" were essential qualities in software that was designed for meetings. The requests of clients and groups and the insights of facilitators over the past twenty years have directed us toward the most productive functions—those necessary for smooth integration with agendas that are difficult and tight.

What Software Needs to Do for Large Meetings

- Control participant screens from a central location
- Collect text comments, instantaneously, from up to hundreds of devices
- Collect poll scores
- Read other participants' data (switchable on or off)
- Organize data for optimal analysis of themes
- Present the group's raw data, themes from that data, or poll results

FRIENDLY SOFTWARE

"We don't want computers getting in the way of real dialogue." We have heard this from time to time and we often think, upon hearing it, (1) this person hasn't ever seen computers used in a group like we've described here, and (2) they can't imagine the benefits of convergence, no matter what they've heard, or (3) they've used a technology in a meeting that was designed or implemented poorly. The assertion begs a good conversation about what real dialogue is and how computers can actually help achieve it.

The purpose of any technology used inside a meeting aimed at convergence must be to promote and enhance real dialogue. The technology should be used as a harvesting mechanism, like flipcharts that "harvest" ideas spoken in a group onto paper. Computers make it easy to capture *and work with* dozens or hundreds of simultaneous small group discussions. So it is important that when any participant picks up an input device, whether it is a tablet, laptop, or smartphone, he or she knows what to do with it immediately and intuitively. There cannot be any question about what to do or even a pause in the flow of the discussion or train of thought.

In the 1990s, the central problem with almost all groupware software was that it was too complicated. Designers erroneously thought that by adding features the software would be sold more widely. It turned out that if it was difficult to use in a meeting, it wasn't used. Designers thought that if small groups entered their ideas into a network of laptops, this would be enough for smart people everywhere to intuitively understand the great value of doing so. This is not what happened, because the essential, thoughtful meeting design that would make it all work lagged far behind the giddy initial uptake of the technology.

User-friendliness was a principle that allowed the concept of technology-supported participant engagement to germinate. User-friendliness extends well past the actual manipulation of device and software . . . to the ease of approaching the task, understanding why it is important, and seeing how the results will move toward the mission of the meeting. It took the experience of hundreds of meetings supported by groupware before it became clear how important the overall process design and facilitation were, and how the use of technology had to be woven into the flow of the meeting with great care.

When we say the software must be user-friendly to serve the purpose of the virtuous meeting, we mean that

- It is easy to see what the focus of the activity is; the focal question is clear.
- It is easy to do the task; the instructions are simple and clear.
- It is intuitive to input text or polling scores.
- It is easy to read what others have written (optional, depending on design).
- It is easy to sort and analyze the whole group's data.
- It is easy to format data for projection to the group.
- It is easy to read the themes and poll results on the big screens.

Software that is designed for use in live face-to-face meetings, used by people whose attention is entirely elsewhere, *must* be very simple. If there are two hundred or two thousand participants in a large meeting and an input screen that is *not* simple and intuitive is sent to all input devices in the room, the negative feedback will be instantaneous. You will be overwhelmed with requests for help. You will have set up the group for wasting time and becoming frustrated. They will quickly devalue the opportunities for interaction that you have so painstakingly sold as a breakthrough. But this nightmare is easy to avoid.

Let's look at an example of how simple the actual screens need to be. In Figure 3.1, we see a common text feedback screen. Let's look carefully at its parts.

The title of each screen catches the eye first and anchors the screen to the task at hand. Below the title are the instructions. The goal there is to write simple instructions for each table exercise and its associated input screen *that will produce no questions!* So they must be succinct and complete, written and rewritten, checked with the facilitator or presenter, and rechecked. Normally, instructions are given first from the stage, but here on the screen they reinforce what was spoken for those who didn't hear it. It is also common for groups

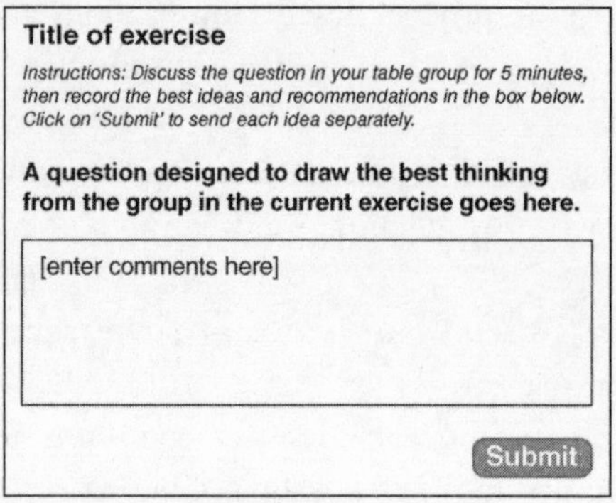

Figure 3.1 Text Feedback Screen

to get deep into discussion and then ask: What were we supposed to be doing? These on-screen instructions are vital for smooth running.

Below the instructions area comes the focusing question. In bolder font to stand out, this question will have been shaped throughout the agenda design process to yield the most satisfying table discussion, together with positive results for the organization. It may also have been modified just a minute earlier based on discoveries within the group only a few minutes before.

The text box is intuitive too: the screen arrives on all input devices with the cursor blinking in the box. Any participant can pick it up and begin to type. Finally, as the instructions point out, click on the big Submit button at bottom in order to send each comment. When you do, the screen refreshes and reappears with an empty text box . . . with the cursor blinking.

There are many different screens that can be used, some with voting, some that show the results for everyone to read in the room. But the principle is the same: Keep the interface as simple as possible. Any additional elements should have a compelling reason to be there.

THE INPUT DEVICES

The current range of input devices includes laptop computers, tablets, and smartphones. Each of these allows users to enter

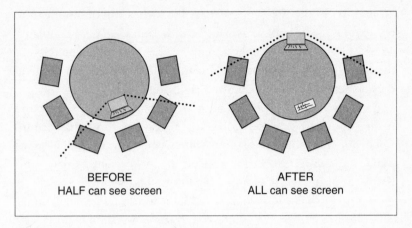

BEFORE
HALF can see screen

AFTER
ALL can see screen

Figure 3.2   Laptop Positioning Makes a Difference

text—the core capability required in participant-centered meetings—though with varying levels of ease. With built-in keyboards, laptops are the easiest for capturing text. And most are large enough for everyone to see what's being written, if positioned correctly. The well-known organization development consultant in France, Meryem Le Saget, had a flash of insight during a three-hundred-person leadership meeting when she suggested we add an external keyboard and position the laptop at each table on the far edge facing the table group, with its back to the stage (Figure 3.2).

When a keyboard is connected and operated across the table (see Figure 3.2, at right), the screen becomes much like a flipchart where everyone can see it, discuss it, and advise on making any changes on it. By simply adjusting the position of the laptop on each table, Meryem Le Saget had invented a way to increase the engagement of everyone in the room.

On the other hand, there are trade-offs. Laptops are the heaviest of the input devices, having a higher cost of renting, shipping, handling, powering, and charging. But this is addressed easily at the beginning of each design process.

Tablet computers have become the popular choice. With their smaller screen, it is more difficult to share what has been written on behalf of the group prior to sending it. But it is still possible. Tablets are light and much easier to both pass around the table and ship around the world. Also, their battery life means you do not need to run power to the tables, as you do with laptops. Their popularity across cultures is undeniable, and people are always delighted to use them—especially when they are designed effectively as a part of high-engagement, participant-centered processes.

Smartphones are rapidly becoming ubiquitous. It is tempting to promote and design feedback processes in very large groups when you know that at least every other person is carrying a smart-phone—a computer—in their purse or pocket. The cost for this hardware approach is significantly lower. And so when budget or logistical considerations make it difficult to use tablets or laptops, smartphones can be the solution. But there are significant design considerations to make them effective in a group setting.

With its tiny screen, a smartphone promotes personal-focused activities more than group-focused ones. Instructions from the stage must steer participants away from personal use of their phones for the duration of the clearly described group discussion segment. Processes favoring shorter, quicker answers are favored. It is also good practice to ask those who are inputting responses which represent the group to read out the response they've written and invite refinements before sending them. And so while sometimes the only choice, and that being sub-optimal, smartphones can be used carefully to support virtuous engagement processes.

Another type of input device is the polling keypad. Polling technology arrived during the 1980s—the earliest of the groupware offerings. These systems have become easy to set up and manage. Typically, each participant is given a small "clicker" device that has as many as ten buttons on it. At certain times, and cued from the big video screens, instructions are given and questions asked that can be answered with a push of a button. Scoring, for example, on numerical scales of 1–5 or 1–10, or voting yes/no, is quick and easy. Results are posted as soon as the polling is closed. It is interesting data to be sure, but it's also a narrow opportunity for input from participants. The "why" of each person's vote is left unanswered, while the aggregate score of the whole group stands firm alongside the question marks in people's minds. It's another example of a trade-off, here between simplicity and depth.

THE NETWORK: LOCAL OR INTERNET?

Choosing an input device goes hand in hand with the design and decisions about how the devices will be networked together. These days, devices are very reliable pieces of hardware. It is the quality of the network that will often determine technical success or failure.

There is a basic choice when planning for a successful network: a) using a "local" network, where the servers that provide the basic software are in the same room (or facility) as the input devices or b) using a "wide-area" network, where input devices are connecting to software through the Internet.

There is a simple way to make the best choice: go local, for the simple reason that you want to eliminate any technical risks in your meeting. A thirty-second slowdown or hiccup on a network during an event can feel like an eternity. And you want the focus of the participants to be on participating, not on the performance of technology.

This is why Covision has made a practice of setting up a local network whenever possible. Other benefits of a local network are that any technical issue can be quickly addressed in the moment, having backup systems ready to take over is an easier task, and the network is often more consistent and reliable than using the Internet and an in-house network provided by a venue.

So if a local network is so reliable and secure, why would you want to involve the Internet at all? There are some good reasons for sometimes choosing to use a wide-area network. You may have participants outside the meeting room that you want to link into the meeting. Or maybe you have multiple meeting rooms, in multiple cities, and you want all participants to be linked together. Covision calls this a "multi-site" meeting, which can be a powerful response in geographically dispersed problem-solving situations, but it does require very reliable Internet service. (See Chapter Twelve for more on this topic.)

You may also have a budget that won't support an in-room network and the technical team it often requires to set up and implement. It might be more economical to use the wireless Internet already in a venue to access the software. If participants are using their own devices and you want or need those devices to be online, then that too calls for utilizing the locally provided Internet and network. However it's important to factor into your process design the effect of distractions as participants will surely connect too with their email and social media.

A third option for the network is a hybrid between local and wide-area/internet networking. In this scenario, a local network is set up, with an onsite server to provide the best reliability for the meeting. But the server is also connected to the Internet so that data collected in the meeting can be shared with other people participating outside the room (Figure 3.3). This option provides the most flexibility.

NETWORKING IN VENUES

If you have chosen either a wide-area or hybrid network, then chances are you'll need to strongly consider the IT services of your venue as an important supplier. Replacing or supplementing the Internet provided at venues is possible, but doing so adds considerable cost.

Therefore, it is important to assess the available internet services at any venue under consideration. If the purpose of the meeting—in

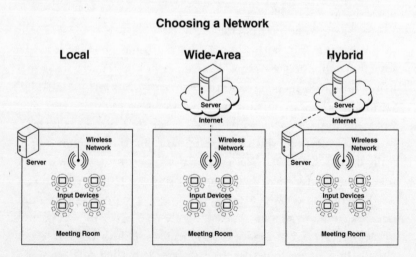

Figure 3.3 Three Types of Networks

terms of participation and engagement—demands it, then network capability and Internet availability should be an important factor in the decision. The following questions can help in this kind of assessment:

1. Does the venue have wireless internet services available in all the meeting rooms that will support the size of your group? Remember that your networking needs will be *concurrent*, meaning that all the participants will be accessing the network at exactly the same time. This is quite different from "normal" use, when people are accessing the Internet at different times.

2. Does the venue have onsite support that can troubleshoot any problem in the moment? Venues often outsource their IT departments, and sometimes the engineers are located in different cities or states and are only able to offer support remotely and intermittently. Ask the venue when they last had a major technical problem and how they solved it. Do they have backup systems in place?

3. If the venue does not have adequate Internet and support, can you supplement it with an external vendor? If the venue is open to this option, and the budget supports the resource, then internet and wireless networking services can be brought in temporarily for an event.

4. If the answer is no to all of the above, can you reconsider using a local network? If adequate wireless Internet is not available, the portable server scenario discussed earlier is your best (and only) option for connectivity. Ask yourself whether the reasons you want to use a wide-area network are a worthwhile trade-off for risking the success of the meeting. Often they are not, and you can leverage process workarounds to allow for the local solution.

5. Do you need the phone cellular network for processes in your meeting?

If you decide on using participant phones as the main input device, you may want to have robust cellular networking available in the meeting space. Phones can be connected to wireless Internet, but most often participants will default to the cellular network of their carrier. When this is the case, you want to be sure that the density of usage will not bring the network to a halt. Depending on the event and number of participants, cellular networks can be temporarily enhanced to get around usage limits and/or limited access to cell towers (i.e., for meeting spaces underground).

THE VIRTUE OF CONNECTIVITY IN LARGE GROUP MEETINGS

If the core of virtuous meetings is *connectivity,* or what is commonly called networking, what does that really mean for the people who are using the technology? It means that the participant's experience is enhanced—actually engaged—and that the whole group is in a much better position to fulfill the organization's objectives for the meeting. This is done by connecting each participant both to the presenters and to the group as a whole through a computer network that is designed, set up, and operated specifically for that meeting to deliver on that meeting's purpose. The technology connects everyone involved, sometimes even remotely. It is designed for it, and rather than asking participants to conform to the limitations of the technology, we design the technology with the goal of connecting everyone. There are many aspects to this connectivity, from technical to logistical to design and cost, but it may help to visualize a meeting that is optimized *for* connectivity. Figure 3.4 gives us a good visual starting point.

This meeting is set up for completely engaging 138 of an organization's brightest and best, who are in hot pursuit of the most difficult and challenging issues facing the organization in a time frame that is too short. It is likely that you have been in a meeting room like this, with the stage in front and the big video screens up high, but let's look at the things that make it different from what you may have experienced.

First, there is a wireless tablet computer on each of the tables that serves as the table group's input device for use during the interactive

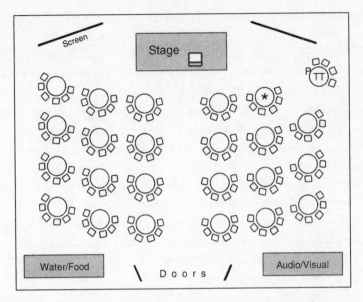

Figure 3.4 A Large Meeting Room, Designed for Virtuous Connectivity

segments. One member may volunteer to do the writing or that task may be passed around. The screens they interact with are like those we've just seen for capturing ideas and polls.

"TT" is the Theme Team table. As mentioned earlier, this is the hub of the designed interactivity. The Participant Engagement Designer sits there, along with two to four members of the client organization who have been specially chosen and invited to contribute their skills and knowledge of the material in the task of distilling. The specialist coaches these team members and guides their work as they use software tools and discussion to quickly make sense of volumes of data from the whole group and then distill the main messages for use in the interactive dialogues. It is these "meta-conversations" that the Theme Team enables that distinguish virtuous meetings from other meeting concepts and that distinguish virtuous meetings from all others. We will discuss the role and responsibilities of this team at length in Chapter Ten.

On the Theme Team table is one laptop computer for each team member, one laptop that controls all the input devices, and another laptop whose screen image is switched occasionally to the big video screens in the room. Under the table is "P," the printer. With as much data, creativity, insight, and good ideas that come from meetings like this, there are frequent requests for printouts. And having the printer literally at your feet is the best position.

Finally, the asterisk (*) marks the ideal seating location for the meeting owner and other executives and presenters. This element is more important than it may appear at first. The position is close to both the stage and the Theme Team table. There are often moments in large meetings when short huddles are needed; for example, for timing adjustments or process refinements. Having the meeting leaders and process leaders near each other saves time and angst when situations beg for quick responses and improvements.

ACTUALLY . . . IT'S NOT ABOUT THE TECHNOLOGY

Technology provides capability. What is needed and what a technology can provide is interesting, but how the capability is fitted carefully to the need makes all the difference. As we know, technologies are pushed on us as new products and, as consumers, we consume them. Sadly, careful attention in applying those technologies after the sale is frequently lacking. We hope we have made it clear that technologies for meetings are a special case. They *require* careful attention. In live meetings, technology can provide disappointments and process breakdowns just as easily as it can provide breakthroughs of insight and learning. With full attention on a meeting's context and objectives, its process design, and the experience of the participant, certain technologies, if well applied, will enable quantum jumps in productivity.

Technology, no matter the type, is a tool. It does not create understanding on its own, just as a telephone does not create conversation. It simply sits there awaiting your inspiration and your impulse to call someone. *Meeting technology* refers to a set of tools that allow for shifting into small group discussion and back to a large group format in short time frames. *Meeting connectivity* is about using this tool to change the way you hold meetings.

> **Meeting connectivity**—a communication capability that allows for shifting into small group discussion and back to a large group format in short time frames.

This new connectivity facilitates harvesting the thoughts from all of the small group discussions. But when and how you make those shifts makes all the difference. This is what makes the agenda design process so interesting and vital.

POLLING VERSUS DISCUSSION:
A Case Study In Why You Can't Have One Key Without the Other

Let's look more closely at the necessity of connecting the two keys of connectivity and the participant-centered approach by examining anonymous polling. This kind of polling has been enabled by technological connectivity, and it has become a common way of making a large meeting "interactive." Or so it seems. Polling definitely serves a purpose in large meetings. However, it cannot accomplish some of the key goals of the virtuous meeting, which instead uses discussions enabled by the participant-centered approach.

Polling is one tool that can be used in the pursuit of a more inclusive meeting experience or to find common ground. But polling does not *generate* anything. Polling gives a snapshot of people's preferences at a given moment across a predetermined set of options. So you don't *find* common ground by polling, you only test or establish it. In the pursuit of convergence, as is the goal in a virtuous meeting, polling is a step toward closure. That is, if you assume you have identified the extent of your options, then a poll will show where people stand in relation to those specific options.

A result of that step may be that you see that you have to revisit the topic, so you are thrown back into the discussion. But the poll itself is only the end of some intermediate process of determining what can be voted on—what options are on the table.

In terms of large group meetings, that means that there is a world of difference between whether the group came up with the options that are going to be polled, or whether the options were defined by some other group or individual in advance of the group meeting. Carolyn Lukensmeyer, who shepherded the creation of the 21st Century Town Hall Large Group Method, was very clear about the limits of polling. In her book *Bringing Citizens' Voices to the Table*, she frames it in terms of public opinion polls. But her points are exactly the same for polling in large group meetings. "Polls do nothing to help individuals grasp and wrestle with an issue's complexity. They don't help people to understand [each others'] views or provide them with an opportunity to develop creative, common ground solutions to significant problems. Finally, polls fail to energize [people] to stand by their opinions or to do their part to make the tough trade-offs embedded in [difficult] decisions."[3]

So while it is relatively easy, and more common, to poll the participants in large meetings, the limits of the function of polling have to be understood. Polling provides an essential view into how everyone is feeling about the destination reached at the end of the journey to find common ground. But polling should not be mistaken for the journey itself—the far tougher task is *finding* the common ground. Polling cannot replace the exciting back-and-forth energy of the small group conversations that are the essence of the participant-centered approach—and the element that takes the group to a new place of understanding.

C CHAPTER THREE • QUICK SUMMARY

- While the evolution of meeting process design has been slow, the adoption of any technology that could transform the routine style of meetings has been even slower.
- Experiments with different technologies in the large group meeting have been flying under the radar for a couple of

decades—driven by the possibility of quantum leaps in whole group communication.

- The technology tools at the center of participant-centered meetings allow for (1) any number of small table groups to input their ideas simultaneously, (2) small group input to be collected in a way that makes it possible for a specially tasked team to distill it in a very short time, and (3) statements of distilled input to be formatted easily for quick presentation back to the group on the large video screens.
- Of the seven capabilities enabled by interactive meeting technologies, the most important is this: It enables shifting from a whole group format to small group and back again in minutes, not hours.
- The software in a large meeting needs to be tuned to the process of the meeting.

Case Story 1: Listening to the City—Rebuilding Lower Manhattan after 9/11

CASE STORY

Let's look at one example of a meeting that exemplifies the virtuous concept in that it used connectivity and the participant-centered approach to create convergence. The example is a meeting that occurred back in 2002 in the aftermath of the demolition of the three buildings at the World Trade Center. The meeting came about as the plans were being made for how to rebuild the site. Tremendous economic forces were at play. The rebuilding would cost tens of billions of dollars, and decisions had to be made about how to spend that money and what to build.

Huge commercial interests weighed in almost immediately. But there were other, less prominent stakeholders as well. Many residents of the immediate area were impacted. And they came from across the income spectrum. Many were low income. There were many small local businesses that were shut down and had to find a way to reopen. And the families of the victims of 9/11 were very concerned about what kind of memorial would be built to honor those who had died.

These less prominent stakeholders were not having much influence on the plans that were being considered. Primarily the commercial interests were driving the discussion, the plans, and, ultimately it seemed, the decisions.

So the question at that point was: How can we give all of these stakeholders a seat at the table in planning how to rebuild Lower Manhattan? Individually, each of these noncommercial stakeholders was insignificant. But collectively, if they could speak with a unified voice, they hoped to influence the plans. They wanted Lower Manhattan to be rebuilt as a place that was a livable mix of residential and commercial property, that retained the iconic magnitude of its former status, and that enshrined a meaningful memorial to those who had lost their lives at that site.

But of course, how could thousands of people, who didn't even know each other—though they might have lived or worked only a few blocks from each other—come to speak with a unified voice? One unlikely scenario would be to have a one-day meeting and craft a unified counterproposal to the plans that were already on the drawing board.

Such an outcome could never be imagined if you thought of 4,500 diverse citizens in a typical town hall–style meeting: crammed into rows of seats, facing a distant stage with random individuals getting up with a microphone and asking a question or making a comment to whoever was leading the meeting from the front of the room. Hours would go by. No one would have a chance to agree on anything. And people would wander away more disempowered than ever. And there would be no change to the direction that the commercial interests were driving.

But a dedicated, highly disciplined band of inventive democracy proponents had a different vision. AmericaSpeaks, the ambitious nonprofit founded by Carolyn Lukensmeyer, took on the challenge of wresting a unified voice from 4,500 New Yorkers in one day. The meeting was called Listening to the City, and the participants included a highly diverse and representative group in terms of race, age, income, and residence. And many of the participants' lives were directly impacted by the events of 9/11 (Figure CS1.1).

Here is how it unfolded . . .

When the participants entered the meeting room, they saw an endless sea of tables spread out over an area larger than two football fields. In the center of the space was a raised stage and above it four huge megatron video screens. They formed a giant

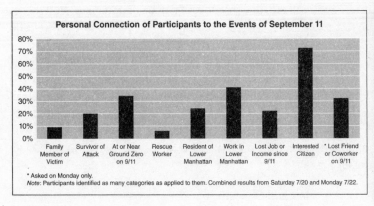

Figure CS1.1 Personal Connections to September 11[1]

cube of video for close-ups of the speakers on stage, who, to the naked eye, were just tiny figures in the distance.

But the focus wasn't primarily on the speakers on the distant stage in the center of the space. The focus was on the 450 round tables, where each participant would spend the day in discussion with eight other fellow New Yorkers and a trained process facilitator.

The groups at the tables were mixed. At a single table, there might be city planners, low-income residents from the surrounding neighborhoods, developers, and small business owners from the area, as well as family members of those who had died at Ground Zero.

Throughout the day, topics were presented from the stage in the center of the space, and participants took thirty or forty-five minutes in their table group to discuss the choices and frame their thoughts about the issue. The thoughts that arose at the tables were then typed into a networked laptop computer at the table and were seen immediately by a dedicated synthesizing group on one side of the hall.

In order to synthesize the input from 450 tables in real time, AmericaSpeaks and Covision put together a synthesizing team that consisted of four subteams of six members each. Each subteam monitored the data flow from a certain part of the hall and fed their preliminary syntheses to a three-person finalizing team. That team looked at the synthesis from all four of the subteams and crafted final themes that captured the ideas and feelings of the whole group. The synthesizing group received thoughts from all 450 tables in real time and worked furiously to craft brief, meaningful statements that captured the choices, feelings, and intentions of the 4,500 participants.

What the group was responding to were *concept plans*—plans that had already been drawn up before the meeting and that were largely influenced by, and oriented toward, the large commercial interests at play. The plans were distributed at all of the tables so that the participants could discuss and respond to them. The meeting was structured so that participants at the tables could give input in seven major areas:

- Hopes and Concerns
- Advice to Planners (About the Concept Plans)

- Economic Development and Employment
- Housing and Civic Amenities
- Transportation
- Memorial Mission Statement
- Memorial

As an example, in the afternoon the participants were asked: Keeping in mind your hopes and concerns about rebuilding [these had been identified and prioritized by the whole group earlier in the day], what advice would you give to the planners about . . .

1. The features you like about the [architectural] program and why?
2. The features you don't like about the program and why not?
3. Other strongly held views?

Participants were given forty-five minutes to discuss it at their tables and to send their thoughts through the laptop to the synthesizing team.

As the question was discussed by 450+ groups out in the main space, the synthesizing group looked through 2,686 comments, trying to discern what was important to the group as a whole. As they read through the input, several concerns began to emerge. People wanted to preserve the footprint of the original buildings. They wanted an extended promenade and ways of making the site pedestrian friendly. They wanted more nonoffice uses.

One of the concerns that showed up repeatedly was about the physical stature of the new structures and the symbolism of the aesthetics. The participants were shown seven different schemas for how Ground Zero might be rebuilt. Figure CS1.2 shows one of the seven schemas.

There were many, many comments that came in addressing the design schemas, and they largely pointed in the direction of a remake. For example:

- Don't be afraid of heights
- No more rectangular column–shaped buildings; let's break out of the box, renew the skyline

Figure CS1.2 View of Ground Zero Proposal[2]

- No signature skyline in any of the plans
- Uninspiring
- Memorial Plaza: looks like any building in any city; lacks distinctive identity
- Buildings are too short and dumpy looking
- None have a clear NYC signature, visually speaking
- Strong feelings that buildings should be taller, skyline enhanced and restored

When the discussion period was over and everyone focused back on the megatron screens in the center of the room, the synthesis that was presented to them included statements about the physical stature of the buildings:

"Buildings should be visually interesting to the skyline."
"Schemas are not ambitious enough—buildings are too short."
"Nothing here is truly monumental."
"Looks like Albany."

The final quintessential sentiment, "Looks like Albany," spoke the poetic truth for the 4,500 New Yorkers in the room and dominated the national media the next day. It had come from simple input from one of the tables, *"Memorial Plaza: looks too much like Albany state government buildings — bland."* But magnified by the clapping and laughter of the 4,500 in the room and broadcast across the country by the media, it was enough to put the brakes on the designs under consideration at the time, and the Lower Manhattan Development Corporation reluctantly took their ideas back to the drawing board. In mid-August, planning officials for the site indicated that they would invite more architects to submit designs.

The meeting that day was a series of this kind of cycle. One of the areas would be introduced, the participants would discuss it at their tables, they would send in their thoughts and ideas, and the synthesizing group would create a statement that captured the essence of what the whole group was saying. The final part of the cycle was that the group would be invited to vote, as individuals, on each of the statements. Everyone in the room had a small hand-held device, like a TV remote control, with which they could cast their individual vote. In this way, the degree of unity could be gauged, and the highest priorities of the 4,500 could be identified.

The unimaginable had been accomplished. In one day this highly diverse group was able to find its voice. Key statements were . . .

1. Develop clear strategies for attracting people back to the city and Lower Manhattan to live, work, and play.
2. Broaden the plan to include all forms of infrastructure, including communications, water, sewer, and technology.
3. Develop a human development plan: physical and metal health issues, posttraumatic counseling for adults and children, child care, housing issues including homelessness.
4. Create an environmental health agenda addressing air quality, hazardous materials, recycling, and green building issues.
5. Ensure that mixed-use plans include public facilities, for example, schools, other education facilities, and child care.
6. Balance quality-of-life and commercial interests.

The unity of the voice was confirmed when 80 percent of the participants responded at the end of the day that they were Satisfied

Figure CS1.3 What Was Finally Built—Not Looking Like Albany Anymore[3]

or Highly Satisfied with the work they had done. And in the end, twelve years later in 2014, the design of the completed buildings embodied the yearnings of the group that had met that day (see Figure CS1.3).

Case Story 2: A Global Manufacturing Organization

CASE STORY

The participant-centered approach utilizing high-speed connectivity can be used in many different kinds of meetings. On the surface the meetings may look very different from one another—the size may be different, the purpose, the type of participants, the flow of the agenda, the content—but what they share is a drive toward convergence and a focus on making the participants active contributors to the process and outcomes of the meeting. Let's look at an agenda segment from a meeting that is completely different from Listening to the City—a senior leadership meeting. This is the kind of meeting that is very typical for large organizations all over the world, and generally is designed as a front-of-the-room-centered meeting, focused almost solely on presentations.

As an innovation company that's been lauded as a "best place to work," the organization that we'll be looking at has been a strong adopter of the participant-centered approach using connectivity. They first experimented with the approach in 2011 at the urging of the senior organization development executive for their global manufacturing division. They originally brought Covision in for their large Technical Leadership Conference, held in January to set the direction for the coming year. This meeting brought together 175 leaders from around the globe, representing several business and support functions.

After two years of designing those meetings as participant-centered meetings with high-speed connectivity, the results were so successful that the same approach began to be used at the leadership meetings of the different functions within global manufacturing and at special meetings of the heads of the manufacturing sites from around the world. Since then it has also been used at the top global leadership meetings for the product development division and the global procurement division.

The adoption of this approach continues to spread across the different parts of the organization. Engaging participants as active contributors in their top leadership meetings is helping to drive core goals at this organization, for whom innovation is key. As the senior organization development leader puts it, "We're an innovation company. It's absolutely essential for us to be innovative."[1] They put a lot of thought into what it will take to have an empowered and collaborative workforce. And they put a lot of care into how they bring their leaders together.

The participant-centered approach allows top leadership meetings to become catalysts for improving cultural norms, by helping with complex issues of participation, democratization, and transparency. In a post-meeting interview, the organization development leader said:

> First it helps us create more participation. In many ways I think organizational experiences in big corporations, particularly in an organization such as ours with eighty thousand people around the planet, are often antithetical to participation. It helps us create more democracy in our organization. People can see that they have an opinion that matters. Leaders have access and insight. People feel a different sense of citizenship in the organization. And it also helps us at the same time with increasing transparency in the organization, because we live in a time where if it can be found out, it will be found out.[2]

Another part of the story is that this organization has put a lot of effort into being a "best place to work," and they have consistently ranked very high in independent assessments of companies worldwide. They place a high priority on sustaining these accolades. But they are beginning to take that momentum and turn it toward the business in new ways. The OD leader has said, "We're moving into a new organizational paradigm, which is, How do we also create a place where people can do their *best* work? And I think when we are able to get out the participant's ideas, particularly those in leadership positions through these large leadership meetings, we're really enabling more of our best work, which then feeds into our innovation."[3]

Adopting high-speed connectivity and the participant-centered approach for senior leadership meetings does not mean scrapping everything you know about meeting design and never doing a presentation again. But it does mean being very precise with the design of each agenda block, and keeping a participant-centered perspective on the activities and outcomes that you are choosing. Let's look at an agenda segment from an early senior leadership meeting that we did with the organization's global technical division as an example.

The agenda segment we'll look at was called Focus on Quality. It had two parts, called Mindset Shifts and Ready for the Next Wave. The company at this time was doing very well and had the best pipeline of potential new products in the industry. In the past year, however, there had been a major, significant, unexpected breakdown at one of the manufacturing sites, from which the company was still working to recover. And in a recent engagement survey, "Effective leadership" and "Ability to make employees feel valued" had come up as low scores relative to the rest of the survey. These shortcomings had the potential to exacerbate the effects of the manufacturing site break-down on morale within the organization if they were not addressed.

In the structure of the meeting, Joanne, the head of Quality, had about two hours, minus a fifteen-to thirty-minute break, to address these quality issues with the organization's extended leadership and try to take the organization down a different and better path for the coming year.

In a traditional front-of-the-room-centered meeting, this would probably have meant

- 30–45 minutes for a presentation detailing what's wrong and what the new direction should be
- 10–20 minutes for the speaker to answer questions from the floor
- A coffee break
- Perhaps 20–30 minutes to have some breakout discussions in adjoining rooms, each involving 25 to 50 participants, depending on the number of breakout rooms

The agenda for the front-of-the-room approach is shown in Table CS2.1.

Because they chose a participant-centered approach, the two-hour section on quality unfolded very differently.

- For the participants, almost half of that two-hour period was spent in active discussion.

Table CS2.1 Front-of-the-Room Agenda

Time	Agenda Topic	Speaker
2:20–3:05	Quality: Looking Back, Looking Forward	Joanne
3:05–3:15	Q&A (Mics in audience)	Joanne
3:15–3:25	Set up task for breakouts and transition to breakout rooms	Jaime
3:25–3:50	Breakouts (approx. 35 participants each)	Alexander 1,2, and 3 Hibiscus 3 and 4
3:50–4:15	Break and transition back to plenary	
4:15–4:30	Report-outs from breakout groups (2 minutes each) Recap	Jaime Joanne

- For the senior leaders, a substantial part of that two-hour period was spent reading input from the table discussions and learning what the participants were thinking.

And the agenda looked very different with the participant-centered approach. The leaders were able to frame the topic, present the issues, give their analysis of the underlying causes, and propose possible solutions. But they did not have to dominate the agenda to do so. The leaders gave very brief and succinct presentations framing the issue and some of the causes. Then they listened to what the group was saying and responded to underlying causes that were identified and possible actions and solutions that were put forward. Plus, no time was spent moving back and forth to breakout rooms.

The agenda for Joanne's segment in Table CS2.2 tracks the structure of the virtuous meeting approach. It tracks what the presenter(s) are doing, both when they are presenting and while the group is in small discussions at their tables. It tracks what the participants are doing: Are they listening or are they in conversation? It also tracks what the synthesizers are doing, when they are listening to the presenter, and when they are reading through the participants' input.

Table CS2.2 Participant-Centered Agenda

Time	Segment	Front of Room	Participants	Synthesizers
2:20 (15)	Mind-set Shifts John P.	Joanne's presentation	Listen	Listen
2:35 (10)	Mind-set Shifts: Small Group Activity	Small groups respond to question *What bold step do we need to take to improve reliability in delivering quality supply to end customers?* Joanne reads input as it comes in.	Participate in small group (three person) discussions.	Scan responses for themes. Keep this data for later use.
2:45 (30)	Reaching Full Engagement	1. Joanne reviews and comments on Bold Steps. 2. She brings Gustav to the stage. 3. Gustav's presentation.	Listen	Listen
3:15 (60)	Reaching Full Engagement: Small Group Work	Gustav sets up table group work (questions below). 1. *In what ways can we reach full engagement through the org? What's the next level of thinking we need to reach in our group?* 2. *Specifically, how can we support the global network in reaching full engagement? How do we foster network thinking?* 3. *What unique contribution can we each make to establishing a mind-set of engrained quality?*	Discuss in groups of six. Include a self-managed break.	Review table group submissions. Create themes for each question.
4:15 (15)	Ready for the Next Wave	1. Gustav reviews themes from the table group discussions with the whole group. 2. Gustav, Joanne, and Surjeet respond to the group's ideas.	Listen	Project themes up on the screen in the front of the room.

2:20. Joanne speaks for about fifteen minutes. Her presentation highlights where things have gone wrong. But it also ties into the engagement survey numbers and the key areas, especially in the discord between the senior leadership team and the extended senior leadership, where the organization needs to improve. After this condensed presentation, participants at the tables break into groups of three and are asked to discuss: What bold step do we need to take to improve reliability in delivering quality supply to end customers?

2:35. Because the discussion groups are small, each participant has plenty of chances to talk. They can focus on what the other two are saying and have time to pursue the different points of view that each of them is holding. Even in the short ten-minute discussion, they are able to go beyond their off-the-top-of-the-head responses and work to find promising answers. And they are having these real-life application discussions with people in the organization that they aren't normally in frequent contact with. This is a catalyst not only for bold action in improving reliability, but also for building trust and rapport among the small group members. Ninety-eight responses come in during the ensuing discussion at the tables, including comments like these:

> Enforce a "freedom to speak up" environment. Means that the "don't whine" can have adverse consequences. It discourages people speaking up.

> Reduce capacity utilization, more idle capacity: improves flexibility, huge sign to the organization.

> Really invest in addressing the vulnerabilities in products that we already know. Resource and empower people to be able to fix the problems. We do well with starting initiatives, but we struggle with finishing them due to resource constraint and focus.

2:45. Joanne comes back on stage and asks to scroll the answers that the groups have submitted up on the large screen at the front of the room. As they slowly scroll, the group gets to see the kinds of steps that their peers have been thinking about.

While the table groups had been discussing the question, Joanne was reading their answers as they sent them in. Now she points out particular ones that she noted and talks about them in the context of what the senior management team is thinking. Joanne scrolls through about the first third of the responses. She lets the participants know that all of the input will be mined after the meeting to help choose priority actions for improving reliability, and then shifts to the next presentation.

Joanne invites Gustav, head of one of the main manufacturing businesses within the organization, up onto the stage. Gustav is another member of the senior leadership team, and his goal is to give the participants a view of what he sees playing out at the manufacturing sites. And he wants to demonstrate that he and Joanne are aligned on how to improve quality at the sites going forward.

He gives a presentation about quality from the business side and talks about the application of the senior leadership team's current thinking to the manufacturing sites and the challenge of engagement among the people working there. His presentation is also relatively short. Then the participants are asked to discuss three questions at their tables:

1. In what ways can we reach full engagement throughout the organization? What's the next level of thinking we need to reach in our individual function?

2. Specifically, how can we support the global network (partners, other functions, etc.) in reaching full engagement? How do we foster network thinking?

3. What unique contribution can we each make to establishing a mind-set of engrained quality and network thinking?

3:15. The participants have heard the senior leadership perspective on how to improve engagement, and now they begin to hear what their peers are thinking about it. The participants have about an hour for discussion and are asked to take a self-managed break. While the participants are in discussion, the synthesizers read through the answers that are being submitted and synthesize all of the input into one slide of themes for each question.

Joanne, and the two heads of the main manufacturing businesses, Gustav and Surjeet, also read through the small group input as it comes in during the discussion period. They get to see what the group is thinking. Whether the responses are a huge surprise or exactly as expected, what might have been assumptions are transformed into something real.

For the organization, false assumptions on the part of the leaders, or differences of opinion between the executive leadership and the extended leadership, which might have remained unknown or been swept under the rug, are exposed and there is an opportunity to rectify these assumptions and arrive at a shared understanding.

4:15. When the small group discussion time is over, these three executives get up in front of the room as a panel. The slides synthesized from the group's answers are projected for the room. In answer to the second question—*Specifically, how can we support the global network in reaching full engagement? How do we foster network thinking?*—the synthesis of key ideas that were gleaned from the table group discussions were

- Shift focus from cost to quality and compliance
- Engrained quality is not a Quality and Operations task— should be understood and talked about by all functions, and across the organization
- Share best practices, lessons learned, and talent (rotational assignments)
- Develop a common understanding of "network" and network thinking. Improve the link between Development and Manufacturing to help preserve and transfer product knowledge (i.e., "Keep Dev representatives on the team longer and be more integrated with Mfg.")

The short list of statements, synthesized from all of the groups' comments, gives Joanne, Gustav, and Surjeet something concrete to respond to. The participants, as a team, reading the synthesized ideas and hearing the executives' responses, begin to achieve a shared understanding of how they want to promote engagement across the global network. This shared understanding creates both a palpable feeling of alignment and a practical foundation for trust between the executive leadership and the extended leadership.

The opportunity for building trust and rapport focuses on the actual business issues facing the organization. This is in contrast to front-of-the-room-centered meetings where, because the participants spend the meeting time as a passive audience, the opportunities for building trust and rapport have to be focused on networking socials or team building activities.

For the participants, the experience of this approach was enlivening, creative, and productive. Two-thirds of the participants scored the meeting a 5 out of 5, and the other third gave it a 4 out of 5. Their comments in the meeting evaluation showed their appreciation of the new format. Here's a sampling:

- "The feedback system was great, eliminating the tedious table report-out sessions."
- "Better team feel than last year. The usage of the tablet and the option to participate via the feedback session was absolutely great."
- "Good mix of topics, very efficient use of technology."
- "Loved the tablet report-outs rather than table group report-outs!"
- "I liked the moving around of seating as it led to meeting new colleagues."
- "I was pleased with the level of candor."

The virtuous meeting has created a participant experience that is becoming integral to the organization's work processes. "One of the changes is that many of our leaders now, particularly in our global manufacturing organization, wouldn't dare to hold a meeting without really considering how we involve participants," Mike explained. "Even beyond the large senior leadership meetings, it's creating (whether they have technology in the room or not) much more of a process in the organization whereby any leaders, when they're holding meetings, make sure that they have got process for honoring participation, democratization, transparency."

PART TWO

ANCHORING VIRTUOUS MEETINGS

CHAPTER FOUR

THE USE OF SMALL GROUPS WITHIN LARGE GROUP MEETINGS

In Part One, we introduced the concept of virtuous meetings and explained how they are different from the much more common front-of-the-room-focused meetings. Before going on to the details of designing this kind of meeting, we want to ground you in a couple of concepts that will allow you to understand the mechanics behind the process. In Part One, we introduced the two keys to convergence in large meetings: the participant-centered approach, and the use of high-speed connectivity. Combining these two elements lets us conduct the meeting simultaneously on two levels. In a front-of-the-room meeting, it is assumed that there is one level of communication—the large group level—and that everyone is hearing the same thing, at the same time, and processing it in the same way. In a virtuous meeting, a second level—where participants spend time in small table group discussions—is integrated with the large group level. This chapter is about designing the integration of the small group level with the large group level. Chapter Five is about using a four-stage Virtuous Engagement Cycle model to design agenda segments that will move effectively between these levels to produce convergent outcomes.

TWO INTEGRATED LEVELS OF PARTICIPANT EXPERIENCE

A primary attribute of virtuous meetings is that the whole group has a shared understanding about the topics that are the focus of the meeting. The key to building that shared understanding is to provide two integrated levels of participant experience in the meeting. When we say "two levels of participant experience," we mean that the participant is a member of two different groups during the meeting: she is a member of both the plenary—the whole large group that has been brought together for the meeting—and a small table group within the plenary, which consists of three to ten participants seated together around a table in the plenary (Figure 4.1).

At certain times within an agenda segment, the participants are focused on the plenary level, and at other times the participants' attention and activity are focused on the table group level. The achievement of shared understanding in a large group depends on harnessing the conversations of the participants in their small table groups. It also depends on being able to share the essence of those conversations with the whole group. This chapter is about understanding that each member of the group is being engaged on two levels—as a member of the whole and as a member of a table group. Knowing the mechanics of how each level works and how they interact with each other is essential to making detailed design decisions for virtuous meetings.

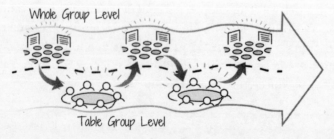

Figure 4.1 Two Levels of a Participant's Experience

What Works in Highly Engaged Small Teams

As we try to expand our imagination around what is possible to achieve in a large meeting, we need a model for what we are trying to create. Robust, small team meetings provide the best model. In this model, the basic elements of highly engaged small group conversations are ideation, exchange, and shared understanding. In small team meetings shared understanding is always seen as a desirable goal, and everyone in the meeting assumes that this goal will be achieved. The essence of a good small team meeting is effective, productive conversation. Let's begin by unlocking the recipe for the conversations that happen in a highly functional small team. What are the constituent elements? How would we define them?

Ideation refers to the individual creative activity of having an insight, or dreaming up an idea. This can happen quite spontaneously, almost from nowhere, or it can happen as a result of stimulation by others in the group. It can also be an idea that has been sitting on the shelf—possibly for years—just waiting to be brought out and passed around in the right conversation.

Exchange is the activity of presenting your own ideas, feelings, and reactions and listening to others present theirs. Exchange is the give and take of team discussion: the group digestion that occurs and that in turn produces greater ideation. Ideation and exchange are the hallmarks of a robust small team discussion, the act of bringing forth your passions, opinions, and insights and allowing others to bring forth theirs within the context of a creative, constructive conversation.

What comes out of that small team discussion may be a decision, a refinement of direction, a schedule or an action plan, or even a whole new concept. But regardless of what the end product of the discussion is, what comes out for all the team members is a sense of *shared understanding.* Whatever product came out of the discussion, all team members got to know what everyone else was thinking about: they became aware of each other's positions and preferences. All of their subsequent discussions are going to be informed by the things that were said in this discussion. The team as a whole is getting smarter and more integrated.

Whether or not there is complete consensus in the end, shared understanding is always the most valuable product of a small team discussion. It is the root of all alignment and ownership. And it is wrought in the warm fires of ideation and exchange. It is the natural by-product of creative small team discussions.

Can Shared Understanding Be Achieved in Large Groups?

Given the definitions above, the big question then is: Can shared understanding be achieved at all in a large or very large group? The answer to that question is the fundamental premise for this book. It may seem as simple as mapping a small group process onto the large group—having the members of the large group go through the same kind of ideation and exchange with each other that would lead to shared understanding (the "processing" that small groups go through). But the simple fact is that *this processing can't happen at the large group level because of the sheer number of participants and the limitations on the group's time.*

> The goal of virtuous meetings is to use ideation and exchange in the large group in order to produce shared understanding in the large group. If it was a small group, that would be done through group discussion. But it can't realistically be achieved through whole group discussion in a large or very large group.

It can, however, happen in a *virtuous* large group meeting that engages two levels simultaneously. The virtuous large group meeting solves the dilemma of how to have ideation, exchange, and shared understanding by (1) accepting that this can't happen in a single whole group discussion in the plenary, and (2) realizing that it can happen if participants are in two groups at the same time, in the same room. They are in the small groups in which they generate their thoughts and exchange their ideas, *and at the same time,* they are in the plenary group where they find out what everyone else is thinking.

The virtuous meeting creates a meta-conversation in which participants at small tables engage with the presenters in front of the room (we'll explore more on meta-conversations in Chapter Five).

Virtuous meetings need to engage participants at two levels in the same meeting—as members of the whole large group and as members of the small table groups. This is the fundamental, oddly counterintuitive requirement for creating shared understanding in large and very large groups.

How the Two Levels Work

You will see in the illustrations below (Figure 4.2 and Figure 4.3) that it is indeed possible to achieve shared understanding in a large or a very large group. Moving the participants back and forth between the two levels accomplishes this. For the participants it is easy. They just sit at their table. At times their focus is directed toward the stage, and at times it is directed to those at the table. The facilitator or presenter directs them when to change their focus.

A table group discussion is always oriented around a focused, topical question, and the group's task is to come up with answers to submit to the whole group. So the participants go through a process of generating shared responses that roughly converges all of their thinking toward a few possible answers.

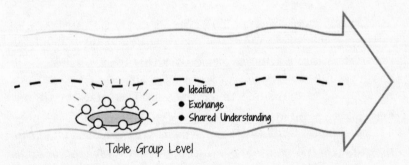

- Ideation
- Exchange
- Shared Understanding

Table Group Level

Ideation: The actual ideas (solutions, questions, etc.) are born here. This is the incubator. The group is small enough that each participant gets to contribute.

Exchange: Because the group is so small, it is easy and fast to exchange ideas with each other and try each other's ideas on for size. And the exchange sparks new ideas.

Shared Understanding: Because everyone is speaking up, each participant fairly quickly comes to understand what the others are thinking.

Figure 4.2 What Happens in the Table Group

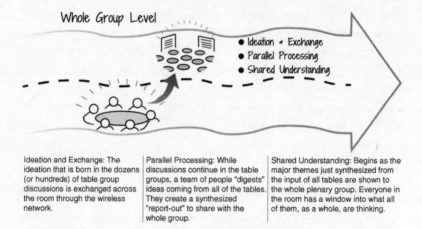

Ideation and Exchange: The ideation that is born in the dozens (or hundreds) of table group discussions is exchanged across the room through the wireless network.	Parallel Processing: While discussions continue in the table groups, a team of people "digests" ideas coming from all of the tables. They create a synthesized "report-out" to share with the whole group.	Shared Understanding: Begins as the major themes just synthesized from the input of all tables are shown to the whole plenary group. Everyone in the room has a window into what all of them, as a whole, are thinking.

Figure 4.3   What Happens in the Large Group

The shared understanding at the large group level is accomplished by the combination of three elements:

- The shared understanding that has already taken place in the individual table groups
- The synthesis of the themes that provides the window into what all of the groups were saying
- The reaction and perspective of the presenter in response to what the groups were saying

The table group discussions—The time spent in constructive conversation in the table group clarifies each person's thoughts about the topic. Then through the exchange of ideas and viewpoints, each person at the table begins to see what is shared and where the common ground and the differences lie. This prepares all the participants to entertain what the whole group might be thinking.

The synthesized themes—When the themes from all the table group discussions get presented, the nuance and detail of what the group as a whole was thinking enriches everything that was experienced in the table group discussions. Each person can begin to see where they "fit" into the bigger picture that is emerging.

The presenter's response to—What the group has "said" provides a reality check on the understanding that is emerging, particularly in organizations that have a hierarchical structure. That reality check grounds the shared understanding that is emerging and further eliminates guesswork or assumptions about where the group is headed.

The key to developing shared understanding in the large group is that these changes between levels take place during the course of an agenda segment. During the time allotted for a given topic, the participants move into and out of the table group level. This is the time frame that allows groups to go through multiple topics in a day. Convergence begins to build when the group gets to see what everyone is thinking and feeling about each topic.

PUTTING A TWO-LEVEL DESIGN INTO PRACTICE

Let's take a slightly different look at the detailed agenda from the case story on the manufacturing organization that we saw in Part One. This time we want to see how the movement between these two layers of participant experience maps onto the process of a real-life agenda segment. Table 4.1 shows the large group/small group interaction in Joanne's agenda section on Quality.

Here you can see the mechanics of shifting the participants back and forth between the two levels. The shift is very easy and simply needs direction from the stage in order to take place. And the shifting back and forth within a topic means that the participants are able to personally engage with the topic as well as experience themselves as part of the bigger picture.

For the participants, the shift between their roles as members of their table group and members of the large group is effortless. But *the whole feel of the room changes* as these shifts are made. During the large group experience, the room is quiet and the focus is all on the front of the room. During the small group experience, the room is buzzing, the feeling is relaxed and conversational, and the sounds of voices and laughter blend together from every table. Often it takes repeated nudges from the front of the room to bring everyone back together. But when everyone is back into the large group experience, the focus is keener and everyone's energy has been reinvigorated.

Table 4.1 Movement Between Large Group and Small Group in a Virtuous Meeting Agenda

	Time	Segment	Front of Room	Participants	Synthesizers
Large Group Experience	2:20 (15)	Mind-set Shifts	Joanne's presentation	Listen	Listen
Small Group Experience	2:35 (10)	Mind-set Shifts: Small Group Activity	Small groups respond to question Joanne reads input as it comes in	Participate in small group (3 person) discussions	Scan responses for themes Keep this data for later use
Large Group Experience	2:45 (30)	Reaching Full Engagement	1. Joanne reviews and comments on Bold Steps 2. She brings Gustav to the stage 3. Gustav's presentation 4. Gustav sets up table group work (3 questions)	Listen	Listen
Small Group Experience	3:15 (60)	Reaching Full Engagement: Small Group Work	Joanne, Gustav, and Surjeet read through the input to get a feel of what the group is saying and to see some of the detail.	Discuss in groups of six	Review table group submissions Create themes for each question
Large Group Experience	4:15 (15)	Reaching Full Engagement	1. Gustav reviews themes with the whole group 2. Gustav, Joanne, and Surjeet respond to the group's ideas	Listen	Project themes up on screen in the front of the room

Designing the Room for Two Levels of Experience

One of the most basic considerations in enabling a two-level meeting process is the layout of the room. The simple question of how people sit in the room has a fundamental power to shape how people will interact (or not interact) with each other in the room. There are two main seating styles for large group meetings. Both are illustrated in the figures that follow. In the first case (Figure 4.4), participants are seated in rows of chairs facing the front of the room. This is still the default style for many large gatherings. It makes sense: it is an efficient use of space, it gives everyone the best view of the front of the room, and it is familiar to us from the movie theater, the concert hall, the church, the PTA meeting. It serves the function of letting the greatest number of people be as close as possible to the front of the room and to whatever ceremony, entertainment, or message is being delivered.

The other major style for seating large groups is at round tables, where the participants face one another, and often a couple of the people at the table have to turn a bit in their chairs to see the front of the room (Figure 4.5). This seating takes up significantly more space and requires a larger room for the same number of people.

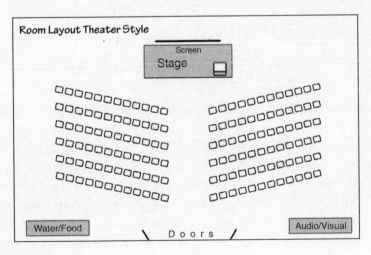

Figure 4.4 Room Layout Theater Style

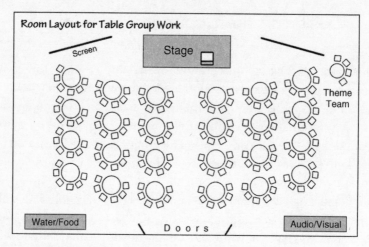

Figure 4.5 Room Layout for Table Group Work

This seating style is used for activities in which you want people to interact with each other. In large venues this style is often used for banquets and meals, where you want everyone to be able to easily talk to each other. No one wants to eat dinner staring at the back of a bunch of people's heads and only being able to speak to the people directly to the right and left.

Seating participants at round tables is an essential element of two-level meetings. When participants are seated at a round table together, they naturally enter the small group experience whenever the attention is released from the front of the room. As soon as they are no longer listening to someone in front of the room, their first instinct is to start conversing with those around them. And being seated around a table keeps the reality of the small group alive with everyone during the periods while they are watching the front of the room and listening to a presenter on stage. Keeping that small group awareness alive during the front-of-the-room periods makes it easy for participants to move back and forth between the two levels. And over the course of the day, it provides a more comfortable and engaged feeling for the participants, letting them feel connected to the larger group in the room but nested with the few people that are sharing their table with them.

The other advantage to having participants seated around tables is that it is easy for the participants to stay focused on their group's discussion. Even in a large hall, filled with dozens or hundreds of tables, participants are able to easily focus on the discussion at their table. Once all the table groups are in discussion, the room has an audible "buzz" that comes from the animated discussions at all the tables. But participants can still be heard by the others at their table without raising their voice. If the tables are round, everyone can always see the face of the person in the group who is speaking.

Perceived Alternatives to a Two-Level Meeting

We characterize the process of having two levels of participant experience as "counterintuitive" because over the years we have seen many design teams forego the movement between two levels in order to use alternatives they are more familiar with. This choice seems to stem from an intuitive feeling on their part that they should keep everything at one level—the whole group level—since they have everyone together in one place.

Even when a design team has decided to have a virtuous meeting and has taken steps to have the infrastructure in place for the participants to have table group conversations, there are often people on the team who think they should forego having the participants spend time in table group discussions. They sense that there are other ways to get to shared understanding that are either quicker or more reliable. Since such thoughts are common, it is worth taking a closer look at these alternatives and examining the predilection to eliminate participants' table group discussions. These other options include

- Option 1: Focusing on the large group level—Q&A or whole group discussion
- Option 2: Soliciting individual responses
- Option 3: Breakout groups with report-outs

Option 1: Let's All Do This as a Group!

Of course, keeping the process at the whole group level and doing Q&A at that level, or even giving the group time for a whole group discussion, is the simplest and quickest way to work with the whole group. This can seem to translate to having the advantages of speed and simplicity in arriving at shared understanding. But if you keep a large or very large group at the whole group level, you will never find out what everyone is thinking. The ideation, exchange, and shared understanding that come out of the table group level are missing. The only ideation and exchange going on at the large group level is a smattering of individuals getting up and saying something to the group. Beyond a certain size, only a few participants will get to ask a question in a Q&A activity, and most participants will also be left out from a whole group discussion. With such limited ideation and exchange, the shared understanding in the group will be very limited as well.

Option 2: We Want to Hear from Every Person!

More difficult to understand are the limitations of having everyone give his or her own response or ask his or her own questions. More often than in the past, we find ourselves designing meetings where all of the participants have a device for connecting to the network and sending in thoughts, ideas, and questions. However, having participants sending in their own questions, or their own thoughts and ideas in response to a presentation, is much less effective for producing shared understanding in the large group. By cutting out small table group discussions, you lose the small group exchange that helps participants understand what they think about the topic and to stimulate a deeper level of ideation. You also lose the shared understanding that is initiated in the table group, which underlies the shared understanding that is developed in the large group.

Option 3: Let's Do Breakouts!

The biggest question is how this two-level process compares to the familiar process of breakouts, with their corollary report-outs. If we say that the goal *of our meeting* is shared understanding within the large group, then we need to provide opportunities for ideation and exchange about multiple topics. Ideally, we would want to provide that opportunity for most or all of the topics of the meeting. Breakouts tend to be used when the goal is shared understanding during *one particular part of the meeting,* or *one particular topic.* Breakouts involve moving the whole group off to different rooms and then gathering them all back together again. Usually it is a significant process and takes up considerable time in the agenda. It is an unwieldy process for creating opportunities for ideation and exchange about multiple topics throughout the day.

Another difference is in the effectiveness of utilizing the smaller group ideation and exchange to create shared understanding with the larger group. With breakout activities there is usually no "parallel processing" of the kind we see in a two-level virtuous meeting. No one has access to what the breakout groups are discussing while those discussions are going on. No one is in a position to synthesize the themes that are coming out of the different discussions. Instead, the process used for exchanging the ideas at the group level and creating shared understanding is some form of report-out. Generally these report-outs are overly long and not very well synthesized, so they do not go as far toward real shared understanding within the larger group as the two-level process does.

Still, because breakouts provide an opportunity for small group ideation, exchange, and shared understanding, they are the closest approximation to the two-level process of the virtuous meeting. As we mentioned earlier in the book, you could think of this two-level process as a series of "micro-breakouts" that:

- Are interspersed throughout the day
- Take very little time
- Don't require moving the group in and out of the plenary room
- Are supported by a "parallel process" of synthesizing the fruits of the discussions
- Present the whole group, including those in front of the room, with the synthesized report-out that is easy to understand and easy to respond to

HOW IT FEELS IN THE TABLE GROUP

Sometimes a design team member will say to us, "That's a lot of work, designing the 'micro-timing' of an agenda segment, and coming up with questions for the participants to discuss. And it's disruptive for them, having to switch gears into small conversations when they've been listening to presentations. Are you sure it's worth it? And that it won't be a drag for the participants?"

A virtuous meeting is focused on the needs of the organization. The means of addressing those needs is to make it possible for everyone to know what the whole group is thinking. The effect for the participants is that it takes them from a simple experience of being just a passive member of the large group, to a far richer experience of being part of two different but integrated groups that intertwine with each other throughout the day. While the single passive role for the participants can become disempowering and draining over the course of the meeting, an integrated two-layer format transforms the experience of the participant, so that it becomes collaborative, constructive, and stimulating.

You Become More Engaged When You Become Part of the Conversation

Participants care about the conversations they are involved in. How often have we heard it said that the "real meeting" always takes place at the breaks? After all of the lecturing and all of the (more or less) sophisticated PowerPoint slide decks, what matters most to the participant is what she was able to say to a couple of other participants.

This isn't because the content of the presentations wasn't important or was uninteresting. Rather, what is most important to the participant is the *processing* of the experience. And whether the conversation at the break was about the content of the presentation or about some other topic of interest to the participant, the act of processing her own thoughts is what is most meaningful.

The real meeting, for each individual, happens in the conversations they are actually involved in.

In a large group, this fact can seem like an invitation to hopeless complexity and divergence. On the contrary, understanding the reality of the participants' interests and predicament is actually the gateway to productivity for the larger group. By channeling the natural energy and appetite of the participant, the great riches of the individual participants—experience, insight, on-the-ground knowledge—can be made available as a resource for the whole group.

You Learn More When You Can Digest the Content

Small group discussion is an ideal way to digest the content of a presentation. No one gets it all immediately. Each person has to connect the different facts, consider the point of view of the presenter, consider any details that were unclear, wonder how it will impact the current reality, and weigh the positives and the negatives. This processing is most easily done with another person, or a few other people, who have just received the same information.

The small group discussion is a way to exercise certain muscles. Hearing others' opinions and insights stimulates one's own thoughts; one's own knowledge is brought forth in response to the statements of others. Someone with an opposing opinion sharpens one's own perspective and begins the internal marshaling of one's arguments and facts.

Each person's past experience serves as one of the filters through which the presentation is heard. That experience can put limits on what a person is willing to entertain, but it is also a rich source of data to contextualize what the presenter is trying to describe or explain. In discussing the topic with other people and hearing about their past experiences, the subject becomes much richer and more nuanced. Each person starts to have a broader view of what was said and the implications.

You Stay Energized When You Are Active

When participants are forced to look across a room and focus on a figure standing on a stage and a slow progression of PowerPoint slides, there is a certain natural fatigue that sets in. A lot of the fatigue is simply physiological: the body is kept still, the depth of focus is kept constant, the lighting is constant and tiring, jet lag is often a factor. And on top of that, the material may be more or less stimulating, and the delivery likewise.

A certain amount of time spent that way is okay. But participant energy levels devolve after a while, and the value of the time to the participant rapidly lessens.

Small group conversation has the opposite effect on participant experience. Talking to someone sitting next to you brings your energy level back up. Focusing your eyes right around you and moving in your chair is stimulating. Usually people start cracking jokes and laughing. Talking raises your energy level and makes you feel active.

Your focus is increased by listening and responding. There is no opportunity for the mind to drift. You have the chance to respond to everything that is said. So you maintain a keen focus on where the conversation is going.

There is always a need to deliver some content from the front of the room at a meeting. The whole group time is the most focused and potentially synergistic. But the small group time is what makes the meeting real, interesting, and creative for the participants.

How It Feels in a Two-Level Meeting

Sometimes a design team member will say to us, "Won't it get kind of dull and repetitive, if we keep doing this same process, shifting them into small group discussions after every presentation?

No one walks out of a meeting saying, "Wow! It was great that they had two levels going on there! I really liked the smooth flow between the small group work and the large group synthesis!" But the participants coming out of a two-level meeting *are* enthusiastic. They just use a different language to describe their experience. It is important that the designer understands that they are talking about the experience of being part of two integrated levels. The following comments came at the end of day one of a two-day leadership meeting for the global procurement division of a

Fortune 500 company, and they are typical of the sentiments that participants voice if they are asked about their experience of a two-level meeting:

- "Great start. I liked the mix of presentation and interactive sessions, plus the breaks were well timed, which all contribute to building networks and a procurement community at the Leadership Team level. Use of technology was great and very successful as well as everyone supporting the conference. All very good!"
- "The use of the technology was great, and the instant collation of data and thoughts so they could be reviewed in real time was a fantastic value-add."
- "I evaluate the day as a tremendous opportunity to create a community and share our vision and role in a strategic way. Excellent presentations, good use of technology!"
- "The technology enables a quicker, smoother data collection and therefore higher quality communications in the limited time."
- "It was great to see so much engagement from all LT members for today's session. On another note, very good interactions and rich discussions at the tables."
- "Informative, interesting, and interactive. Much appreciated opportunity to understand and fully digest the strategy, plus network with new colleagues."

All of these comments, which came in from a single meeting, point toward a tremendous appreciation of the new role that the participants enjoyed in the meeting. Participants don't experience multiple rounds of going in and out of their small group as tedious or repetitive. They enjoy getting a break from the constant presentations. They welcome the chance to talk and to add constructive ideas to the topic that is being discussed. And they are thrilled to feel that they know and understand what the large group is thinking.

But the real winner is the organization. Virtuous meetings recast the role of the participant in order for the organization to become flexible, innovative, and collaborative, so that it can flourish in a dynamic, volatile environment. In an integrated approach like this, small group processes efficiently and effectively transfer the ideas of the participants to the large group level. And those in front of the room are in a constant state of discovery and feedback. This enables the large group to go deeper, entertaining conversations that otherwise would seem too difficult. A meeting becomes more iterative, and there is the possibility for creating new ways forward for the organization or the stakeholders. Using small group discussions to provide comprehensive input to the larger group is the mechanism for leveraging all of the assets of the larger group in setting direction, making choices, and planning action.

The participants feel the potential for convergence as a virtuous meeting unfolds. The participants start to experience the rhythmic movement from the large group level to the small group level and then back out to the large group level. They start to experience the contribution that their small table group is having to the whole. This rhythmic movement from one level to the next we call the Virtuous Engagement Cycle. It is the way of structuring an agenda segment to take advantage of a two-level design approach.

C CHAPTER FOUR • QUICK SUMMARY

- Highly engaged small groups use a process of ideation, exchange, and shared understanding.
- The virtuous meeting is a two-level process that allows the participant to be a member of the large group and a small table group *at the same time.*
- The intertwined engagement of the large group and small group creates a shared understanding between the group and the front of the room.
- Highly engaged participants are active, energized, and able to learn more because they are involved in the conversations with each other and with those in the front of the room.

VIRTUOUS ENGAGEMENT CYCLES:

CREATING A META-CONVERSATION

I n large group meetings, the participants no longer need to be silent partners to the activity that is going on. They can play an active role. The active role of the participants is the doorway to convergent group outcomes, in even the largest and most distributed of meetings.

In this way, the process of virtuous meetings goes beyond the participants being active. And it also goes beyond the participants contributing. The real purpose of active participation in virtuous meetings is to create an inclusive *meta-conversation* in the room. This meta-conversation is a dialogue between the group and the front of the room. In order to achieve this meta-conversation, the group must have a voice, and those in the front of the room must listen to the voice and give a response.

Meta-conversation—the exchange of thoughts and ideas between the group and those in the front of the room; an ongoing dialogue process between these two parties, throughout a meeting.

As we saw earlier, an agenda segment in a two-level virtuous meeting looks quite different from the same agenda segment in a front-of-the-room-centered meeting. The use of small table group discussions distinguishes virtuous meetings from legacy-style

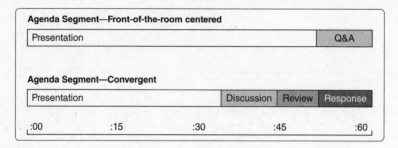

Figure 5.1 Designing the Agenda Segment

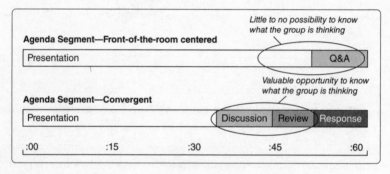

Figure 5.2 Finding Out What the Whole Group Is Thinking

meetings, where participants generally do not converse with each other during the plenary sessions (Figure 5.1)

THE REVOLUTION: KNOWING WHAT THE GROUP IS THINKING

Small group discussions are the means for giving participants back their voices in large meetings. Small group discussions allow the participants to "think out loud," digest what they have been presented with, and bring their own knowledge and experience to bear on the topic. They keep participants energized, focused, and in a learning and creative mode.

But more important, small group discussions are *the only way* to know what the whole group is thinking. This is the revolution. You *can* know what the group is thinking (Figure 5.2). In a virtuous meeting

- The group can know what they themselves are thinking (the mirror of shared understanding).
- The presenters or experts in front of the room can know what the group is thinking.
- The leadership or conveners can also know what the group is thinking.

Because of the table group discussions, every participant is able to have a voice. And because of the parallel processing of the synthesizers and the presentation of themes back to the group, everyone's voice can be heard.

When it becomes possible to know what the group is thinking, then all new potentials open up. Once you know what the group is thinking, it becomes possible to directly address the group's questions, ideas, and reactions.

THE VALUE OF META-CONVERSATIONS

In most organizations, particularly large ones, different people have access to different information and experiences. The meta-conversation with the greatest potential in a large organization is the one between those who have the broadest possible overview of the whole organization and those who know more about the day-to-day details of accomplishing the work of the organization. One group has more access to information regarding what needs to get done, and one group has more information on how to do it. Both groups want to succeed and do what is best, and they both need each other's perspective in order to be most efficient and effective.

Typically, the group who knows more about the overall environment and has the broadest view of what the organization needs is a smaller group leading the meeting from the front of the room. The larger group made up of participants knows about the reality within the organization and how to most efficiently accomplish those broad goals. Each one is a resource to the other. Generally, the information and perspective of the smaller group has been available at large meetings, and legacy-style meetings focus on disseminating this information and perspective to the larger group.

The goal of virtuous meetings is to make this a two-way street, where both groups are able to help each other. The meeting goes from being an information download (for which there are many other more resource-frugal alternatives) to being a dialogue, or even a conversation, in real time between these two groups. There is no resource-frugal alternative for this real-time conversation.[*] Everyone has to be together for it to happen. Especially in today's constantly disruptive environment, the value of this conversation is extremely high. More and more, such a conversation is seen as a necessity, and the question is not whether to have it but *how* to have it—how to catalyze it and maintain it.

VIRTUOUS ENGAGEMENT CYCLES: FOUR STAGES

The method for having a meta-conversation in the room is the same as for having any kind of dialogue. One party has to say something, another party has to listen to what's being said and say something back, and then the first party can make a response to that. In a large meeting that back-and-forth dialogue represents the orchestrated movement of the group from the large group experience to the small group experience and back.

We call this sequence the ***Virtuous Engagement Cycle***. The Virtuous Engagement Cycle is very simple. It comprises just four stages. And those four stages are very natural and intuitive to grasp: Present, Discuss, Review, Respond.

We call it a cycle because it has a sequence of four steps, and all of them need to be completed to create the meta-conversation in the room. We call it virtuous because it creates repeated opportunities for engagement and response, and responses in each iteration are that

---

[*]In Chapter Twelve, we will look at meetings held in several locations simultaneously—a development that will create a resource-frugal alternative to the time and travel invested in large group meetings.

View from Inside a Meeting

Conversation with a Larger Group

When eight members of a start-up company meet in the founder's garage around a wooden door laid on its side across a couple of sawhorses, they power through many animated cycles of dialogue. Every time there is a new topic somebody puts out a point of view and people respond to it. Everyone absorbs that response, and it becomes the new stimulus that people respond to. In small groups, dialogue moves swiftly and is unnamed—no one has to pay attention to it or direct it; it flows with a life of its own.

Difficulties emerge when that start-up has succeeded and now has 150 people in a meeting trying to work effectively together. All of a sudden it doesn't work the same anymore. There is a difference between the smooth give and take of a small entrepreneurial group and the "conversation" or "dialogue" that a large group can have. The small group discussion is fluid and passes from one person to the next every time someone speaks up. In a large group, the means to conversation is more formalized. There isn't enough time for everyone to speak up one at a time to the group on each topic. The actual steps that the group goes through must be thoughtfully designed, so that in the end everyone feels that they have been heard, and everyone feels they have had a chance to respond to what they have heard from others. Without the form in place, the opportunity for dialogue with the whole group is squandered.

The form we've identified is the Virtuous Engagement Cycle, and the cycle proceeds through identifiable stages. Knowing what those stages are, and being conscious in moving the group through them, allows that larger group of 150 to work as collaboratively and innovatively as they did when it was just the eight of them sitting around a makeshift table in a garage.

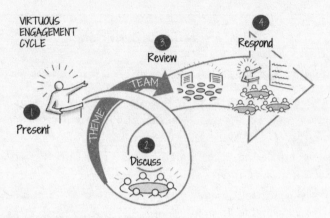

Figure 5.3 Virtuous Engagement Cycle

much richer and more powerful because of the responses from the last cycle. Repeating the sequence with each new agenda topic, enabling the meta-conversation to continue throughout the meeting, is what generates an experience of convergence for the whole group.

Figure 5.3 shows the four stages of the engagement cycle in interaction.

Stage 1: Present

If we look at the Virtuous Engagement Cycle as a whole, it begins with something being presented to the large group. This may be a lengthy presentation or a short one to just set the context. It may involve a single presenter, a panel, or even a video.

Participants listen with directed attention to the speaker. Their attention is directed by the question that they know they will be discussing in response to the presentation, and their attention is increased by knowing that they will have the opportunity to discuss the content with their colleagues immediately after.

The question allows the meeting conveners to focus the participants' discussion toward what is most useful for the participants, the leadership, and the organization as a whole. The question can be used to fully mine the experience and the day-to-day operational knowledge that the organization's best and brightest bring to the table.

Stage 2: Discuss

A lot is happening during the discussion stage. For the participants, now in small groups, this is the time of ideation and exchange, where they react and respond to a focused question about what was presented to the large group. This period of ideation and exchange brings about a shared understanding at the table group. Everyone starts to know what the others at the table are thinking and feeling about the topic of the presentation.

At the same time, all of the table groups are producing answers, or ideas, in response to the focusing question. The task of formulating a shared response is a constructive, creative act that puts the small group into a positive and problem-solving kind of mentality. This stage gives the participants an opportunity to take a concrete step to move the organization forward on the topic that was presented.

While the small groups are in discussion, another small team of people read through the ideas and reactions that are coming in from the tables and synthesize that input into an "executive summary" of what the whole group is saying.

Stage 3: Review

In the next stage the participants go back to the large group experience, looking again to the front of the room, and the synthesis of all of the tables' ideas is presented back to the whole group. Seeing the key ideas that were being exchanged across the whole room begins a sense of shared understanding among the large group. Participants are highly interested in what the group as a whole is thinking. Knowing how the group is trending keeps everyone at a heightened level of attention. Also, this is a time of growing awareness about how the participant's own thoughts and feelings intersect with the group as a whole.

Stage 4: Respond

The cycle is completed when the person(s) who made the presentation comes back in front of the group and responds to what the group has put forth. The person in the front of the room adds value to what the group has come up with by integrating the group's ideas and reactions with the content and direction of the original topic. Even greater shared understanding is achieved in the group as they see how the presenter reacts to and incorporates what they have come up with. And when the presenter shows the group that those in the front of the room are listening and want to converse, it adds value to their efforts and also gives the group more energy to embrace the next cycle.

If the group goes through several engagement cycles in a day, and each time someone in the front of the room responds to what the whole group has said in their multiple table-group conversations, a true sense of dialogue develops. This isn't the stilted interchange of some brave soul getting up and taking a roving mic to say something to the presenters in the front of the room and then sitting down and listening to the answer. Rather, it is a genuine response from the front of the room to a synthesized "voice" of all of the participants. No one knew what the group would say, and the presenter's response is equally spontaneous and directed exactly at the participants' ideas and concerns.

PUTTING ENGAGEMENT CYCLES INTO PRACTICE

If we look again at Joanne's agenda section on quality in the example from the Case Story in Part One, we can see from the two left-hand columns that there were two Virtuous Engagement Cycles in this part of the meeting (Table 5.1). One Virtuous Engagement Cycle was designed around quality issues and discussing how to improve reliability, and a second cycle was designed around the manufacturing site's strategies and how to improve engagement.

In the first cycle, Stage 1 (Present), Joanne gave a short presentation on quality missteps and the results of an engagement survey. Then in Stage 2 (Discuss), the group went into a short discussion around a single focal question identifying a bold step the organization needed to take. In Stage 3 (Review), Joanne scrolled through some of the ideas that the group had generated. And in Stage 4 (Respond), Joanne gave her reactions and the context to some of the ideas that she had preselected while the group was working.

Table 5.1 Agenda with Virtuous Engagement Cycles

Cycle	Stage	Time	Segment	Front of Room	Participants	Synthesizers
Engagement Cycle 1	**Present**	2:20 (15)	Mind-set Shifts	Joanne's presentation	Listen	Listen
	Discuss	2:35 (10)	Mind-set Shifts: Small Group Activity	Small groups respond to question. Joanne reads input as it comes in.	Participate in small group (3 person) discussions	Scan responses for themes Keep this data for later use
	Review Respond	2:45 (10)	Mind-set Shifts	1. Joanne reviews and comments on Bold Steps. 2. She brings Gustav to the stage.	Listen	Listen
Engagement Cycle 2	**Present**	2:55 (20)	Reaching Full Engagement	Gustav's presentation		
	Discuss	3:15 (60)	Reaching Full Engagement: Small Group Work	Joanne, Gustav, and Surjeet read through the input to get the feel of what the group is saying and to see some of the detail.	Discuss in groups of six	Review table group submissions Create themes for each question
	Review Respond	4:15 (15)	Reaching Full Engagement	1. Gustav reviews themes with the whole group. 2. Gustav, Joanne and Surjeet respond to the group's ideas.	Listen	Project themes up on screen in the front of the room

In the second cycle, Stage 1 (Present), Gustav gave a lengthier presentation about engagement strategies from the perspective of the manufacturing sites. The group then engaged in Stage 2 (Discuss) with longer table discussions focusing on three aspects of engagement: the organizational aspect, the global network, and personal contribution. During the discussion period, the input to each of the questions was synthesized into a PowerPoint slide. Also during that discussion time, Joanne, Gustav, and Surjeet read through the input as it came in, so that they could see the detail of what the group was saying.

When the group focused back together again for Stage 3 (Review), the slides were projected in the front of the room. The three senior leaders responded in Stage 4 and shared their reactions and thoughts about the synthesis and the detail that they read in the raw input of the group. They also engaged in dialogue with each other onstage as a panel.

If you look at these two Virtuous Engagement Cycles, each of the stages was handled differently in each cycle. The presentations were different lengths. The discussions were different lengths, they contained different numbers of questions, and the discussion groups were different sizes. The review process was different for each one. And the response process was also different for each: in the first one Joanne was responding to a few of the raw ideas of the group; in the second one Joanne, Gustav, and Surjeet responded as a panel to a series of slides synthesizing the answers to a series of questions.

But despite how the stages were executed, the important thing is that the cycle was observed and completed. Every agenda will look different. There are a multitude of ways that each stage of the cycle can be carried out. The key is to identify the stages and ensure that none is missing.

COMPLETING ENGAGEMENT CYCLES

When engagement cycles are completed, the participants' energy is heightened, they are interested in going into the next cycle, and they feel that their input was valued. When engagement cycles are begun and not completed, participants become confused about the value of their input, and they have less enthusiasm for the next cycle. After a couple of uncompleted cycles, they lose interest in the process, their energy begins to lag, and the volume and quality of input goes way down. They feel like a promise has been broken. Participants in hierarchical organizations may feel like their belief that no one wants to hear what they have to say has been confirmed.

> It is important to complete engagement cycles!

Why Cycles Don't Get Completed

There are three main reasons:

1. The designer wasn't aware of how engagement cycles work and hence didn't design a complete cycle.
2. The designer didn't allow enough time in the agenda for the cycle to get completed, and so the group ran out of time before the end of the process.
3. A presenter uses up much more time than they were allowed by the design so that there isn't enough time for the group to complete the cycle.

Where Engagement Cycles Get Interrupted and the Impact

Engagement cycles can get interrupted in one of three places:

1. After the group's input stage: The cycle is interrupted if there is no synthesis or presentation of what the group has done, and no response to it. The result is that the group feels as if this has been just a big "data dump" exercise.
2. After the synthesis stage: Even if the group's input gets synthesized, there may be no presentation back to the group and no response to the synthesis. Again, the feeling for the group is that this has been a "data dump."

3. After the presentation back to the group: The cycle is inter-
    rupted if there is no response to the group's input by anyone in
    front of the room (presenter or leader). This is not nearly as
    disengaging for the participants as the first two scenarios. At
    least the group knows that their input was valued, and seeing
    what the whole group is thinking raises their interest and
    energy. However, they are left wondering what the leadership
    is thinking about what they said, and there is a sense of a
    conversation not being completed.

If any one of these interruptions takes place, the group as a whole
is missing opportunities for shared understanding and the meta-
conversation never takes place.

Ten Potential Missed Opportunities in Virtuous Meetings

Missed opportunities in completing engagement cycles can be mistakes in design of the agenda or feedback process, as the three types
of interruption indicate, or they can be mistakes in understanding the
two-level, participant-centered approach. The following are potential
missed opportunities to be aware of when thinking about engagement cycles.

1. *Not giving the participants any (enough) small group conversation
time.* If the agenda is packed and the design team is looking for
something to cut in order to make it all work, small group conversation may seem expendable. However, if the time for the small group
conversation gets reduced too much, then it becomes ineffective.

Where that dividing line is—between enough time and not enough
time for discussion—varies with the design of each session. If you are
going to give the participants the opportunity to actively contribute, you
don't want to make that experience so constrained that they start to
wonder whether the discussion is really valued from the front of the
room and, as a consequence, whether they should value it themselves.

2. *Not giving enough time to distill and synthesize the input from the
small group.* This is a simple, but common, mistake that comes from

not thinking through what it will take for the synthesizers to complete their task. The amount of time will vary, and there are no hard and fast rules. But there are variables that you can pay attention to that will help you be realistic in the amount of time you design in for this critical process. These variables include how many small groups are contributing, how long the discussion period lasts, and how many questions the group is answering. All of these variables will determine the volume of input that you will receive from the room. The more input you receive, the more you need to process, which means either more time for the processing or more synthesizers to do the processing. In practice, the number of synthesizers may go up and down throughout the day, depending on the needs of the agenda section.

3. *Not coaching presenters on how to utilize the synthesized ideas of the group.* More often than not, most of the presenters at a meeting haven't been part of the inner circle of the design team. That means that they may be relatively unfamiliar with the concept and application of the convergent approach. But they are critical to delivering it. It is part of the role of the design team to give the presenter enough coaching on the process and the presenter's role, so that she isn't left "winging it" once she's onstage. Where this mostly occurs is in responding to the synthesis of the group's input. The presenter needs to be clear about what format the synthesis will be presented in and how the designers want her to use the synthesis in responding to the group. Also it is helpful to let her know that she can have access to the input as it is coming in. She can then review some of the actual language from the table groups or look at it with the synthesizers if she wants to.

4. *Not focusing the small group conversations enough.* It is easy to assume that quantity equals quality and, as a result, come up with too many questions for the group to process or have questions that are too broad. The effect is that the conversation is not directed enough to be productive in the time frame given and doesn't result in something that can be synthesized.

5. *Missing opportunities to prioritize.* Whenever the group has generated a list of what is important to them about a topic, it is possible to take that list and prioritize it in the moment, with every member of the large group having an anonymous vote. This gives everyone a quick view of which of the group's ideas are most important.

6. *Defaulting to quantitative questions and polling.* This pitfall is really the opposite of number 5: in this case, you are quick to prioritize with quantitative questions or polling but fail to have the discussion. Also, in contrast to number 5, the polling questions invariably are created by the designers, before the meeting, rather than being ideas the group has generated.

7. *Missing opportunities to harvest refined thinking.* This occurs at the very end of an agenda block, when you fail to use the table group conversation for a "harvesting" process. In this case, there are only a few minutes left in the agenda block, and the group could be asked to have a short discussion and input their final takeaways from the session they have just done. There is no time for distilling the input, presenting it back, and responding to it. The leadership simply takes this input and saves it to look at after the meeting. If you use this process, it can feel very fulfilling to the participants. But the key is to be very clear to the group about who will look at the input after the meeting, and how they will use it. If this is clear, the participants will be satisfied.

8. *Not understanding the difference in participant experience between (a) listening, (b) formulating their own thoughts, and (3) formulating thoughts with others.* For the participant, these are three very different experiences. They differ because of the amount of processing, or digestion, the participant gets to do with the material. When the participant is only listening, any process that's possible has to take place while she is listening. If she gets a chance to formulate her own thoughts—this usually means participants individually sending in responses to what they've heard—she gets to reflect on it, but it is only her own perspective she can bring to bear on it. When she gets to discuss what she's heard with others, then there are multiple perspectives, and she gets to try out her ideas on others. The three experiences produce very different results, and they should not be seen as equal processes.

9. *Equating live Q&A from mics in the room to participant questions sent in by everyone through the network.* Using the network of input devices to gather participants' questions about a presentation is a very particular process. Often an input screen is made available to the participants while they are listening to the presentation. Then if any question

occurs to them, as they listen, they can write it into the software and send it to the team of synthesizers. The synthesizers receive these questions in real time during the presentation. They sort through them and determine the few questions to which the whole group seems most interested in hearing the answers. These answers are given to the presenter when the presentation is finished. In this way the presenter can immediately address the most pressing questions of the group.

Many times an executive presenter will say, "Let's just cut the interactive thing; I can take Q&A from the audience for a few minutes and we can wrap it up." To the presenter this makes perfect sense: she's done it before a hundred times and it has always worked. But the difference is that with Q&A from the floor, you have no idea if the questions that are getting asked are really the questions the whole room wants to hear the answers to. If the participants are able to send in multiple anonymous questions, then the synthesizers can get a pretty good idea of what the whole group wants to know more about. If the presenter just responds to whoever raises a hand, there is a chance that many of the questions may not feel very important to many of the people in the room.

10. *Believing an open "back channel," like a projected Twitter feed, can make a meeting participant-centered.* Having an open back channel has become almost commonplace in conferences that are designed for the public, or loosely affiliated individuals, to network and learn. By and large, these processes tend to divide focus, and the focus they do throw is on the individual more than on the group as a whole. Virtuous meetings achieve convergence by having people work in small groups and by synthesizing the input that comes in from those small groups. Just putting up a Twitter feed does not move individuals toward conversations, nor the group toward convergence.

℃ CHAPTER FIVE • QUICK SUMMARY

- The expression of convergence in a virtuous meeting is the all-inclusive meta-conversation: a dialogue between the group and the front of the room.

- The Virtuous Engagement Cycle is a kind of feedback cycle that, each time it is completed, results in a deeper level of trust and shared understanding for the group, which in turn allows the next cycle to have even greater convergence.
- The four stages of the Virtuous Engagement Cycle are Present, Discuss, Review, and Respond. When completed, they create the meta-conversation.
- Each agenda segment is an iteration of the engagement cycle.
- Care must be taken to avoid interrupted or incomplete cycles.

Case Stories 3 and 4: Anchoring Virtuous Meetings

CASE STORY

The process in virtuous meetings creates a meta-conversation in the room. This meta-conversation is a dialogue between the group and the front of the room. In order to achieve this meta-conversation, the group must have a voice, and those in the front of the room must listen to the voice and give a response.

CASE STORY 3: LEADERSHIP MEETING FOR A GLOBAL PROCUREMENT ORGANIZATION

An example of such a meta-conversation took place in the extended leadership meeting for the procurement division of a successful Fortune 500 company. In this case, the meta-conversation was built into the design as a decision-making process. The meeting took place over two days. On the first day, along with updates on the business, there had been agenda sections on Best in Class procurement and on Strategic Focus Areas. The group had explored both topics in small group discussions and had identified seven Best in Class capabilities, as well as drilled down on the seven Strategic Focus Areas. The second day they had discussed actions to strengthen their community and had developed five actions.

So on the afternoon of the second day, they took time to prioritize what they had developed. As a whole group, they selected the three most important Best in Class capabilities and then discussed in small groups the question: "Now, based upon these top three priorities, what, specifically, do we need to do to be successful in the next year?" As a whole group they decided, "Out of the seven Strategic Focus Areas that we discussed yesterday, which are the two that should be *deprioritized*?" and determined, "Out of the actions to strengthen our community that we developed today, which are the two that would deliver the most needed value to our organization?"

The whole time that this process was going on, the leader of the division was on stage with two of his senior executives, responding to the prioritization and to the comments about what specifically should be done in the next year. As the group chose their priorities, the three on stage would discuss it and then sign off on taking those priorities away from the meeting to inform their work over the next year. This was a meta-conversation carefully built over two days that resulted in strategic priorities being set from ideas identified in small group conversations and prioritized at the large group level.

CASE STORY 4: LEADERSHIP MEETING FOR A U.S. INSURANCE ORGANIZATION

On the other hand, a meta-conversation can sometimes be sudden and profound. At a top leadership meeting for a midsize insurance company, the meeting started off with a welcome and then a brief small group discussion around participants' expectations for the summit: "What's the single most important expectation you have for this meeting?"

The company was at a crossroads. They were unprofitable and had been acquired by a large European insurance corporation and given some time to get back on their feet. They had listened to their customers and identified where they were too slow and complex to compete with newer companies that had come aggressively into their markets. From this they had developed a new strategy to straighten out their processes internally so that they would be competitive again in their markets. They were focusing on renewing IT and simplifying their touch point with brokers. The meeting graphics showed a train rolling toward the new future that had been envisioned in the strategy work the group had done.

The participants discussed the question and sent in a range of expectations. The synthesis had about eight major expectations that summarized all of the group's input. One of these was: "What to do in order to meet our Plan." About twenty minutes into the first day, the CEO picked up on that comment and pulled the emergency brake. He said, "Let's stop right now and understand where we are."

He carefully explained that his experience since coming on board was that the culture was top down, and that people, out of fear and out of habit, waited to be told what to do. He felt that the sentiment voiced in the comments from the table group conversations sounded like another case of people (the extended leadership of the company) waiting to be told how this renewal would take place and what they were supposed to do.

He said that nothing could be further from the truth and that to think that way meant that the train was rolling down the tracks, but most of the passengers were back at the last station. He was emphatic that the whole purpose of the work they had done over the last year was to drive decision making down into the hands of the people in this room, so that they could make the client and IT changes that were needed quickly enough and advantageously enough to make up market losses in a time frame that would ensure survival. He said that this had to be very clear before going any further with the meeting.

The group spent about an hour responding to this point and working it over. So the real agenda didn't get started until about two hours into the meeting, but the rest of the meeting was colored by that first morning. And the enthusiasm of the participants, and their sense of ownership of the meeting, was palpable.

These case studies confirm one key idea that we want you to hang onto as you go into the design part of this book: If you embrace the spirit and principles of the participant-centered approach and the idea of the meta-conversation that can take place between the large group and the small groups, you can have carefully planned moments of spectacular success as well as completely surprising moments of profound change and revelation.

PART THREE

DESIGNING VIRTUOUS MEETINGS

GATHERING THE FORCES:
THE PROCESS OF DESIGN

C onvergence in a large group meeting is a wonder to behold, even after you've become accustomed to it. It is an uncommon event when so many people can have a voice in an important discussion, which in turn informs important decisions. It is so uncommon that for most it is hard to believe and even harder to visualize. This feat is challenging to achieve, but not difficult. The energy it creates easily repays the energy it takes, if it is planned and designed with care. This book makes the case that while virtuous meetings do take more work than a "normal" meeting to produce, the results far outweigh any costs.

So how is designing a virtuous meeting different from designing a legacy-style, front-of-the-room-centered meeting? Now that we have discussed the anchoring concepts of virtuous meetings (Part Two), we need to ask: What do we need to think about? What is involved in designing a virtuous meeting? In Chapter Six, we introduce you to some overarching considerations and concerns that the Design Team will be faced with when transforming a large group meeting into a meta-conversation between the front-of-the-room and the participants in their table discussions.

The design for a virtuous meeting begins with a concerted effort by a small group of spirited, dedicated people working with the concepts and tools we've just covered. They transform the meeting owners' purpose for the meeting into achievable steps that leaders, presenters, and participants alike can use in order to achieve convergence. The group might be more accurately called the "convergence team," since whatever convergence is finally achieved is a result of their

119

work. Or they could more generally be called "the planning team," since their work is nothing if not planning. We will call them the Design Team (DT).

But why *spirited?* Most would agree that *every* large meeting needs a design team to sort out all the questions about content, focus, who will speak, timing, and format (which we will address in Chapter Eight).

What makes the Design Team of a virtuous meeting unique is the spirit of their endeavor. The critical element among the members of the Design Team of a virtuous meeting is a sense of wonder, curiosity, and anticipation about the voice of the participant. That spirit of inquiry and service to the understanding and contributions of everyone in the meeting (participants, especially) is what makes the role so fulfilling. Looking back at the virtuous cycle from the Introduction that forms the foundation for our definition of the virtuous meeting (Figure 6.1), we can see that these elements also serve as the guiding principles or aspirations of the Design Team.

Full engagement, shared understanding, ownership, and trust—the Design Team members must embrace and pursue all of these. We can't create value and convergence without them.

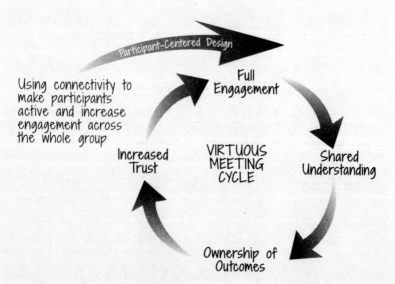

Figure 6.1 The Virtuous Meeting Cycle

THE ROLE OF THE DESIGN TEAM IN A VIRTUOUS MEETING

Most of us have experienced large meetings, one way or another. There is an excitement in walking into a meeting room for the first time. But there's even more excitement, albeit slower building, in being there at the beginning in the designer role, imagining that room full of people ready to connect and converse about the goals and plans that will shape the future of the organization. The Design Team designs the flow of content, activities, and energy in that room in the future. Best of all, the Design Team will be there in the room, both behind the scenes and in front of the participants, watching and directing how it all unfolds.

Specifically, the Design Team is responsible for what happens at the plenary and table group levels of a virtuous large group meeting. Serving at the pleasure of the meeting owners, Design Team members are the masters of the agenda—the constantly refined document that builds the engagement cycles, introduced in Chapter Five. Engagement cycles order the "the flow of the show" toward the best possible outcomes for the organization. They are the organizing structure of activities from which the meeting "magically" springs forth one day.

When the Design Team does an excellent job, people notice. A given participant may never know that the meeting they were in was designed as a "virtuous large group meeting"; they may never be privy to the imagination, heart, and decision making that it took to create this positive, productive experience. But they will know how they *feel* about it, that they experienced something different, and that it was transformative and unique. How to produce that experience is the subject of this chapter.

As we begin to go into more detail about how the Design Team is best shaped, let's be clear too that all designs are different in practice. All kinds of cultures, leaders, and situations naturally produce the widest variety of approaches to planning important meetings. Here we describe what has worked best over decades of experience in the widest variety of meetings. And so, let's look at the big picture first . . . How does the Design Team determine its

mission? In broad strokes, what are the key steps for the Design
Team in the birth process of a virtuous meeting?

SEQUENCE OF DESIGN
TEAM ACTIVITIES

The following are key steps in the evolution and work of the Design
Team:

1. *Leader determines the need for a face-to-face meeting*—This step
   entails the initial purpose, topics, and outcomes framework.
2. *A Design Team is formed*—The DT leader is tapped and the
   initial charter for the DT is given; members are chosen; the
   purpose and scope of the meeting are refined with the meeting leaders; the date and time for the meeting is set; major
   topics are set; the tentative production schedule is proposed;
   agenda design commences.
3. *The DT works for two to four months*—The DT co-leads the site
   check visit along with the Logistics Team, and the Audio-
   Visual Production Team participates. Each DT member takes
   on the tasks that they are best suited for. Roles are determined, such as advisor, member of the Theme Team, presenters' coach, timekeeper, guest speaker host, and so forth.
   The roles are assigned and the agenda segments are contin-
   ually refined.
4. *Onsite preparations for two to four days*—Before the meeting
   starts, the DT runs the rehearsals.
5. *During the meeting*—DT members bring the Virtuous Engagement Cycle stages, as described in Chapter Five, to life. Participant engagement goes into high gear, according to the agenda
   and roles. Agenda huddles are held each evening to ensure that
   the DT members and meeting leaders are on track and fulfilling
   their roles.
6. *After the meeting*—DT members return to their "day jobs." At
   this stage there are various opportunities for carrying forward
   the work of the meeting. For example, the Design Team

might morph into a Momentum Team and oversee the application of the plan after the meeting and help the group ensure that goals established at the meeting are being met and that momentum is not lost.

INTEGRATING DESIGN, PRODUCTION, AND LOGISTICS

The need for a virtuous-style large group meeting begins with a vision and people with skills to influence others. The goals of the meeting are among the very first decisions that must be made. Design and production can commence only from that point forward. But if the choice is convergence and full engagement, a concept so little understood by traditional meeting production teams (audio/visual production or meeting planners), it is important that the leader or meeting owner gives clear direction and proper decision-making authority to the various planning teams right from the start.

The team that carries out the meeting is actually three teams, each with a different purpose. Their ability to work together for a smooth production process will determine the success of the meeting.

Three Key Teams

The Design Team. The DT is responsible for what happens in the meeting rooms—the content, process, and room layout.

The Audio-Visual Production Team. This team is responsible for producing what the Design Team wants to happen on the stage and screens in the meeting rooms.

The Logistics Team. This team is responsible for everything involving the participants, but outside the meeting rooms.

With those boundaries made clear, it is then up to the leaders of each team to create seamless working relationships among the teams as a whole. But the leader needs to help us here too—how will he or she know what to say? This is where coaching and expertise are critical in the process of producing a virtuous meeting. After a leader has gone through such a production a number of times, he or she will practically feel the right message from the inside out. But on the first try, this is the time for coaching and consultation. The Design Team and the leader must come to a deep understanding, together, of the imperatives of this meeting, the hopes and dreams, and the current realities, and then craft the message that will set all the design ships sailing. Concepts such as participant-centered, high-speed connectivity, two levels of meeting (whole and table group), full engagement, shared understanding, and so on, will all be useful in explaining to the teams what their charter is for this meeting and the importance of their roles in it.

Building an Effective Design Team

While each Design Team is different, the functions that we've seen as most effective in producing a large, virtuous meeting are shown in the following list. Some functions may be played by one person, while others may be split among two to three people.

Design Team Leader: reports to the meeting owner, who owns the meeting purpose and has deep knowledge of the culture and relationships with most of the key players; is relatively fearless and a good manager, and is a content/process generalist

Representatives from *Key Departments:* content specialists; team players

Participant Engagement Designer: large group process specialist; external consultant, at least at first; expert in convergence

Presenters' Coach: process specialist; part psychologist!

Meeting Facilitator: if there is one, a process expert

Internal Organization Development or Leadership Development Professional: development specialist, if possible

Internal Communications Professional: content specialist, if possible

Note on the Participant Engagement Designer

The role of Participant Engagement Designer will be a new one for most organizations and design teams. It is someone who has seen, participated in, and designed multiple other meetings in which the two-level process with participant-centered design was used. He or she is a key person on the team and the holder of the keys to interactivity and engagement. In countless discussions about the process design of whole days, segments, or even minute to minute, this specialist will bring together best practices and practical advice while representing the collective mind and feelings of the participants. He or she will often be a teacher in this regard. Slowly, others on the Design Team will come to see how this specialized meeting designer thinks and from where the advice comes. Through many iterations of the Purpose → Outcomes → Process → Agenda design sequence, which you will learn in Chapter Seven, this designer will flesh out the active role of the participants and, together with the rest of the team, design the process that leads to convergence.

FORMING THE DESIGN TEAM: IMPORTANCE OF THE FIRST STEP

Right from the start, the conversations around forming the Design Team are highly predictive of the way the meeting will turn out in the end. These conversations are personal ones between leaders who know each other well. A few words in these cases can shape the whole meeting design and production effort. Here's one example of an informal charter for the Design Team: "Mary, I want you to shake things up this year. We can no longer afford to do this meeting the way we've always done it. You've got to come up with something that is a lot more productive, really engaging, and with *much* stronger outcomes. I want people to come flying out of this meeting and hit the ground running back in their areas." That, in counterpoint to this: "Bill, it's that time again. Time to get the team together for the Annual Strategic Retreat. I'll send you my thoughts about content. Pretty much like last year . . . possibly a big-name speaker this year, maybe a motivation expert. See what you can find. And send me periodic updates."

It is rarely this hot or cold. Here is another scenario—lukewarm. The Design Team gets under way, and since their mission is to design the best meeting outcomes that they can, they somehow come across this "other approach" (the participant-centered one). Despite the initial charter for the meeting (like the cold one, above), the Design Team leader feels that there is merit in the idea of getting the participants really involved but then has to go to the leader/meeting owner and extol the benefits of this other approach without really understanding it. Lacking expertise in participant-centered design, this can be a rough discussion, with many questions from the meeting owner going unanswered. Convergence as a possible meeting purpose will twist slowly in the wind unless or until a convergence *specialist* can be brought together with the meeting owner. If this new approach is chosen, then the chartering of teams and decision rules must be reiterated and with a fresh start. A restart, but with a giant leap forward.

THE WORK OF THE DESIGN TEAM

On a practical level, the work of the Design Team is best conducted between and within weekly meetings or conference calls. The team members can then think together about how various elements of content and process can fit together and see where the challenges are. Assignments can be given for individual or subteam work between the design meetings to address these challenges.

The difference between normal planning for traditional large group meetings and designing virtuous large group meetings is in how you hold the participant's role—either passive as the recipients of everything presented or active as contributors and shapers of the outcomes from the meeting. When designing a virtuous meeting, you must hold the participants as present and active in each agenda segment. The focus is less on "*What* will we show them?" (although it's still important) and more on "What will we *ask* them?" and "How will we engage them to yield the best outcomes for the organization?" This requires constant thought-cycling

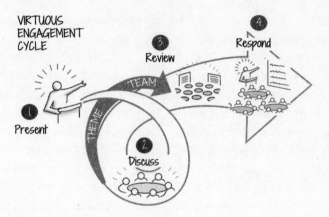

Figure 6.2 Virtuous Engagement Cycle

through the Purpose → Outcomes → Process → Agenda sequence, enough times so that all team members believe they've done the best possible job at delivering on the Purpose of the meeting.

As each segment in the agenda is considered, the Design Team must decide whether the purpose of the segment is served better with the participants' active engagement or not. In some segments, the purpose is only to inform, and a straightforward presentation is fully sufficient. Other agenda segments will naturally beg for small group discussions and a full engagement cycle (or more) that is designed especially for it. This process of bringing the agenda to life (to the participants) is helped by referring often to the Virtuous Engagement Cycle. It makes it easy to consider the four primary activities in the meeting room against the requirements of each agenda segment. Let's look at Figure 6.2, which we saw in the previous chapter.

As the Design Team evolves its thinking on each segment, it is important to record it in the agenda. For each segment, the agenda should show clearly stated desired outcomes and how the process will unfold, as it does in Table 5.1 in the previous chapter. During this phase, the agenda will be read often by many stakeholders—including leaders, presenters, and other associates. When the desired outcomes of each segment are clearly stated, and the process is described with enough detail that those new to convergence can follow the flow, all will have enough information with which to make the most constructive contributions. The agenda is thus a living document, containing the best, up-to-the-minute thinking of all contributors. It is not uncommon for it to go through many versions before the meeting is ready to start.

Consider the following thinking exercise from professional photographers, which Design Team members can borrow when designing the agenda: Photographers over time develop a knack for *imagining* a photograph before they ever lift a finger or before they consider moving their position or grabbing a camera or a certain lens. They can look outward and imagine a photograph as if it were taken with a wide-angle lens, or a telephoto, or from this position or that, and decide in a second if it's worth taking the first step toward creating it. Similarly, as Design Team members consider over and over again various segments in a meeting designed to achieve convergence, they can *imagine* a process, they can run through the stages of the Engagement Cycle and see if a certain process achieves the intent of each stage, touch back to the purpose, review the desired outcomes, reread the instructions and framing for the exercise, and come back again to the process, trying this variation and that—all without lifting a finger. How can the process be improved? Does it complete an engagement cycle or leave it hanging? Does it flow logically into the next segment? Does it deliver the outcomes we want? How can we focus it better? Is the time sufficient? Practicing this "wide-angle thinking," Design Team members can become proficient at thought-cycling through the steps toward convergent outcomes. It is perhaps the best way to arrive at a design that leverages the Virtuous Engagement Cycle fully.

A final note on the work of the Design Team is the importance of timing. There is no more important resource in a large, important meeting than time. How often have you felt like "there wasn't enough time" in a portion of a meeting that you attended? In designing virtuous large group meetings, managing the minutes is critical. As we said earlier, this type of design is challenging but not difficult. We'll look at the process levers more closely in Chapter Eight—they are the "moving parts" or steps that must be followed in order to deliver convergent outcomes. If a previous presenter blows past his allotted time, it can disrupt the rest of the meeting in terms of what can be accomplished. During the design process, the Design Team needs to consider even the smallest time segments and think about what is necessary—what could rob those moments?—and what to do to protect them.

In a Virtuous Engagement Cycle, as we've seen, you won't get much value if you don't complete the cycle. Not only foregoing value, you'll breed discontent among the participants if you don't complete the cycles. It's like asking a friend a rather significant question, watching him think about how to respond, and then walking away just as he begins to answer you. Everyone is better off if you don't start a cycle at all than if you start a cycle (a presentation) and then don't finish it. In many cases, ten minutes is all that is needed to complete a cycle. If small chunks of time are skipped in the planning—like the time for going to break or moving back from breakout meetings—those precious ten minutes could be lost. During the actual meeting, it often falls to a Design Team member to be the "time cop" signaling to presenters when their time is passed.

CRITICAL DESIGN DECISIONS

In designing virtuous meetings, some important decisions need high-lighting. In each case, the decision criteria are whether participation, engagement, and convergence will be enhanced or not. Even the best process design can be undermined by pressures from inadequate meeting space, or missing facilitation, or ineffective members on the Theme Team.

Choosing the Room Design

This is both a critical and a sticky issue. It is critical because how the room is laid out, the positioning of the participant tables and Theme Team table, where the leaders sit, the distance to break-outs, and so forth, all can have an impact on how well the meeting process will work. The room design is potentially sticky because the meeting rooms may be booked one or two years in advance of an important meeting, and participant-centered, two-level design may not have been considered. If it wasn't, then the size of the general session hall will have been specified based on require-ments for "normal" (front-of-the-room) meetings. Thankfully, it is increasingly common to use round tables for participants in these meetings. "Rounds" are fundamentally necessary to conduct the virtuous large group meeting we are describing. If there is not room for them, as is often the case in typical European conference halls, for example, the possibility of convergence is severely dim-inished. The same is true when "schoolroom" or "classroom" style tables and seating are specified. When it is difficult to conduct frequent small, table group discussions for any reason, then the outcomes of a virtuous meeting suffer.

So it is important, early in the life of a Design Team, to survey the "givens" in terms of meeting space and time. Are the meeting logistics planners constrained in any way that could become a problem later for the meeting process designers? Will there be breakout rooms? If so, where are they? How distant? Are there elevators to reach them? Will food be served nearby or far away? Are participants being bussed from the hotel to the meeting site and back? Often the actual decision about room design becomes dozens of smaller decisions over a few months. The question of who has the final decision in these matters is helpful to resolve early. It is painful when site logistics, or persons without any knowledge of the purpose of a virtuous large group meeting, dictate what is possible (or not) in the meeting. For this reason, it is best if the Design Team leader or the Participant Engagement Designer makes those final decisions. Bottom line: Anything that could possibly impact space utilization and timing must be surfaced as early as possible, before the design of the meeting process can begin on a solid basis.

Using a Professional Facilitator

A skilled process facilitator can make a significant difference in important meetings—no question. They have studied process design and facilitation. They typically have scores of meetings worth of experience under their belts, and they are adept at seeing where to "intervene" in possibly difficult situations and where to step back. But there is often a countervailing force in this decision—executives and leaders often prefer to be on stage and dislike ceding apparent power to an outside person (or even to an inside person), no matter what their skills are. It's hard to argue with that position. In the next section, Part Four, we will look at facilitating virtuous large group meetings in some detail. Without a professional in the role, the facilitation task will fall to a number of people, like presenters, as they naturally appear on stage for other purposes. So it is critically important for members of the Design Team to orient and support anyone who will be on stage *and* who will take any part of the task of facilitating the group and process.

If the situation does lean toward using an outside, professional facilitator for the meeting, then it is best to include that person on the Design Team at the earliest opportunity. The process design, the meeting, and the organization overall will surely benefit by that person's knowledge and experience.

Recruiting the Theme Team

What is the Theme Team? In virtuous large group meetings, the Theme Team is critically important. The team is responsible, as a group, for reading the data from all participants at various times during the meeting and distilling it into the main messages—the themes—running through it. Who should those three to five people be? What are their backgrounds, motivations, and skills? Who invites them and for what reasons? How will they be oriented and trained? And how will they be introduced to the group? These questions and more should cause good discussions in the Design Team and possibly with the meeting owners as well.

Theme Team—is responsible for reading the data coming in live from all participants at various times during the meeting and creating quick summaries of the main messages—the themes—running through it. The summaries are usually shown immediately to the whole group.

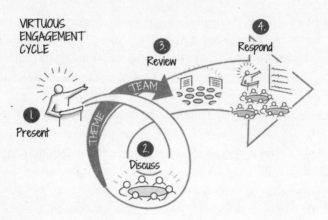

Figure 6.3 Virtuous Engagement Cycle with the Theme Team

Key Attributes of a Theme Team Member

The first step in recruiting a Theme Team is finding the right people for the job. Ideally, a Theme Team member will possess the following traits:

1. Quick reader, synthesizer
2. Doesn't get tripped up in the details; naturally looks for the big picture
3. Good with words and expressing meaning (like a journalist or a communications specialist)
4. A passion for the organization and for learning
5. Trusted or trustworthy by most participants

It is a huge opportunity for those invited to serve in this capacity, as they will impact the outcome of the meeting and benefit the organization if they wildly succeed in their task. We say sometimes that it is "the best seat in the house," especially for those who may not have been invited to the meeting otherwise. For example, for high-potential, mid-level employees it can be a fantastic learning and development experience to serve the highest-level executives in their organization in this way. Similarly, assistants to divisional leaders or internal communications specialists have a lot to gain from the exposure to senior-level issues.

Regarding the composition of the Theme Team: diversity is best. Representatives from different divisions, countries, or market segments can provide the Theme Team with multiple "lenses" through which to analyze the participants' data for themes. Similarly, members from different age groups, customer types, management levels, or cultures can add perspective. For clues about which categories and what mix of people would serve best on the Theme Team, look at the topics and issues the meeting is focused upon. Which perspectives will be able to give shape to the participants' contributions?

The process of selecting the best members should be managed within the Design Team and result in a short list of people to invite. Once chosen, Theme Team members are fully supported and coached from before the meeting until the end, primarily by the Theme Team leader. We will look more closely at the role and tasks of the Theme Team in Chapter Nine, but for now think of this metaphor: If the meeting is a vehicle for getting the organization to a new place, and the participants' ideas and input are the "fuel," then the Theme Team is the engine and the Theme Team members the pistons. Who those people are is important to the success of the trip!

The Leader's Role

In a virtuous large group meeting, the role of the leader(s) is much more visible and active than in front-of-the-room-type meetings. It's easy to assume that the front-of-the-room-style meeting gives the leader the greatest visibility, but this is not the case. Because engaging in a large-scale dialogue takes a different kind of preparation than making a presentation, effort and engagement are both much higher in a virtuous large group meeting. In order for leaders to feel comfortable and effective in this enhanced role, they should work as closely as possible with the Design Team. In talking to the Design Team, leaders will have sparks of insight about their role and message(s) with each and every interaction. Weekly teleconference calls can provide a way for all parties to get the full benefit of each other's perspective and insights as the meeting design evolves.

The desire and commitment to have a virtuous large group meeting must come from the leaders as soon as possible in the design process. It is they who will be in dialogue with a large group of the organization's top people, and it is they who understand most keenly the organizational impact of a concerted effort toward convergence.

The big difference between the planning process for a traditional, front-of-the-room, large meeting and a virtuous large group meeting is the focus on encouraging the voice of the participants. Months before the meeting, the Design Team will essentially build both sides of those dialogues-to-be. They will build the framework of the dialogues and address questions like

- What questions are the participants likely to bring to the meeting?
- What content is critical to get across to the participants?
- What questions of the participants, and discussions, will be most useful to the leaders and the organization?
- What do we suppose might be the range of the participants' answers?
- How can we leverage the value this group brings to the organization?

Answers to these questions will help shape the design of the meta-conversation.

When the actual meeting begins and the agenda is set in motion, the leader(s) will be coached by the Participant Engagement Designer and others on the Design Team. Most process details will be planned for, but some will arise spontaneously. This is where the Engagement Designer earns his or her keep and where the leaders will earn their stripes. In working closely with the Theme Team during the meeting, leaders have an immediate grasp of what the whole group is thinking. The first few times through the process, leaders should have the best possible support while the meeting unfolds. Later, of course, they will know the process and take to their role much more naturally. We discuss the full spectrum of the leader's role in more detail in Chapter Eleven.

For leaders who are new to participant-centered, two-level processes and engagement cycles, it is important to reiterate the need to be in closer touch with the Design Team throughout the design process. That is where the interactive dialogues are designed. All stakeholders benefit when the participating leaders are inside the thinking about those processes. In fact, we see this active participation by leaders in large group dialogue *as visible acts of leadership*. People notice when leaders take risks to be authentic, vulnerable, and fully constructive in plain view. And the secret key to doing this well lies in the relationship between the leader and the Design Team.

Inviting the Participants

And last but by no means least, the invitation message to participants is a great opportunity to get the wheels of convergence turning, long before the actual meeting. If the organization has experienced many participant-centered meetings in the past, then the purpose of the invitation is more to bring invitees up to speed on the content and features of the program and to get them thinking in the right direction. They will already know the passion and participation part. If the organization is experiencing its first virtuous large group meeting, then the invitation has a further purpose—to *enthuse* invitees about the opportunity in store for each of them. The message of "Why are we doing this meeting differently?" needs to be carefully designed. It's an opportunity to get people not only thinking about the meeting and its topics, but also *feeling* the new opportunity that the meeting represents.

The invitation is also a time for leaders to begin speaking in their new voice about the purpose, outcomes, and process of the meeting. Leaders can articulate the importance of the meeting and why full engagement is so necessary, as well as mention the guiding principles of shared understanding, ownership, and trust and how we will strive to achieve these through full engagement. It signals to participants that they are being invited to a very different kind of meeting. The Design Team will of course help craft this message, but the leaders must personalize it. Further, there can be advice about what participants might be thinking about, or looking for, before the meeting and how to prepare for contributing to the meeting once they are in it.

In this chapter, we have examined some overarching considerations for the Design Team. In the next chapters, we will delve deeply into the actual design elements and sequence.

☾ CHAPTER SIX • QUICK SUMMARY

- The Design Team is responsible for transforming the meeting owners' purpose for the meeting into achievable steps that leaders, presenters, and participants alike can take in order to achieve convergence.
- There is a virtuous cycle at the heart of a virtuous meeting: full engagement → shared understanding → ownership of outcomes → increased trust → (fuller) full engagement . . .
- Clear decision-making rules are necessary at the start between the three primary planning teams: Design Team, Audio-Visual Production Team, and Logistics Team.
- The Participant Engagement Designer fleshes out the active role of the participants through many iterations of the Purpose → Outcomes → Process → Agenda design sequence.
- The Design Team has to make three critical decisions about (1) the layout of the meeting room, (2) whether to use a professional facilitator, and (3) who should be on the Theme Team.

CHAPTER SEVEN

UNDERSTANDING THE POSSIBILITIES:
THE DESIGN ELEMENTS

Virtuous meetings don't necessitate any particular overall structure. Over the years we have supported every possible kind of meeting structure, from highly defined large group methods to unique, creative large group simulations to very common and efficient strategy and leadership summits. Neither is it the subject matter that distinguishes a virtuous large group meeting from any other format of large meeting.

Rather, virtuous large group meetings embody new processes that are markedly different from the processes of legacy, front-of-the-room-centered meetings, or other large meeting formats. As we have seen, the agenda looks quite different. It details a process that moves fluidly between presentations and small discussions, and it uses the Virtuous Engagement Cycle to guide how those discussions go on to inform the larger group. The goal of virtuous meetings is convergent outcomes.

This chapter will look at the nature of convergent outcomes and the convergent processes that achieve them and how they take the group beyond the normal outcomes of a front-of-the-room-centered meeting. We will also look at how the purpose of the meeting can be more robust in a virtuous large group meeting. By achieving convergent outcomes, virtuous meetings make it possible to reach for the kind of collaborative and generative purposes that are familiar to us from small team meetings.

137

THE DESIGN SEQUENCE

The design sequence is important because it defines the role each element plays and how each one relates to the others. The design process has to begin with a purpose. Once the purpose is clear, the Design Team can define the outcomes that the meeting needs to accomplish. The Design Team then selects processes that will accomplish those outcomes. And the agenda is created to structure those processes, so that they can be effectively carried out in the given time frame. This simple sequence is shown in Figure 7.1.

Even though we say that the design process begins with deciding the purpose, in reality the design process is iterative. The purpose, the outcomes, and the process all impact one another, and adjustments are made to each one as the design evolves. The Design Team is always going back and asking:

Does this process accomplish this outcome?

Does this outcome really fulfill this purpose?

Is the purpose as ambitious and mission-critical as it could be?

As you make concrete decisions about any element of the sequence, you begin to see adjustments that need to be made to other elements.

If you reverse the sequence, as we see in Figure 7.2, you can understand how new process possibilities, and bold process choices,

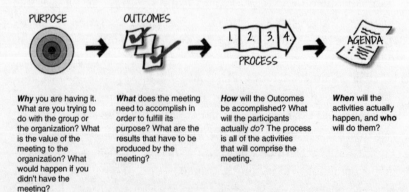

Why you are having it. What are you trying to do with the group or the organization? What is the value of the meeting to the organization? What would happen if you didn't have the meeting?

What does the meeting need to accomplish in order to fulfill its purpose? What are the results that have to be produced by the meeting?

How will the Outcomes be accomplished? What will the participants actually *do*? The process is all of the activities that will comprise the meeting.

When will the activities actually happen, and **who** will do them?

Figure 7.1   Basic Design Sequence

have significant influence on what outcomes are possible and the types of purposes that can be attempted.

This implementation sequence—the sequence that produces the results—holds the key to greater value in meetings and helps illustrate the power of the convergent processes in a virtuous meeting. In a very real sense, the process is always driving and defining the outcomes and, through the outcomes, defining and enabling the purpose. But for the purposes of this chapter, let's focus on the stages of the design sequence, and we'll use the awareness of the implementation sequence to see the underlying value at each stage.

DETERMINING PURPOSE

Several years ago, we did a series of quarterly all-hands meetings for a U.S.-based clothing manufacturer. The meetings were only a couple of hours long and usually covered just a few topics. The participants included most of the people working at the headquarters building. People from offices in Canada and Mexico also dialed in. They watched the events in the room over video, gathered in small groups so that they could contribute their thoughts to the whole group through the synthesizing process.

At the time we were doing these meetings, they were planning and then gradually rolling out a conversion to SAP® software. So one of the topics that was usually on the agenda was the SAP® implementation. The background buzz on converting to SAP® software was that

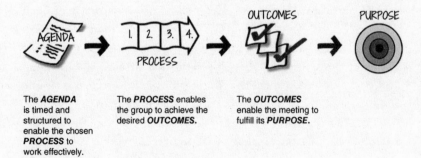

The **AGENDA** is timed and structured to enable the chosen **PROCESS** to work effectively.

The **PROCESS** enables the group to achieve the desired **OUTCOMES**.

The **OUTCOMES** enable the meeting to fulfill its **PURPOSE**.

Figure 7.2 Design Implementation Sequence

everyone was very nervous about it. People were afraid that things wouldn't be in place in time and that the changeover would be too difficult in the ultra-fast-paced environment they were working in— trying to discern the fashion trend, design to it, get it built, and get it into stores while the trend was still viable. There was a lot of negative anticipation among the workforce.

Unfortunately, the people working on the design of the meetings were overstretched. They didn't really have the bandwidth to focus on the design of these meetings, even though they were holding them regularly every quarter. We weren't able to get much time with them to discuss the agenda or provide insight into their process choices.

Even though they had the technical capability in the room to pursue convergent outcomes, with regard to the SAP® software implementation, they chose to keep the purpose simply informational. The implementation team dressed up in costumes and created skits to try to lighten the image of the transition and reassure everyone that things would work out well. They gave reports on the timetables they were creating for the rollout. They gave updates on how the initial mini-steps of the rollout were playing out in Asia.

But they never once asked the participants to discuss it. They never asked what was creating the fear, or what people thought were the weaknesses in the organization that might jeopardize a smooth rollout. And they never asked them to generate any solutions or intermediate steps that could be taken to counter the problems they were anticipating.

When the North American implementation hit, things went very badly. Order fulfillment collapsed, and the company had tremendous financial problems. It was as if all of the fears that had been lying underneath were realized. We kept thinking about the missed opportunities in those all-hands meetings. Of course, the whole implementation couldn't have been turned around just through the activities of a few meetings. But it still stands as a clear example of the importance of the decision about the purpose of the meeting.

The fact that the SAP® software implementation was on the agenda each time means that the designers knew that it was a key topic for the all-hands meeting. But deciding to limit the purpose to informing and inspiring the participants disregarded the value of what the participants might have known and been able to offer in terms of making the conversion work "on the ground." Rather than seeing the purpose in the meetings as being to identify the weak points and generate solutions—which these participants were in a unique position to do—they saw the purpose as being to convey optimism and energy to overcome whatever hesitation or worry the people were experiencing. Generally, more resources were put into making sure all the aesthetics were right than were put into thinking about what value the participants could provide to the key business issues. This is fundamentally a question of purpose: choosing to focus on entertaining the participants, rather than on learning from them and having them learn from each other.

Part of the reason for choosing entertainment and information in this case was a lack of awareness about what the purpose could be instead. This is actually an understandable mistake. If the meeting designers have always seen large meetings focused on the front-of-the-room, they don't have much of a model for what kinds of purposes could be achieved using other methods.

THE SMALL TEAM MODEL:
Generative Versus Informational Purpose

What should be the model for virtuous meeting purposes? The purpose of a virtuous meeting is to generate new insights, new understandings, and probably new plans (or revisions). The normal purposes of smaller team meetings can serve as the best model for virtuous large group meeting purposes. Small teams, by carving out time and meeting together for a couple of days, can set new direction, develop implementation plans, and create solutions in the moment to operational or structural problems. And they always come out of those couple of days as a more integrated, efficient, self-aware team, able to leverage their different strengths and areas of expertise to create a whole that's more than the sum of its parts.

Small team offsites can be held for many different purposes. But despite the differences, we can say that the purposes are *generative*.

The purpose of the meeting is to generate something new, not just to inform the participants and send them away. And this is a worthwhile distinction, because the common approach for a large meeting is to consider the purpose to be primarily *informational.*

A seat-of-the-pants example of a meeting purpose might be "To get reset for the coming year." In a team of eight, that will be a *generative purpose.* It won't primarily be about transmitting information, it will be about thinking together, envisioning what is coming, and creating a response to it. Whereas in a top leadership team of two hundred, "To get reset for the coming year" will probably be construed as primarily about transmitting information, "getting everyone on the same page."

> **Generative purpose**—the purpose of the meeting is not mainly to deliver content, but to be a vehicle for the group to generate alignment and commitment. This sort of purpose drives a situation where the participants not only receive information, but they also generate new information for themselves and for the organization.

For example, in the clothing manufacturer's situation with a rollout of SAP®, there were undoubtedly conversations going on all over the organization about what was coming. A lot of those conversations would have been about hearsay data points, discussed behind closed doors by apprehensive employees. But some of those conversations would have been in meetings, deliberately designed and scheduled to talk about the progress of the rollout. And in these smaller, planned meetings, the topics were probably: How is the rollout coming along? What have you been hearing from people around the organization about how they're feeling? Do you think there really will be problems? What do you think they will be? What should we do? Anything?

The purpose of those smaller planned meetings would have been generative: to figure out how the organization is responding to the news of the rollout and to see what, if anything, could be done. The processes might include generating an accurate picture of the current reality, generating a list (or sense) of what kind of problems or issues are likely to surface, coming to consensus on whether it is worthwhile to take action, and then, if it is worthwhile, generating some first action steps.

But when it came to having all of the headquarters staff, along with people in Canada and Mexico, meeting together, then the purpose was substantially narrowed. No one was able to imagine forming a picture of current reality with so many people, or aligning on what were the key trouble spots or the kinds of actions to take ahead of time. And unfortunately, in this case we were not invited to be in the design meetings. As a result, the purpose did not end up fitting the most urgent needs of the organization.

Any small meetings that were held—to identify rollout problems ahead of time and to plan responses—didn't involve the people at the all-hands meetings. So any problem identification and solutions from those smaller meetings "came down from above"; they weren't created and owned by the people who had to face the problems and implement the solutions. And the opportunity to include them was lost mostly due to a lack of awareness of what was possible in the all-hands meeting.

CLARIFYING OUTCOMES

We have said that the goal of virtuous meetings is convergence, and that convergence is the integration of the thoughts and ideas of everyone in the room. What shape does that convergence act- ually take? As we move from purpose to desired outcomes we use a model that has slowly developed over twenty years of designing virtuous meetings.

The model shown in Figure 7.3 describes a way of achieving real convergence: What steps do large groups have to move through in order to arrive at alignment and ownership? Nested inside an outcome like alignment or ownership are a number of other outcomes that provide the "stair steps" to the final outcome. Few participants are able to get from the bottom stair to the top stair in one wild jump. Figure 7.3

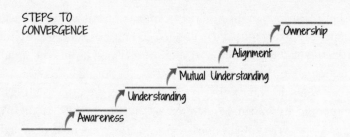

Figure 7.3 Stair-Step Model: Pathway to Convergent Outcomes

shows the steps participants need to move through to get from "here," dawning awareness, to "there," alignment and ownership:

Awareness—that there is an issue to be resolved, or a new direction to be taken

Understanding—of what the issue or the new direction is

Mutual Understanding—knowing that the group knows about the issue or direction and knowing how the group feels about it

Alignment—the group gains a common perspective and accepts the validity and wisdom of a proposed resolution to the issue or a proposed road map for moving in the new direction

Ownership—each individual feels that he or she had a hand in creating or influencing the final resolution or road map, and that executing it is in their personal interest

Having this model in mind allows you to delineate the different steps so that you can be more nuanced about what you need to accomplish. You will also realize that what it takes to accomplish certain steps is fundamentally different from what it takes to accomplish other steps. For example, Awareness and Understanding can be given to participants through well-designed and well-delivered information, whereas Mutual Understanding, Alignment, and Ownership have to be achieved by the participants themselves. These higher-level outcomes are *generated by* the participants, not *supplied to* the participants through information.

Achieving outcomes is dependent on process. And while presenting information and letting participants ask clarifying questions is a certain kind of process, it will not readily lead to an outcome like alignment. To achieve an outcome like alignment you need to use processes in which the participants themselves generate information and reactions to the information.

For example, if a large group wants to align around a suggested strategy, one process option would be to have the participants discuss the strategy, let each table group name the three most crucial things that the organization needs to stop, the three it needs to continue, and the three it needs to start in order to make the strategy work. And then let them prioritize the ideas that the synthesis shows to be the most widely held choices across the larger group. Once it's clear from the prioritization what the group feels should be stopped, started, and continued, the leadership could put those priorities into the context of the current and near-future operations and environment. As a final step you could take an anonymous Confidence Vote to see the group's overall level of confidence about whether the process had successfully identified and prioritized the things that would give the strategy the best chance to succeed.

Such a process is only one choice out of many possibilities. But the point is that in a virtuous meeting, it can be undertaken by a large group. Through these kinds of processes, the meeting can be the best way possible to get a large group aligned about what they think and feel and about the best way forward.

Figure 7.4 illustrates the movement of participants up the steps toward Alignment by executing processes like the one we just described.

As Figure 7.4 indicates, not everyone starts at the same point of awareness or understanding, and not everyone gets to the same level as everyone else. The goal of the meeting is to bring as many participants as far up the steps as possible. The group is made up of individuals, and their circumstances, ambitions, and capacities will vary. The aim is to use the process to "move the center" of the group toward greater convergence.

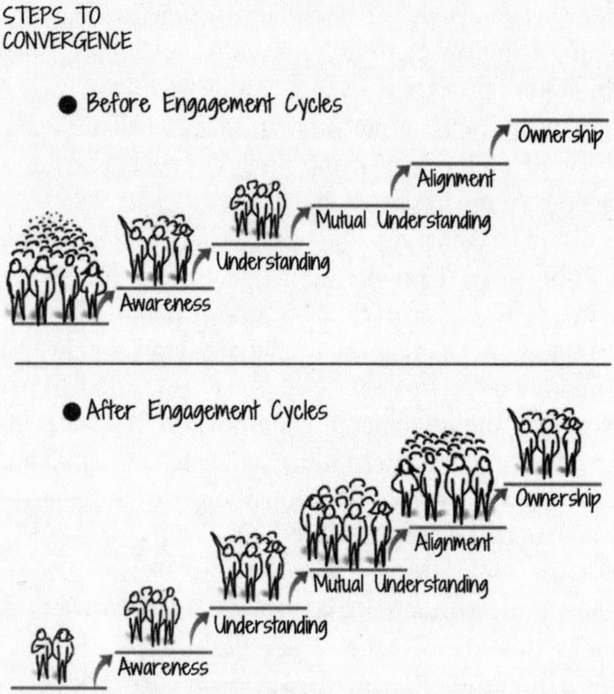

STEPS TO
CONVERGENCE

● Before Engagement Cycles

Ownership

Alignment

Mutual Understanding

Understanding

Awareness

● After Engagement Cycles

Ownership

Alignment

Mutual Understanding

Understanding

Awareness

Figure 7.4   Group Moving Toward Alignment

Defining Convergent Outcomes

If we consider *process* in the case of people designing front-of-the-room-centered meetings, no matter what outcome they say they desire to achieve, they create an agenda that is limited mostly to presentations with Q&A from the front of the room. Does that mean that they think they can achieve their desired outcomes using this process choice? A lot of confusion exists because Design Teams don't describe the outcome they are seeking in detail. Instead they just say "alignment" or "ownership" or "commitment," etc. Then the different members of the team can walk away and each imagine the outcome that they want to imagine. And the outcome they imagine often isn't tied to what can realistically be achieved through the process they have chosen. Language is the key here.

If the Design Team says the outcome they want at the end of the meetings is alignment, what do they mean? It could be: "They'll be

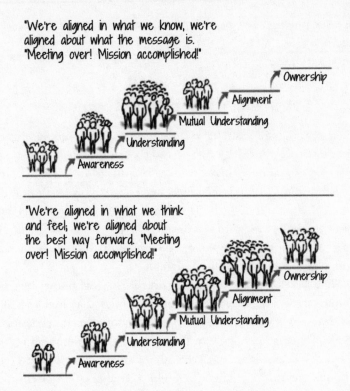

Figure 7.5 Two Interpretations of Achieving "Alignment"

aligned in what they know; they'll be aligned about what the message is." Or it could be: "They'll be aligned in what they think and feel; they'll be aligned about the best way forward." The difference between these two versions of alignment is huge. So huge, in fact, that it requires quite a different process to accomplish each one (Figure 7.5).

If the designers say the outcome they want is alignment, but they provide only passive processes for the participants, what they really mean is, "Let's give them our best reasoning, and our clearest vision of the future, and hope that most of them go along with it." You can call it "building alignment," but it is really an attempt to give enough information to be convincing. In these cases, the designers are really aiming at getting everyone aligned in what they've heard, and therefore, what they know. These kinds of processes only get the participants up the first two steps, so that participants are aware of the proposed strategy and understand what it is (Figure 7.5, top).

Achieving Higher Outcomes

Achieving ownership among a large group takes multiple engagement cycles over at least a day or two, because there has to be an opportunity for the participants to "work with it" on both the table group and whole group levels. They need to try it on, see how it fits, see how they would tailor it. They need a chance to consider how realistic it is, assess the implications to everything else they're doing, get a sense of support from their peers, and probably have some kind of input on the details of the design.

What this looks like in actual practice is highly variable. For example, there are several engagement cycles that build on one another in a sequence that takes the participants through coming to their own understanding about the proposals, and then seeing how the group understands and feels about them. And as the cycles continue, they are designed to build a common perspective on what will work, and finally incorporate enough necessary modifications, generated by the participants, so that the participants know it will be in their personal interest to make it happen.

Certainly an agenda aimed at ownership includes discussions about the future state the proposal will create, the direction things need to move in, the issues or problems that are being overcome, and the nature of changes to individuals' roles in the group that will result from doing things differently. The details of what is being proposed need to be considered in all of these aspects. And it is most conducive to generating a sense of ownership if the details are subject to modification based on the results of these different discussions. It's very helpful, as well, to test the group's confidence about the proposal all along the way, using voting tools that let each individual have an anonymous vote so that everyone gets a true picture of how the whole group is trending.

When large meeting designers say the outcome they want is ownership, and the process for achieving it is a series of presentations with Q & A, then the "ownership" they are talking about really means: "Let's give them as compelling of reasons as we can, and hope that they see how right it is and start to think that way." In reality, there is little chance of the participants coming away owning this new idea or direction. Figure 7.6 and Figure 7.7 show the two meanings of "ownership."

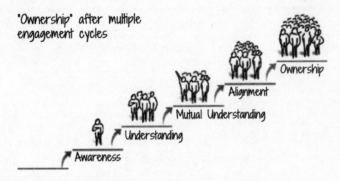

Figure 7.6 "Ownership" after Multiple Engagement Cycles

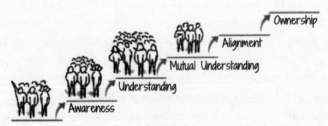

Figure 7.7 "Ownership" after Presentations with Q&A

Process Drives Outcomes

As you begin to articulate outcomes, think ahead and consider whether there is a viable process for actually achieving the outcomes you are entertaining. This seems simple enough on the face of it. However, in sitting in meeting design sessions for over twenty years, we've found that often Design Teams overlook one of the crucial

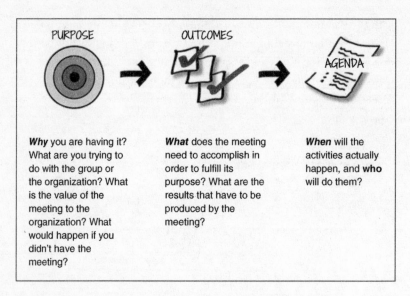

PURPOSE

Why you are having it? What are you trying to do with the group or the organization? What is the value of the meeting to the organization? What would happen if you didn't have the meeting?

OUTCOMES

What does the meeting need to accomplish in order to fulfill its purpose? What are the results that have to be produced by the meeting?

When will the activities actually happen, and **who** will do them?

AGENDA

Figure 7.8   Process Goes Missing from the Design Discussion

steps. Figure 7.8 represents the way executives and Design Teams often think about the design process.

This is a very frequent scenario. They simply decide on their desired outcomes and start building the agenda. They don't even have a conversation about the process. How will the Outcomes be accomplished? What specific process will enable the participants to align with each other (or to achieve a sense of ownership)? The designers do make process choices, but they are so used to choosing a certain process, they no longer think of it as making a choice. They don't question whether it will be effective; they just assume that the choice they've always made, the process they've always chosen, is the only way that it can be done.

Two missing design conversations need to be brought into focus. Every time a desired outcome is entertained, it should be discussed *before* it is given a name (like alignment or commitment), so that everyone understands the detail about the quality of experience that is desired. And once a clear outcome has been decided upon, then another conversation should follow that asks, How will we achieve that outcome? The further challenge, of course, is to help designers realize that there are different process options.

Without these conversations, executives and Design Team members leave design sessions imagining that they are going to achieve outcomes that can never really be achieved with the process they are planning to use in the meeting. It's very, very difficult, for example, for a large group to achieve a real sense of alignment around a new strategy, if their experience is only listening to a PowerPoint presentation about it and listening to some Q&A.

And yet this difference can go unnoticed by the Design Team because they don't spell out the meaning of alignment. To take the example of an offsite strategy meeting, if we probe deeper about what they mean when they say *alignment,* a typical statement from a Design Team member might be, "We want them to understand the new strategy, be aligned with it, committed to it, and feel like they own it—and to go out from this meeting and act on it." Crowded inside the original notion of alignment are several outcomes the group needs to accomplish in the course of the meeting. And those steps have a sequence to them. You have to accomplish one outcome to get to the next.

When considering outcomes, of course you need to know what purpose the meeting is trying to fulfill. But you also need to keep returning to the implementation sequence, asking, *How* will we accomplish this? What kind of process will we use to produce this outcome? Trying to decide on outcomes without discussing process possibilities is inefficient and can lead to mistaken expectations. Understanding what process options you have available is the best way to make good decisions about the outcomes you will try to accomplish.

Cases When Convergence Isn't Needed

This is not to say, however, that meeting designers should always choose convergent processes for their meetings. On the contrary, the process choices should be chosen based on what outcomes need to be achieved. There may be some meetings where delivering information is the main outcome that is desired. Some Design Teams might say, "We'll get them up to speed and make sure everyone hears the same message in the meeting. And then over the next several months we'll work with everyone to get them to commit to the new strategy and to own it." In that case, presentation with some Q&A may be the *best* process to use. Also, within virtuous large group meetings, there may be agenda segments that are primarily about delivering content—a special one-hour slot for an outside speaker, for example. And in these cases presentation with Q&A achieves the desired outcome. Good meeting design, of course, focuses on the agenda segments, or topics, and treats each one individually: What outcomes are needed for that segment? What process will produce those outcomes?

That being said, we want to emphasize that the days are numbered for conceiving of a large meeting as solely an opportunity to deliver content. If simply delivering the message is the main goal, then technological aids are becoming better and better for doing that without pulling all the people away from their daily responsibilities and flying them all somewhere. In the future, bringing everyone together just to deliver information will seem wasteful. The greater cost and inconvenience of bringing people together argues for making those people active contributors and designing processes that leverage that convergent potential.

PRACTICAL CONSIDERATIONS ABOUT PROCESS

As with any design practice, paying attention to the details of a particular application is essential for ensuring that the design is effective. Part of thinking about the purpose, outcomes, and process of a meeting is to consider whatever givens and constraints are already defined for the meeting, the number of participants and the length of the meeting, and the particular culture of the group that is meeting.

Making the Design Work

Designing a virtuous large group meeting doesn't depend on any particular structure for the meeting. The design process is quite flexible within whatever givens and constraints already exist for the meeting. But it is important to understand what has already been decided or put in place, so that the processes in the agenda segments are realistic and workable. For example, there may be three important speakers that have to be squeezed into a ninety-minute slot before the morning break because they are all flying out after that. Rather than try to have a discussion after each speaker and end up with almost no time for their presentations, it might be better to let each of them have thirty minutes to present, let them leave, take the morning break, and then design a discussion for the participants after the break that addresses some shared aspect of all three of the presentations from the morning.

> The important point here is to be fluid with the process so that it enables the group to get the most value out of each activity that they engage in.

Also, the number of participants and how long they have for their meeting are extremely important in calibrating the design. We will look at making those calibrations in Chapter Eight. Also, in many ways this consideration has to do with scaling, and we will look at the scaling possibilities in detail in Chapter Twelve.

Considering Culture

Many of the design decisions at the process level, decisions about how to structure the agenda segments, will depend on the culture of the group that is meeting. All groups fall along different points of a continuum with regard to openness, honesty, sense of urgency, willingness to speak up in front of superiors, awareness of themselves as a group, and trust. Each group is different, and their reaction to being given an active contributing role in the meeting will vary.

> The important point here is to assess the culture as well as you can before making design suggestions, and always give credence to people's input about how the group will respond to the process activities that are being designed—both how participants will respond and how leaders will respond to their new roles in the meeting.

There may be people who are nervous about any change in the purpose, outcomes, or processes of their meeting. And they will argue against holding a virtuous large group meeting or argue against the process decisions at the agenda segment level. To the extent that it is just doubt about the unfamiliar, these voices can be a resource for plumbing the cultural constraints that will need to be accounted for in designing particular activities. Large meetings can have a profound effect on the participants, and it is worthwhile to treat every reservation as an insight into how the culture functions. The reason for doing this kind of design for large meetings is to transform the role of the participants, and by doing that, to transform the role of the leaders or conveners as well. That transformation is always an interesting and nuanced metamorphosis, and a key aspect of it is paying attention to the group's culture and adapting the convergent processes to be safe and to make sense to everyone who will be at the meeting.

Concerns of Trust, Safety, Respect, and Learning

When you take participants from being an audience to being active contributors, you can begin to envision meetings that have purposes and outcomes that are more similar to small meetings: purposes like generating strategy or defining and catalyzing new actions.

Part of what this means is that the designer has to address the dynamics and concerns that would normally be encountered in designing and facilitating a small meeting. The participant-centered approach to large meetings has the advantage of accomplishing outcomes that normally can only be accomplished in small meetings or groups. It also has the responsibilities that go along with working with a group of people actively engaged with each other. The concerns that surface when participants in a large meeting become active contributors include

- Trust
- Safety
- Respect
- Learning

These are the types of concerns that a designer or facilitator would expect to encounter in planning a meeting for a group of twenty or thirty participants, where much of the time will be spent in open conversation. But at first this may seem like quite a departure from the usual concerns of someone designing a meeting for several hundred.

In reality those concerns are there for any meeting of any size. They are obvious in a smaller group, where everyone, by default, interacts with each other. In a large or very large group, they become more readily obvious in a process in which every effort is being made to create real-time interactions among the participants. When you are asking participants to discuss critical topics and provide ideas or formulate solutions, and when you are asking leaders to get up and respond to what the group is thinking, then you begin to realize that issues of trust and respect and safety are going to be important to everyone.

In front-of-the-room-centered large meetings there is so little interaction that trust and safety aren't obvious issues. No one is putting him- or herself at risk of very much. The learning is highly structured. And the respect for the participant is supposedly conferred by the invitation to attend in the first place.

But although these concerns seem far less important in a front-of-the-room-centered meeting, in actuality the same concerns do exist. They just aren't being addressed directly. We have to return to the concept outlined in Chapter One: the meeting *is* the message. The process of the meeting, the format, what people are actually doing and *not doing*, is a clear and compelling communication about how these concerns are being handled by the group.

When interactivity is kept at a minimum, it can communicate that trust and safety are actually major concerns of all of the players, participant and leaders alike. Keeping learning as a one-way channel from the expert or leader to the audience underscores a disempowering and de-energizing view of how learning takes place and who is involved. And the value of people's time and the respect for their experience and knowledge is called into question quite forcefully by asking them to sit and play a passive role all day.

Let's look at how virtuous meeting design addresses such underlying concerns in large meetings. A critical part of striving for more ambitious outcomes and purposes in large meetings is addressing these concerns by building trust, ensuring safety and respect, and creating the opportunity for active learning. The issue of trust is addressed by making sure that the things participants and presenters are asked to do are safe (meaning they are not being asked to take reckless risks).

Safety for Participants

For the participants, safety comes from anonymity. In most cases, all of the input from the small table groups is kept anonymous. This means that the participants, in their small discussion groups, can feel free to communicate whatever truth they feel they are seeing. Anonymity may seem counter to candor at first, but experience shows that it actually promotes candor in the long run.

It is completely normal for participants to be afraid to speak their mind in front of a large group, particularly in an organizational setting. And it's not because they are being weak or malicious, but rather because they're being smart in the face of real or perceived hierarchies and the threat of reprisal. Anonymity in the input system allows the whole group to get difficult issues out onto the table safely, without identifying the people who were bringing the issues up. Often, once the ideas are out there and the group sees them, individuals are more empowered to address and own the issues (and the solutions). It is common for individuals to be voicing challenging concerns into microphones by the end of Day 1 of a meeting that has employed multiple Virtuous Engagement Cycles (and anonymity) from the start.

Anonymity is often the quickest way to get participants to open up and bring their most honest and constructive experiences to the discussion. When honest feedback is asked for and given—albeit gingerly at first—and it is responded to with increasing honesty and transparency by leaders, then participants are more willing to give honest feedback in subsequent cycles as well.

Safety for Leaders and Presenters

On the other side, leaders and presenters need to have safety, too, in order to embrace a process in which they don't know what the group might say. Two principles are important here. First, the input from all of the participants is filtered through the group that is synthesizing. This means that there is a filtering mechanism so that what the presenter or leader is responding to is meaningful and succinct. Second, she can have access to the synthesis before going on stage to respond to it, so that she is not surprised or taken off guard by what she has to respond to. There are many different ways to structure how the input is synthesized and how and where in the process the leader or presenter is kept informed, but the principle is that the person who has to get up in front of the room and respond to the group should never be surprised and should be comfortable with the process that has been designed. The issues of trust and safety are further addressed by making sure that what participants are asked to do, and the process as a whole, is constructive and gets them to new places that they want to go.

Constructive Contribution

Often during the design process we are asked, "What if they [the participants] start sending in negative or offensive comments? Does that happen?" And the answer really is that it doesn't. But that is a result of the design principles of a virtuous meeting. One part of it is that the participants' contributions are valued and the participants are respected. Asking the participants for their input, and giving them thoughtful and meaningful questions to discuss—questions that they can see have a value for the organization—confers respect on the participants. And when their ideas are reflected back to the group through synthesizing them with all of the other participant ideas, and responded to by the leadership, that confers value on their contribution. Under those conditions, the conversations become very constructive. Issues and problems may be identified, but they are identified in a constructive way that is aimed at solutions and the more effective operation of the whole organization.

Another design principle that keeps the conversations and the input very constructive is that these are small group discussions. This is nothing like the sniping by nameless individuals in online comment sections that have become all too familiar. When people from an organization sit with others of their colleagues, often people that they don't see on an everyday basis, and discuss the real issues facing them, the conversation is critical to them, and there is no time for petty diversions. Because the input comes from a group, it keeps one individual's sour grapes from becoming exaggerated into a statement.

Respecting the Participants

The underlying question of respect for the participants is addressed through valuing the participants' time and their contributions during the meeting. This means respecting the work of the participants in their small group conversations. It means making sure cycles get completed, so that participants aren't asked to give a lot of input and then hear nothing back about it. It means making sure the discussions only last as long as they are valuable to the participants, but also making sure that they don't feel that they are so short that many participants can't get their thoughts voiced. The key to conferring respect is using the participants' input well. Part of that is making sure there is meaningful and focused response to their input.

Learning as an Interactive Process

Finally, learning has to be embraced as an active experience. Virtuous meeting design is focused on creating learning that is empowering and energizing. The participant is learning at each step. Whether the activity is active listening, engaging in a discussion, generating an idea, or hearing what the group came up with and what the presenter thinks of it, at the core of each step is discovery—learning about oneself, the group, the presenter, and the issue.

The greatest value of virtuous large group meetings is that they can make it possible to bring large groups together for purposes that in the past would have been attempted only in small groups. And they can fulfill these types of generative, collaborative purposes within the time frame of a normal large group meeting. The key to achieving these purposes is bringing the group step by step to higher and higher outcomes. And the ability for the group to cross the threshold from individual understanding to mutual understanding, and beyond, rests with the process and the choices that are made to shape that process. In the next chapter we try to give a comprehensive overview of those process choices, and we offer some insight into the criteria for choosing different options that are available at each stage of each Virtuous Engagement Cycle.

ℭ CHAPTER SEVEN • QUICK SUMMARY

- The design sequence includes four elements: purpose, outcomes, process, and agenda.
- Virtuous meetings allow you to aim for more generative purposes, similar to the purposes that would seem natural in small meetings.
- Virtuous meetings achieve outcomes that involve all of the participants being able to hear and understand each other—outcomes such as mutual understanding, alignment, and ownership.
- Outcomes are produced by the processes that you use in a meeting. It is important to identify outcomes very specifically and concretely, to be sure that the processes you are using in the meeting can actually achieve the outcomes you desire.
- Large group virtuous meetings are similar to small group meetings because everyone has a voice. As a result, it is important to pay attention to issues of trust, safety, and respect.

CHAPTER EIGHT

MAKING CHOICES:
THE DESIGN LEVERS

M utual understanding, alignment, and ownership aren't given to the participants through presentations. Rather, they are *achieved by participants* in the meeting—in a small meeting through simple open conversation, and in a large or very large meeting through a two-level convergent process that focuses on creating and completing Virtuous Engagement Cycles in the various agenda segments.

Virtuous Engagement Cycles proceed through four stages. At each new stage of the cycle there are different design choices available to us. These design choices, or options, are like levers that we can pull in order to shape the cycle in the way that will be most productive and effective. As designers, when we look across an engagement cycle, we decide which levers to pull for the presentation stage, which levers to pull for the discussion stage, and so on.

> **Design levers**—design decisions that help us shape the format, tools, timing, roles, and content of the meeting; they can include presentation levers, discussion levers, focusing question levers, input levers, and response levers.

The choices are finite; there are only a few levers for each stage. As we design one stage, we want to keep the other stages in mind. We want to be able to see what levers are available to us and make sure that the lever we are pulling at one stage supports and is coordinated with the levers we are pulling at the other stages.

161

All of these levers are commonsense choices, but some may be unfamiliar to designers who haven't designed large two-level meetings that utilize high-speed connectivity. In this chapter we will lay out all of the levers in a chart, so that you can see them in relation to each other. And we will take a focused look at each lever, providing more detail about what the choices are and what considerations are relevant in making those design choices.

Paying attention to these levers is critical. While the new connectivity makes the engagement cycle efficient, it doesn't make the cycle effective. Making thoughtful design decisions about which levers are needed at each stage is what makes the method effective.

STAGES AND LEVERS: THE BUILDING BLOCKS

In Chapter Five, we introduced the Virtuous Engagement Cycle. Let's review the stages of the cycle again in Figure 8.1.

Let's break down the stages again so that we will know where to use the design levers that we discuss in this chapter:

1. **Present.** Something is presented to the group.
   The group is given a question.
2. **Discuss.** The table groups go into small focused discussions (micro-breakouts).

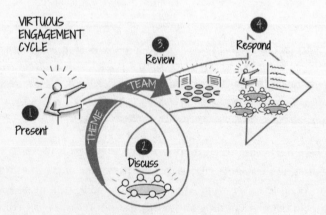

Figure 8.1 Virtuous Engagement Cycle

The groups send the ideas from their discussion to the synthesizers.

All of the groups' ideas get synthesized.

3. **Review.** The themes from the synthesis get presented to the whole group.

4. **Respond.** The presenters, or others, respond to the themes of what the group is saying.

Table 8.1 is meant to serve as a reference for large meeting designers using the Virtuous Meetings approach. We have attempted to be as comprehensive as possible in laying out the different levers at the designer's disposal. The purpose of this table is to look at all of the levers in one view, so that it is easier to consider what implications the different decisions have on each other. The Participant Engagement Designer on the Design Team will be particularly focused on keeping the choices for these decisions in mind and in front of the team, so that by the time of the meeting there will be a specific and realistic plan for how to handle each of the agenda segments throughout the meeting.

You can read this table column by column, thinking about the levers in relation to each unfolding stage of the Virtuous Engagement Cycle. Or you can read across the chart horizontally, considering who is involved at each stage, what everyone will be doing at each stage, what all the timing will look like, and so forth.

PERSPECTIVES ON DESIGN VARIATIONS

Before we go into the detail of the levers available at each stage of the engagement cycle, it may be useful to take an overview of the design perspective. At the core is the principle of small group conversations producing large group understanding through the Virtuous Engagement Cycle. But virtuous large group meetings may look very different depending on what kind of purpose and which kind of participants they are designed for.

Table 8.1 Decision Levers in the Virtuous Engagement Cycle

In these stages of the Cycle, → you have these decisions ↘ in these areas ↓	Present		Discuss
	Presentation Levers	**Focusing Question Levers**	**Discussion Levers**
Who	Who will present?	. . .	Who will be seated together?
Content (What)	What will be presented?	What question(s) will be asked?	. . .
Timing and Duration (When)	How long will the presentation last?	When will the group hear the question(s)?	How long will the discussion last? How will their time be allotted?
Format (How)	. . .	How many questions? Will the whole group answer the same questions?	How many people will be in each small group? Will anyone facilitate the conversation?
Tools	. . .	. . .	. . .

		Review	Respond
Input Levers	**Synthesis Levers**	**Review Levers**	**Response Levers**
Who at the table will have the role of entering the input?	Who will do the synthesis?	Who will review the synthesized group input?	Who will respond to the synthesis?
What type of content will participants be entering?	. . .	What will be reviewed?	What will the response be?
. . .	When will the synthesis happen? How long will they have to do the synthesis?	When will the synthesis be reviewed?	When will they respond? How long will the response be?
How much content will they enter?	What synthesis method will be used?	How will the synthesis be reviewed?	. . .
What tool will be used for entering their thoughts?	What tool will synthesizers use?	What tool will be used to review the synthesis?	. . .

The different stages—Present, Discuss, Review, and Respond—may play out differently in different kinds of virtuous meetings. If we compare three major kinds of large group meetings—organizational, multi-stakeholder, and civic—we can examine what the needs of each kind of large group would be, and how that would play out in terms of designing the stages of the Virtuous Engagement Cycle.

If we focus on the participants, their relationship to each other, and what they are trying to accomplish through a large meeting, we see that there are certain differences that will influence the design of a large-scale meeting:

Organizational meeting participants know each other and are organized in a hierarchy. They share a common goal of organizational success.

Multi-stakeholder meeting participants may know each other, but they don't work together and there is generally no formal hierarchy. They are experts and have a common interest: finding the best, mutually agreeable way forward.

Civic meeting participants don't know each other and there is no hierarchy. There are no experts, and their goal is to define interests and find common ground.

Let's look at the general design considerations for each stage of the Virtuous Engagement Cycle in these three types of meetings:

·   *Organizational meetings.* Presentations are often key in these meetings, and would tend to be the dominant mode of activity in traditional front-of-the-room-centered meeting design. In virtuous meeting designs, the presentations are necessarily briefer, so that some of the agenda block can be spent in discussion at the tables. The presentations therefore tend to be more focused and concise than usual (a more limited number of PowerPoint slides), but they still form a significant portion of most agenda segments.

Because organizational meetings have such a need for presentations, we often have shorter discussion periods, with fewer participants in the discussion group. Even if you have tables of six participants, you may break them into two discussion groups. The smaller the discussion group is, the more "air time" each member gets. So if you have limited time for discussion, the smaller the groups are, the more each member of the group will get to be active in digesting what was presented, and they will all have more opportunity to express ideas and formulate the tables' input to the larger group.

The synthesis that is presented back to the large group is often a bulleted list that is easy to understand. Sometimes there will be prioritization (vote) of the list, depending on what the next step in the meeting process is. But more often the list will be a way for everyone to see what the group is thinking and a volley into the leadership's court, so that whoever has been presenting can respond to the group's ideas and concerns.

The response by the leadership from the front of the room in organizational meetings is extremely important because of the hierarchical nature of most organizations. To achieve a sense of shared understanding in the room, the participants need to know how the leadership feels about what the table groups came up with. How this response is handled gives a candid picture of the culture of the group. If, for example, a change in culture is sought, this is a marquee moment to illustrate that change—to "walk the talk." We will talk more about this in Chapter Eleven where we discuss the leader's role in virtuous large group meetings.

Multi-stakeholder meetings. Presentation may or may not play a big role in meetings where a group of stakeholders is trying to come to convergence. There may be information that needs to be shared in order to work together, or the options may be well known but the challenge is to find a common way forward. Presentations can also take the form of expert panels, such as those at international summits, whose members interact with each other to create a new set of perspectives for the participants to consider in their table groups.

The discussion tends to be the focus of such meetings, and having more participants in the discussion groups is advantageous because the goal is to bring many points of view to bear on what is being discussed. Also these discussions tend to be longer than those in organizational meetings. Partly this is due to less need for presentation time, but mostly it is because the discussion is more of an exploration, taking the group through new and uncharted territory.

Also, although everyone at the table may share a common interest in getting to a convergent solution, they may all be coming from different stakeholder realities, and it takes time to wade through what keeps the group separated and what brings the group's thinking together.

The synthesis in this case can take many forms, and it tends to be more detailed and perhaps more complex than the synthesis for an organizational meeting. Often there is a need to prioritize what the large group has come up with, in order to find and work further with the most commonly shared subset of ideas. One of the outcomes that is frequently needed from this kind of meeting is an agreed set of actions, priorities, or perspectives, so that the conveners can take the next step in trying to create a solution.

Response to the synthesis is less critical in these meetings. However, if an expert, or a panel of experts, set up the topic for discussion, the participants are usually eager to hear what that person, or people, have to say about what they came up with and how they prioritized it. The presenters at this point in the process can give valuable input to the group about the reality of what they are proposing and the things they may need to pay attention to heading off in the direction they have chosen. Often the group itself will be asked to respond to the synthesis, by voting on to what degree the synthesis represents what went on at their table.

Civic meetings. Civic meetings are similar to multi-stakeholder meetings in many respects. However, in most cases, citizens come to a meeting representing themselves, and maybe those at home who are most like them. And their common interest is more grounded in their own life and needs, rather than something that they are trying to accomplish for an organization or for the world. Civic meetings using the two-level process with Virtuous Engagement Cycles are truly democracy in action; participants stand for their own point of view—one voice, one vote per person.

Presentations are generally best kept to a minimum. They can be invaluable for setting the context of the discussion and inspiring the participants to bring the best of themselves to the deliberations. But they are not a good place to try to "bring everyone up to speed." People are at too many different levels of familiarity with the topics, and the presentation will either be too simplistic for many of them, or if you go the other way, too complex for many of the other participants.

What we have seen work best is to have comprehensive materials premade and staged at the tables. These materials create an even playing field no matter what level of familiarity a citizen has with the topic. Although the presentations may be kept to a minimum, time needs to be built into the agenda, in place of the presentations, for the participants to look through the materials at the table and think about them a bit. If the materials are broken into bite-size chunks to go with each topic, it reduces the time that people need to review them, and we've found that it does not seem to interrupt the flow of the meeting.

As with multi-stakeholder meetings, the discussion is the center-piece of the Virtuous Engagement Cycle in civic meetings. Discussion periods tend to be lengthy, and a larger discussion group actually helps everyone to work their way through the discussion. In these meetings one of the needed outcomes is for participants to hear views that are different from, or even opposite, their own, and then come to some kind of understanding of that point of view and a way to incorporate it into their view of the topic going forward. So having more people in the discussion group—and people from different walks of life, ages, professions, life experiences, and so forth—is actually part of the process that can deliver the needed outcome.

However, there is a need for caution here. A small group conversation goes very easily with three participants. With six participants it still goes fairly easily, and most people are able to assert themselves and play an active role in the discussion when they want to. But when you get up to eight people or more, there is the real possibility that some members will not have their say. And above eight people, it becomes more important to have someone playing a facilitation role in the table group. Once you get to ten or more participants, you are really talking about a small meeting of its own, and it is important to define a role that is looking out for the process within the group and making sure that everyone's voice is heard.

In presenting back the synthesis in civic meetings, the aim should be to keep it simple, knowing that you want it to be as accurate and comprehensive as possible. Often there will be voting on what is presented back to the group if it has been an ideation type of process. In this way, you get an instant read on how the whole group feels about the ideas that were proposed. This doesn't always lead to further work with those ideas in the next section of the agenda, but it lets the group, policymakers, and the media see where things stand.

Response to the synthesis is generally not as important in these meetings, unless it comes from someone who is in a policymaking position relative to the topic. Often politicians will be invited and asked to tell the group their response to what has been generated. If the politicians are people who have some power to affect the group's proposals, obviously the group is very keen to hear their feedback.

BECOMING FAMILIAR WITH EACH LEVER: Design Considerations for Each of the Levers

What follows is a more complete articulation of design considerations, organized by the different levers that are shown in Table 8.1. Please refer to Table 8.1 as you use this section. This section is not meant to be read through as a part of the text, it is meant to serve as a reference for designers, something that you can come back to as needed. As you find yourself facing different design challenges, you can use the specific details in the following pages to get perspective on what your choices might be and criteria that might be useful in choosing between them.

The following discussion of levers has been arranged according to the different stages of the cycle. This arrangement is designed to be helpful in thinking about the design implications of each choice.

Stage 1: *Present* → Presentation Levers

Who	Who will present?

Choices

- The person who will respond to the participants' themes during the Response stage.
- One of the people who will respond to the participants' themes during the Response stage.
- A different person than the person who will respond to the participants' themes during the Response stage.

Considerations

- The ideal is to have the person who will respond to the groups' input be the one who delivers the presentation. That works just as well if the response to the group will be from a panel and the presenter is a member or the moderator of the panel.
- If someone else is going to respond to the group's input, then it is best for those two people to have time to talk about the presentation, the scope, the details, and the purpose, so that the presenter can calculate what information to deliver and the person responding to the group understands the detail of the information and the key goals in presenting it.

*   *   *

Content	What will be presented?

Choices

- The key considerations for this lever are the amount of information to present, the choice of what to present, and what level of detail to include.

Considerations

- What makes presentations different in virtuous large group meetings is that the group will be discussing what was presented and then respond to it. And the presenter will have an opportunity to react to the group's responses.
- Often this means that the ideal will be to condense what the presenter might originally think to present to the group. This accomplishes two things. First it allows the group to have time to

discuss what they've heard. Second, it allows the presenter to have an opportunity to spend some of the agenda time more exactly focused on what the group is most concerned about with regard to the topic. In a normal presentation, the presenter never really finds out what the group cares about most. It's really up to the presenter to cover as much of the topic as she can, in as much detail as time will permit. In addition, she has to try to provide *all* of the content that the group might want to hear about in detail. If, instead, the group gets to discuss a shorter presentation, the themes that come out of that discussion will tell the presenter what details the group needs to hear more about. Then, in the response stage the presenter can be very accurately focused on the specific details that the group cares most about.

- Rather than thinking of the presentation as one event, the presentation should be thought of as a two-part sequence: (1) the presentation, and (2) the response to the participants' input. The presentation time that is sacrificed so that the participants can have a chance to converse is recouped by being more specific and accurate in the follow-on detail of the Response stage. This is also much more tailored and interesting for the participants.

*   *   *

Timing and Duration	How long will the presentation last?

Choices

- This follows on from the last lever. The length of the presentation should be calculated based on how much material there is to deliver, how long you want to allow the participants to discuss it, and how long you want the Response stage to be (including the review of what the participants have come up with).
- The presentation can take as much time as desired, as long as there is enough time for a meaningful small group discussion (which can be as little as a few minutes in a group of three participants) and time for the presenter to respond to the fruits of that discussion.

Considerations

- It is always good to err toward shorter time at the front end (the presentation) and allowing more time to respond to what the group is saying. Of course, that has to be balanced by the amount of material that needs to be delivered. But if you consider the value that the participants will get out of their table discussions, many times it will make it worth it to cut out some of the material that was being considered.
- Often the amount of time traditionally left at the end of an agenda segment "for some brief Q&A from the floor" is a little less than is needed for the engagement cycle to be completed well. So a good suggestion is to try to condense the presentation a bit and cut it down to more essential points—assuming that you will get to deliver relevant detail in the Response stage.

Stage 1: *Present* → Focusing Question Levers

Content	What question(s) will be asked?

Choices

- More general or more specific.
- Tapping into what everyone's already been thinking about versus exploring an area or idea that is new to everyone.
- Tied directly to the content of the presentation versus a more general subject that incorporates what was presented.

Considerations

- Designing the best possible question is paramount. But that is balanced by the fact that there is no "right" question. The question both focuses the table group discussions, so that they are productive, and determines the scope of what the group will learn about itself when it sees the synthesis of all of the "answers."
- You need to think: What would be most productive for this group to have a discussion about? The definition of "productive" will depend on what outcomes you are after. But generally in a convergent meeting you will want to mine the wisdom,

experience, and on-the-ground knowledge of the assembled participants. You want the synthesized answers to the question to give you a window into the thoughts and feelings of the group that would otherwise be unavailable. And you want the collective realizations of the answers to benefit the operations of the organization.

- If the purpose of the meeting is generative, more like a small team meeting would be, then the answers to the question have to produce some new information—information that the larger group can work with and respond to.

* * *

Timing and Duration	When will the group hear the question(s)?

Choices

- Before the presentation (or any presented material in any form).
- After the presentation, as the group is about to go into their table group discussions.

Considerations

- If you give the group the question before or during the presentation, they can focus their attention more precisely as they are listening. This makes for more active listening.
- If you want them to be more neutral during the presented material, and not be overly focused in any particular direction, then you can give them the question as they go into discussion.
- The middle route is telling them, "After this presentation, we are going to give you an opportunity to discuss xyz in your table groups" so that they are aware of what the upcoming discussion will focus on, but they don't have a specific question they are thinking about as they listen to the presentation.

* * *

Format	How many questions? Will the whole group answer the same questions?

Choices

- A single question answered by the whole group—the default and most commonly used lever.
- When you have a large group, there is the temptation to have them cover multiple topics at once by assigning part of the room to discuss one topic and other parts of the room to discuss other topics. This is similar to what designers often try to accomplish through having a few large breakout groups.
- A different scenario is to have the whole group discuss a couple or even several different questions during a single discussion period. This is generally used to cover different facets of a single topic (e.g., What are the three things you think will be most difficult for us to overcome in order to do xyz? And what do you think are the three things that will most readily leverage what we already have in place?).
- Of course, the fourth choice is the combination of the other two, where different parts of the group discuss different topics and they discuss more than one question.

Considerations

- The considerations here are a bit tricky. All of your levers have to be coordinated. As you get into multiple questions to discuss, and particularly different topics for different parts of the room, you begin to have a lot of repercussions throughout the engagement cycle. These choices will affect
  - How much time the table groups have for discussion
  - How large the table groups are, and whether there is anyone playing a facilitation role in the table group
  - How large the synthesis team is, how well planned the process is for that team, and how long they have to do the synthesizing
  - How long the group has for the Review stage of the cycle, as well as for the Respond stage
- Generally, either multiple questions or multiple topics add time to the table group discussions. They also add complexity to the allocation of time to the task at the table—requiring

more facilitative focus either at the tables or from the front of the room.

- Multiple questions require either more time or more teammates at the synthesis team. Generally, multiple topics require both more time and more teammates, although if there is just one question for each topic, it can be done just with more time.
- And the more different questions (and topics) get synthesized, the more time it takes to review those syntheses, and the more material there is that must be addressed in the Response stage of the cycle.

Stage 2: *Discuss* → Discussion Levers

Who	Who will be seated together?

Choices

- There are many choices, but a key question is whether you want to assign participants to specific tables (assigned seating) or let them self-select their table (unassigned seating).
- If you are going to assign the seating, the question is whether you want to have diverse groups working together at the tables (e.g., cross-functional groups), or you want to have groups with something in common working together (e.g., participants from the same function).
- A corollary question is whether to have the groups change during the meeting, so that for certain topics they are sitting in more diverse groups and for other topics they are seated in more homogeneous groups.

Considerations

- You want to think about what you are trying to accomplish in a particular agenda segment and try to figure out who could have the most productive conversation. Usually this is from the point of view of the large group or the whole organization. Is it more important to get people talking together who never get to interact? (Which configuration might be helpful for topics that address the whole organization or the environment it operates in?) Or is it more important to home in on specific details in the discussion that only the people from a certain function know and care about?

- Also, you may want to change the table assignments at lunch, or at the start of the second day, in order to allow participants to meet and have discussions with more people.

*   *   *

Timing and Duration	How long will the discussion last?

Choices

- This is wide open. Less than a few minutes, even with a three-person group, will not seem satisfactory.
- After about forty-five minutes, people's attention starts to wander and the group loses focus.

Considerations

- How many participants are in the group will make a big difference in how long they will need for discussion—the more participants in the group, the more time you need to budget for their discussions.
- Having multiple questions will increase the time the group needs.
- If the discussion is about a topic that the participants are already thinking about every day, then the discussion can be relatively shorter than if the participants have to spend a while just "opening up" the topic in their own minds and the whole discussion is more exploratory and creative.
- If the table groups are asked to come to consensus, for example, what is "their one most important idea," getting agreement at the table will take additional time.

*   *   *

Timing and Duration	How will their time be allotted?

Choices

- Just have one set time length for the discussion and let the group manage their own time.
- Decide how long you want them spending on each stage of the discussion, or on each question (if there are multiple questions), and create a very simple structure for the discussions.

Considerations

- You may want to create some sort of structure for these table discussions, if
  - The group is large (eight to ten participants)
  - The group is answering more than one question during the course of a single discussion period
  - The time you are giving them for discussion is relatively long

*   *   *

Format	How many people will be in each small group?

Choices

- The group size can vary anywhere from two to ten participants; with fewer than two, there's no discussion; with more than ten, it becomes difficult to seat everyone at the same table in the plenary.

Considerations

- You have to be able to seat the number you choose at whatever tables are available to you in the venue (or bring the size tables you want into the venue).
- The fewer participants in the group, the more "air time" they each will have to express their views and ideas. So a discussion will go more quickly with a smaller group.
- The more participants in a group, the more different viewpoints will be represented in the discussion. So a discussion will include more diversity and "processing" with a larger group.

- You can always break a table group up into smaller groups for the discussions. We commonly have tables of six for leadership meetings. Often we will have them work independently as two groups of three, so that they can participate actively when there is only limited time for discussion. Then at other times during the day, when we want more perspectives in the discussion, we will budget a little more time and have them work as a group of six.
- A group up to about five or six participants can facilitate itself. Once the table group gets bigger than that, it is helpful to have someone in the group playing a facilitator role.

* * *

Format	Will anyone facilitate the conversation?

Choices

- Have the group self-facilitate.
- Have the group identify a volunteer in the group to play a facilitative role.
- Supply a facilitator for each table.

Considerations

- Mostly it's a question of how big the table group is. Once it starts to be seven or eight participants or more, it becomes it's own "mini-meeting," and having someone to look after the process of the discussion, and make sure every voice gets included, becomes very helpful.
- If you can supply the facilitators, then you can design a more intricate process at the tables, because you'll have the opportunity to communicate with them and brief them ahead of the meeting.
- If you have to rely on a volunteer from the table group, then it is best to keep the process at the table simple and try to have an efficient way to convey your expectations of the role to the volunteer.

Stage 2: *Discuss* → Input Levers

Who	Who at the table will have the role of entering the input?

Choices

- The group selects a volunteer.
- The group selects a volunteer, and after a while someone else in the group relieves the original volunteer.
- A person is assigned to that role by the conveners.
- Whoever is facilitating also takes on the role of recording the input.

Considerations

- Usually the group selects the volunteer. This happens naturally in a table group of three or four. The process is a bit more formalized if there are ten people and an assigned facilitator.
- Usually the role gets passed between different people in the table group during the course of the day (if they all stay together in the same table group all day).
- It is usually difficult for someone who has taken on the role of facilitator in a larger table group (eight to ten) to also be the one recording the input. The facilitator can be more effective in their role if they can keep close attention on the conversation dynamics of the table group and not be distracted trying to capture the group's thoughts on a device.

* * *

Content	What type of content will participants be entering?

Choices

- A single word or two.
- Brief phrases or sentences.
- Multiple sentences—complex answers that incorporate several details of a solution or a direction.

Considerations

- This is largely determined by the nature of the question(s) that are asked.
- If you want it to be synthesized quickly—particularly if you are working with a very large group—then you probably want to keep answers as phrases or single sentences.
- If it's more important to have a detailed record after the meeting, and the topics are slightly complex or multistepped, then you might want longer, more involved responses that capture all of the detail you need to understand exactly what the group was thinking.

* * *

Format	How much content will they enter?

Choices

- Only one comment or idea if you restrict them in the instructions: "Talk together in your table group and come up with the one action we need to take next year in order to . . ."
- Several ideas or comments.
- Many ideas or comments.

Considerations

- The more content entered at each table, the bigger the job is for the team that has to synthesize all of it in real time.
- Generally, the size of the group does not determine how much content gets entered.
- The longer the discussion period is, the more content will come in—to be more thorough, budget longer discussion periods; to make the content easier to synthesize, keep the discussions somewhat shorter.
- Despite the length of the discussion period, you can control how much content comes in through the instructions you

give: "Discuss in your table group and send in . . . your top three . . . a handful, as many . . . as you can think of."

*   *   *

Tools	What tool will be used for entering their thoughts?

Choices

- Hardware
  - Smartphone
  - Tablet
  - Laptop
  - Monitor with keyboard
- Software
  - Software that was designed and built for harnessing the free text input from many different sources
  - Software that has some sort of function for posting a question that people can answer in a text format
  - Any kind of software that enables the user to write a free text comment

Considerations

- Hardware
  - Readability of the screen—with larger table groups, having a larger screen is helpful, although usually the only one who has to be able to read the screen is the person typing in the group's input. But often other people in the group like to watch what is going in. Phones, of course, can really only be read by the typist.
  - Comfort in typing the group's input—because you want the groups to be able to put in plenty of detail when they need to, comfort in typing is important, particularly in a multiday meeting.
  - Portability—devices with long battery life, and which are smaller and lighter, are easier to work with logistically for the conveners and the participants.

- Availability—which device is most readily available for the group to use is a factor, but ready availability should not force the group into using devices that are uncomfortable or less effective in some way for the group.
- Software
  - The main criteria are that it is easy for the participants to use (zero learning curve), it is available on any hardware device the group chooses to use (without having to download or install anything), and the interface is extremely flexible to accommodate multiple questions, multiple subgroups within the room (with separate questions), and other media that might need to be used or referenced by the participants. It is especially important that the manner in which the data comes in from the table groups makes it very easy for the synthesizers to access the data quickly and be able to divide it, so that the synthesizing team can assign members to look at different parts of the data simultaneously (see the section below on synthesizing).
  - At Covision we always work with software that we have developed that is designed specifically for free text entry (and voting) from large numbers of table groups or individuals in a meeting. It is browser based and can be used just as easily across multiple locations, as we discuss in detail in Chapter Twelve. It supports any number of users no matter how many, is a simple interface, and makes the parallel synthesizing process very easy that takes place while the table groups are in discussions and sending in the fruits of those discussions.
  - If you end up having to use software that was not designed for this purpose, take time to evaluate how the data would be retrieved (by a synthesis team) during the discussion period as the table groups are sending in their thoughts. Also evaluate how easy it is for participants to understand what to do to operate the software, and whether the interface has the flexibility for the kinds of processes that you are considering doing with the group. While it is tempting to think you'll just use Twitter to get the table group input, or

WebEx for a multi-site meeting, you may find that their limitations make it worth pursuing a more sophisticated software that is more directly aimed at supporting real-time convergent processes at a large and/or distributed scale.

Stage 2: *Discuss* → Synthesis Levers

Who	Who will do the synthesis?

Choices

- A synthesis team made up of people from the organization that is convening the meeting.
- A synthesis team made up of people external to the organization convening the meeting.
- Someone in the front of the room facilitating the meeting.
- The group itself.

Considerations

- If the amount of input from the group is small enough, then the group itself can review everything that was submitted and create the synthesis itself (with the assistance of a process facilitator in the front of the room guiding the synthesis). A group can synthesize a few dozen ideas or comments themselves. But it has to be a group of manageable size—probably fewer than fifty participants.
- If the amount of input is low, the facilitator in front of the room can read through what's come in and either help the group synthesize it or synthesize it him- or herself, using a flipchart to write up the themes and keeping a dialogue going with the room to make sure the themes are right.
- If you have a large amount of input coming in, then you need to have a coordinated, well-briefed team to do the synthesizing. That team can either be from the convening organization or outside professionals. But the former is by far and away the better choice. Individuals from within the

convening organization know the idiosyncrasies, the buzz-words, the culture, and the issues of the organization. They also know a lot of the people in the room. They are the best choice for synthesizing, coordinated and coached by others who are expert on the synthesizing process.

*   *   *

Timing and Duration	When will the synthesis happen?

Choices

- During the table group discussion.
- During a break.
- Later in the meeting.
- After the meeting.

Considerations

- During the group discussion is the best time to do the synthesis, because it can be presented back to the whole group the most quickly.
- Sometimes a break (like a coffee break) can be used in addition to the discussion period to provide more time to finish the synthesis. In very large group meetings, where there is a huge amount of input to synthesize (and a large, coordinated synthesis team), we often use the breaks as a design element to give the team more time for the synthesis. If we are thinking about designing in a break, we try to look for a time when the synthesizers will be most in need of extra minutes to get their work done.
- If the synthesizing group is unavailable during the discussion period, or if you want to involve other people in creating the final themes from the inputs, then you can also postpone the synthesis and do it later in the meeting. This means postponing the completion of the engagement cycle. This is a viable option as long as you tell the participants that you will be returning to the topic later to see what the group has submitted and see what the reaction is from the front of

the room. But this sort of postponement in completing the engagement cycle only works as the exception—using it only once or twice during the meeting—not the rule. If you start consistently postponing the Review stage, participants' energy for the discussions will wane.

- You can collect the table groups' input at the meeting and then synthesize it after the meeting, but then you are essentially extending the engagement cycle until the synthesis has been completed. And then you are faced with how to review that synthesis with the whole group and how to communicate your response to them. Again, this can be done, and it is the best choice sometimes for complex issues that an internal leadership team needs to review in detail. The only precaution is not to do it too often and to be very, very clear with the participants when and how the cycle will get completed. "You'll hear back from us on x date, via y mode."

*   *   *

Timing and Duration	How long will they have to do the synthesis?

Choices

- A few minutes, while short table discussions take place.
- Fifteen to twenty minutes, while longer table discussions take place.
- Up to an hour, including the table discussion period and an accompanying break.

Considerations

- How long it takes to do the synthesis depends on how much input is coming in and how many people are on the team doing the synthesis (and how well organized they are).
- The more input, the longer the synthesis will take.
- The synthesis will also take longer if you are trying to create a refined list of themes that the whole group can vote on.

- Generally, if there are multiple questions the table groups are answering during their discussion, the synthesis will take longer.
- But any of these factors that normally would make the synthesis take longer can be overcome by having a larger and more coordinated synthesizing team.

*   *   *

Format	What synthesis method will be used?

Choices

- Someone, or some people together, have to look at everything that has been submitted by all of the table groups and synthesize all of it into the main themes that express the essence of what the whole group was "saying."
- You have a choice about who will do this task, as mentioned above. In most large or very large convergent meetings this is a team of people from the convening group who know the subject matter. Alternatives for smaller groups are having a facilitator lead the group through synthesizing the input themselves, or having the facilitator do it him- or herself, live, in front of the group.
- You also have choices about how to structure the team. Will everyone look at the same input, or will you divide it up and assign certain team members to work on separate parts? Will synthesizers work individually? Will they work in pairs? Who will craft the final themes that are shown to the whole group in the Review stage of the cycle?

Considerations

- If it is a relatively small large group, and the amount of input from the table group discussions has been modest, then you could consider having the group itself, with the help of a facilitator, read through the input and generate the themes. But as soon as you get very much data, or a larger group, then you need the parallel processing of a separate synthesis team. Also, the parallel processing of the input as it comes in during the Discussion stage of the cycle enables the group to move through topics at a practical pace, even though the group may be quite large.

- Generally, in order to have the synthesis happen quickly, you need to first divide the input that is coming in from the table groups between the team members. This allows the team to look at a lot more input at once. The second step is to consolidate the findings of the different members to create themes that reflect what the team has been seeing. But even with this second consolidation step, the synthesizing process is still much faster than it would have been if all of the team members had to read through all of the input.

*   *   *

Tools	What tool will synthesizers use?

Choices

- The software that is being used for the table groups to enter the results of their discussions.
- A second software.

Considerations

- In most cases what the synthesis team will use is the software that the participants are using in their table groups to send in their thoughts. This is the only truly efficient way to do the synthesis quickly. We've already pointed out that when you are choosing a software for the participants to use, one of the most critical criteria is how well the synthesis team will be able to work with it. Ideally, the software would enable you to divide up the group's input as it comes in, so that you could have team members reading through different parts of the input simultaneously. One of the functions we have designed into the Covision software is the ability for the team members to send rough draft themes back and forth to each other from the same screens that they are using to view the table group input, so that they can start to build themes that reflect what everyone in the team is seeing, even while more new input is coming in.

- The key criterion is that the input coming in from the table groups is easily viewed and managed. One temptation, if the software you are using for table group entry isn't very well suited to the synthesizing task, is to use a second software for the synthesis process—one that is better at managing the input. The caution about that approach is that you then need to "move" all of the data coming in from the table groups into this second software. This can make it very difficult to keep up with the real-time cascade of input from the tables. Before focusing too much on the functionality of a second software for synthesizing, make sure you have evaluated the time and effort necessary to bring the data across from the one software into another one.

Stage 3: *Review* → Review Levers

Who	Who will review the synthesized group input?

Choices

- The person who presented to the group during the Presentation stage.
- A facilitator who is running the process part of the meeting.
- A leader of the group, or some other role, who is the one (instead of the presenter) who will respond to the synthesis in the next stage.

Considerations

- Someone needs to play this role. You can't just flash the themes up on the screen in the front of the room and leave it up to the participants to read them solely on their own.
- The important thing in this stage is that the person reviewing the synthesis or the raw input with the group
  - Takes the role seriously
  - Is clear and thorough in presenting it to the group

- Makes it clear that it is a direct reflection of all of the table groups' input taken as a whole
- Allows the group enough time to take in the content—doesn't rush through it
- Of course, the obvious choice would be whoever is going to be responding to the review material in the next stage. But sometimes that is a group, a panel for example, or sometimes the person responding to the input won't be very aware of the process and may not fulfill the role well. So sometimes it's better to have another person or the facilitator take on the role of leading the group through the review.

* * *

Content	What will be reviewed?

Choices

- The raw input as it came in from all of the table groups.
- Synthesized themes distilled from all of the raw data by the synthesizing team.
- A combination of these.

Considerations

- Reading the raw input—that is, simply scrolling the input verbatim in the order it was submitted on the big screens in the front of the room—can be grounding for the group, as it enables everyone to see the detail of the actual input and get a sense of how the room is "feeling." Of course, the larger the group is, the less input you would be able to scroll through in a couple of minutes. If the group is large, this option is just used to give participants a sense of the detailed input.
- Unless the input is small enough to scroll through in a couple of minutes, and usually even if it is, what you need to review with the group is the synthesis of everyone's input. Usually that synthesis is captured in a list of six to ten bullet statements for each of the questions that the table groups were asked to discuss.

- The option of scrolling some of the groups' raw input is often only done in the first one or two cycles. It serves to let the participants see how the process works and where their input goes when they send it off from their table over the network. After a couple of cycles, the group understands the process and has a good mental picture, and the review can focus on just the shared ideas identified in the synthesis.

* * *

Timing and Duration	When will the synthesis be reviewed?

Choices

- Immediately at the conclusion of the table group discussions.
- After a further discussion or other activity that the group does, or after a coffee or meal break.
- At some point later in the meeting, for example, at the end of the day or at the beginning of another topic the next day.
- After the meeting, by some means that distributes it out to all the people who attended the meeting.

Considerations

- Directly after the Discussion stage is always the most desirable time for the Review, because the participants' energy has been activated by the discussion period, and they are curious to find out what was discussed in the rest of the room.
- It's also perfectly fine to do the Review after some sort of break, or after another agenda segment or discussion. The participants are surprisingly able to refocus on a topic that they have spent some time discussing.
- It's not as ideal if the Review has to be put off to the end of the day, or after the meeting. It can work well later in the day, if the Review and Response are the lead-in to another topic that the group will discuss. But if it just seems like the group keeps on with their discussions and doesn't hear what was said, the enthusiasm to keep discussing and to keep entering the table group's ideas will diminish quickly.

- If the Review has to be in some other format after the meeting, most of the sense of shared understanding and engagement will be lost. The discussions will seem like data dumps, with no real belief that the ideas that are being generated are ever going to be considered.

*   *   *

Format	How will the synthesis be reviewed?

Choices

- Spoken by the person in front of the room.
- Displayed on big screen(s) in front of the room and spoken (and/or commented on) by someone in the front of the room.

Considerations

- Even if the main thing you are going to show the group is the raw input (because it's a small group, and there is not too much input), someone should still speak to it from the front of the room.
- In most cases, someone will be presenting themes that have been synthesized from the input. The list(s) of themes are projected onto a large screen in the front of the room. Generally, whoever is leading the review will lead the group through the list, either reading it aloud or commenting on it and letting the group read through it themselves.
- The exception is if the person reviewing the themes with the group is also going to respond to the themes and wants to have more control over the review. Sometimes a leader in front of the group will just want a handwritten list of the themes. And instead of projecting the list to the room on the screen, the person in front of the room will go through the themes one at a time by reading one out to the group and then giving a response to it. One advantage of this is that if the list is too long, the speaker can just review those themes that he or she has time to address. The disadvantage is that

the group doesn't have as complete a picture of what they are collectively thinking and feeling about the topic.

* * *

Tools	What tool will be used to review the synthesis?

Choices

- PowerPoint slides or some other presentation software.
- The software that the group is using for input (i.e., for scrolling the raw data).

Considerations

- This is pretty straightforward. If the software that the group is using for sending in their input has a good display function, then that is the easiest tool to use for themes. Also, if you are scrolling some of the raw input, you should try to use the software that the participants are using for input. That is one of the criteria you can use in choosing what software to use.
- If you need to, you can create theme slides in PowerPoint or some other display software. But the time for synthesizing is often very limited, so you will want to use software that enables very quick slide creation and editing.

Stage 4: *Respond* → Response Levers

Who	Who will respond to the synthesis?

Choices

- The presenter from Stage 1.
- A leader or other person in the appropriate role.
- A panel of people in the appropriate role with the group.

Considerations

- It's best to have the person whose opinions and observations will have the most significance to the group be the one who gives the response. The person with greatest significance, for example, could be the person in the highest decision-making role for that topic, the person who everyone considers knows the most about the topic, an outside expert who delivered the presentation, or a few people (as in a leadership team) who play a significant role in the organization.

- Most often it is the person who delivered the presentation in Stage 1 who ends up giving a response to the synthesis of what the group is "saying." Frequently, he or she is joined on stage by others whose opinions are important for the group to hear. The response is a critical step in developing a meta-conversation between the group and the front of the room, so it has to be done by someone who has a real interest in having that conversation.

* * *

Content	What will the response be?

Choices

- The choices are wide-ranging and depend on the desired outcome of the particular agenda segment to
  - Let the participants know that their "voice" has been heard
  - Respond directly to their suggestions
  - Put their suggestions or ideas into a bigger context
  - Decide something based on their input
  - Link their input to other topics that will be or have been covered in the meeting

Considerations

- As far as the content, think about what is the most valuable thing you can give to the group in response to what they will be "saying." Be as detailed as you can. And think about what outcome you are hoping to achieve in this particular segment.
- The important thing here is the opportunity to influence the trust, openness, and feeling of respect in the group so that even more interesting and important subjects can be tackled by the

large group, not only in the meeting, but also as they all work together day to day in some form of large distributed team. Here is where you will reap what you sow. When you give them what they most value, that will confer respect. Similarly, openness in the response will confer trust and respect for the participants and a willingness to engage with them and think with them.

- Think of the Response stage the way you would think about responding to someone's opinion or ideas in a small group setting. Honesty, information, and perspective is what the person speaking (in this case, all of the participants) wants to receive in return. It is possible to arrive at a shared understanding with a large group of people if the response in Stage 4 is genuine, considered, and focused on what the group has said.

*   *   *

Timing and Duration	When will they respond? How long will the response be?

Choices

- As soon as the group has reviewed the synthesis or raw input.
- At some point later in the meeting.
- The response can be as long as needed—minimally enough to be a satisfying response to what the group has "said" through their discussion. Generally, if the Presentation is kept very focused and succinct at the beginning of the cycle, the Response stage can be the opportunity for conveying the detail that is most interest and value to the group (based on their input).

Considerations

- Directly after the Review stage is always the most desirable time for the Response, because it enables the meta-conversation between the group and the front of the room to take place in real time.

- A second choice is to have it follow some brief interruption in the cycle, like a coffee break, or another discussion period. This doesn't necessarily break the sense of meta-conversation in the room, unless it becomes the norm, and most agenda segments end up having the cycle interrupted. It's better to have those sorts of interrupted cycles be the exception.

- Having the Response separated from the Discussion and the Review by even more time makes the meta-conversation that much more difficult to maintain. Again, this should be done as an exception, and the person doing the response should be very deliberate about revisiting the Review material when presenting the Response.

- Promising to get back to the group at a later date with the Response is the least desirable option. Unless you have done this with them before, they have no reason to believe you, and their doubts will drain some of their energy for the conversation. This option is usually adopted when a leadership team feels they need to consider the groups' input more seriously, and they need time to figure out their response. This is a perfectly appropriate response, but it should be presented as a response, by the leaders, to the Review. In other words, acknowledge the Review, explain what position that puts the leadership in, and give them a sense of what you need to deliberate on, and what kinds of responses might be forthcoming so that the group has enough understanding to see how and why to stay in the conversation.

C CHAPTER EIGHT • QUICK SUMMARY

- There are many choice points in designing a Virtuous Engagement Cycle. Each of these choices is a lever that you can use to shape the cycle.
- Each choice you make impacts the other stages of the cycle.
- The nature of your choices will vary depending on what type of meeting you are designing, what the purpose of the meeting is,

and who the participants are. An example of that variation can be seen in the differences between organizational, multi-stakeholder, and civic meetings.

- Being aware of your choices at each stage of the cycle enables you to build virtuous cycles that give the group the most benefit from being together.

Case Story 5: Clinton Global Initiative

CASE
STORY

In its first four years, we supported AmericaSpeaks[1] in running the interactive processes for the Clinton Global Initiative Annual Conference in New York City. The meeting took place each year in September and lasted for three days. During Days 1 and 2, there were multiple interactive sessions with the participants. Each day four simultaneous tracks were running, each on a different policy issue: Climate Change, Governance, Poverty, and Religious Conflicts. Each track was like a separate meeting: about two hundred participants, seated at tables of ten, and a panel of experts and luminaries in the front of the room, as well as a high-profile moderator.

Each track met six times over the two days, and each time they met, they had a new topic and a new panel, and they went through a single engagement cycle. The process was structured like this:

Present. The panelists each gave a talk about their perspective on the topic. During the panelists' talks, if any of the participants had a question, they sent it in to the Theme Team. The Theme Team synthesized these questions as they came in and crafted a handful of questions that captured the essence of what was being asked in all of the participants' questions.

Discuss. The participants then discussed the topic in their table groups and sent in their thoughts and ideas about the topic. The Theme Team synthesized the input from the tables and created a short list of compelling ideas.

Review. When the participant discussions ended, the moderator posed the questions distilled by the Theme Team to the panelists, and let them give some answers back to the group. Then the most important new ideas, drawn from the input of the participants, were shown up on screens in the room, and the moderator read through them.

Respond. The moderator drove a discussion of these new ideas, getting the panelists to weigh in with their reactions and perspectives. The sessions would wrap up with announcements of awards or of challenges taken up within that topic area of the Initiative.

The design was very good, and the cycles were well arranged to allow the participants to have maximum contribution while keeping the sessions within a ninety-minute time frame. But a design issue arose during the Response stage of the engagement cycle. From our perspective, the response from the panelists to the participants' ideas wasn't as focused as we knew it could be. At times panelists were only giving brief reactions to the participants' ideas that had been shown up on the screens, and they were returning to the subjects that were most interesting to them about the topic. They weren't addressing and responding to the ideas the group had generated as fully as they could.

From a design point of view, we had to look at what lever to pull in order to make the panelists better able to focus on being responsive to the specific ideas of the participants. The meta-conversation would break down if there wasn't enough real "back and forth" between the group and the front of the room. Still, the group was far too large, and the time too limited, to facilitate any kind of meaningful whole group discussion. We had to use the engagement cycle methodology. But somehow we had to influence the behavior of the panelists in that last stage of the cycle.

The panelists were of a very high caliber. There were heads of state, in some cases, heads of large corporations, famous authors, and world experts in their fields. They had a lot to say, and they were very interested in meeting each other and in the whole social and political environment that the Initiative created. So why weren't they responding to the ideas of the participants— who themselves were a very select and important group?

What we determined was that the panelists weren't able to pay attention and assimilate the themed ideas of the group that were projected up to the group during the Review stage. The ideas that were projected during the Review stage were necessarily condensed. They had to be able to capture the brainstorming of many tables in a sentence or two, so that we could distill several of these compelling ideas back to the group. For the participants, these condensed statements represented the details of the in-depth conversations they had all been having at their tables. For them, the statements of these new ideas, even though they were condensed to be part of the list, were highly resonant, reawakening the nuances of the discussion at their table.[2]

But for the panelists it was completely different. During the participants' discussion period, they were in the offstage lounge meeting and talking with each other, or making calls, and taking care of the other details of their lives. They had no idea what specific question was being discussed in the table groups. Their minds were on other things. Then all of a sudden, the participants' discussion period was over and they were brought back on stage.

First, the moderator posed some questions to the panel, and they took turns answering those. And then the compelling ideas that had arisen from the tables were put up on the screen and read through by the moderator. Sometimes a panelist resonated strongly with a certain idea and would want to respond to it and explore it, thinking aloud back to the group. But just as often, the panelists listened as the moderator read what was up on the screen, considered it briefly, and then went back to thinking and talking about what they had originally presented to the group or what they had been talking about with the other panelists offstage.

So what was the solution? What stage and what lever would affect how the panelists responded to the participants? Assuming that the panelists really wanted to respond to the participants' ideas, the question became: Why are they not fully prepared to respond? (Rather than, "Why won't they respond correctly?") And the stage at which they had the opportunity to become prepared was the Discussion stage. After that stage, they were back on-stage for the Review, and then they were into the moderated discussion of the Response stage. So we had to focus on the Discussion stage and how to prepare them for the Review and to be able to respond.

If we looked at the panelists' activities during the Discussion stage, they were removed from the groups' work in the room. They left the room, they didn't think about the question the participants were discussing at their tables, and they became engrossed in conversations about other things with their fellow panelists. So when they returned into the main room, they weren't very aware of everything that had been going on there.

The solution was simply to supply the panelists with laptops in the offstage lounge that were on the network with the room, and ask them to read through the ideas that were coming in from the participants—the same task that the Theme Team was doing out in the room.

But whereas the assignment to the Theme Team was to try to discern the themes from all of these ideas and craft some condensed statements that represented the best thinking of the group, the assignment to the panelists was merely to look through some of the material coming in from the tables. They didn't have to look at all of it, and they didn't have to spend the whole time in the offstage lounge doing it. But they had to spend some amount of time becoming familiar with the question that was being discussed and getting to see some of the nuances of what the table groups were sending in to the Theme Team.

So when they returned to the stage and saw the compelling idea statements that the Theme Team had distilled, they would understand some of the detail and thinking that went into those ideas. Rather than seeing the ideas for the first time in a rush, they would see the ideas as the synthesis of many more detailed statements that they had read through in the offstage lounge. In this way, the design took responsibility for preparing them to respond to the participants' best thinking with their own best thinking and passion.

In the Climate track we adopted this new process in the Discussion stage, and it had the anticipated effect on the quality of the panelists' response to the group in the Respond stage. However, we found that even with success, it was difficult to explain it to the designers and facilitators of the other tracks. The difficulty was that it was counterintuitive. The problem was happening in the Respond stage, but the solution had to be found and implemented in the Discussion stage (a stage when the panelists supposedly didn't even have a role).

There was a moment in a large design circle where we proposed the idea for the process change, and one of the other people in the circle immediately rejected the idea, saying that was what the Theme Team was for and that was what they were already doing, so we shouldn't ask the panelists to do the same thing. In fact, no amount of discussion was able to dissuade him from his belief that it was unnecessary and that it was duplicating the work of the Theme Team. Eventually the design issue was resolved, but more because of results than because of the process being embraced.

This particular design dilemma highlights the interconnectedness of the different stages of the engagement cycle. The different stages of the cycle depend on one another. And the decisions made in one stage affect the outcome in subsequent stages. Choices that could seem intuitively right, after years of designing front-of-the-room-centered meetings, may not adequately account for everything that will result from that choice in the course of the whole cycle. Designing virtuous large group meetings requires understanding the engagement cycle and always looking at it, and designing with it, from a holistic perspective.

PART FOUR

FACILITATING VIRTUOUS MEETINGS

THE CRITICAL ROLES IN A VIRTUOUS MEETING

O nce the decision is made to go for high engagement in a large and important meeting, the Design Team is formed and the journey begins. It is a journey of discussions, focusing, and choice making. And like any large event, a virtuous, participant-centered meeting takes many hands to produce. How do all those process choices get made? Who does each step? How does it all get accomplished? There are roles in producing a virtuous large group meeting that are key, and we describe each and what they need. We covered the role of the Design Team in Chapter Six. Chapter Ten focuses on the specific role of the facilitator—the person charged with managing the smooth interaction of all the roles in the meeting. Chapter Eleven looks inside the pivotal role of the leader. In this chapter, we look at the roles side by side (see Figure 9.1).

The people taking on these roles typically have broad talents and are known to handle multiple responsibilities well; they are comfortable with the challenge. Furthermore, performing these roles brings temporary high visibility and broad access to anyone in the organization. It is something of an honor to be chosen to serve the organization in this way. So what are these roles?

Figure 9.1   Roles in a Virtuous Meeting

ROLES AND NEEDS IN A VIRTUOUS MEETING

The most important role in a participant-centered meeting is . . . yes, participant. Almost hidden in plain sight, this role can now be fully developed because of the high-speed connectivity we've described, together with good design, which integrates and leverages the connectivity. The participant can finally be allowed to engage fully, even in a very large group, because leadership and the meeting purpose and design allow it, and the imperatives of the sponsoring organization demand it.

The Role of the Participant

The participant is invited to bring his or her whole self to the meeting— experience, knowledge, ideas, insights, feelings, solutions—and contribute that during numerous discussion opportunities. Participants are asked to trust the process, become satisfied that it's working, and fully engage with other participants and leaders alike as the group moves through the meeting agenda designed to include the best thinking of all.

Participant-centered design is centered on the *experience* of the participants. All steps in the process design are shaped to stimulate them, giving each participant valuable insight and understanding while keeping all fully engaged in the flow of the meeting. And the design and facilitation should make participants' perspectives available step-by-step to the leaders and to the group as a whole. Here is what they need:

Participants need to know how the process will work during the meeting. As they sit down at round tables, with a networked laptop or tablet computer on the table, participants will naturally wonder what is in store for them. This initial feeling of strangeness always comes with a little excitement and curiosity. So the setup of the room will signal to participants that the day may not end up as ponderous as they had assumed.

Of course, they need to be told what will be happening: how the day will work, why they are seated the way they are, what the networked device is for, and so forth. A brief overview of the process is usually enough to quiet their curiosity so they can relax and participate. More specific details can be given at the right time.

Participants need to know why this process is being used and what the anticipated outcomes are. Most participants will be unfamiliar with this way of working. It is important to explain what the group is going to try to accomplish in this meeting. Once the participants have a sense of where they are going (and this takes just minutes), they will be more invested in this new process to get them there.

Participants need to know exactly what they should be doing at each stage of the engagement cycle. Once the group goes through a couple of cycles, they will feel the rhythm and the process will make sense to them. But during the first cycles especially, participants will need clear instructions on what their task and role are at each stage.

It is less important that the participants know it is a Virtuous Engagement Cycle that they are going through. They only need to be clear about what to do at a particular time.

Participants need to know how much time they have for whatever part of the cycle they are involved in. While in their table group discussions, participants have little ability to pace themselves to accomplish what they need to do. Times allotted need to be realistic and clear, and the facilitator—or whoever is driving the process—needs to give periodic instructions about how much time is left and where in the process the groups should be.

Participants need to feel safe to express themselves openly and understand the role of anonymity. The participants have to be assured that whatever input they submit as a group will be anonymous, so that they can feel safe being honest. They need to know too that the leaders *want* their honesty—as it will pave the best way forward. Participants need to feel that the leadership trusts them and has adopted this process so that they will be able to hear from everyone and to hear the truth.

Participants need to feel that the conversations they are having are worthwhile, effective, and leading to some positive end. This is largely accomplished by choosing good focal questions for the participants to discuss. The participants will know immediately if the topic they are discussing is of value to them and to the organization. The better the overall design of the meeting is, the more value the participants will see in each conversation as the day progresses.

Participants need to feel that someone is looking at their input, and that it matters. It is important that the leader establishes at the beginning of the meeting that the input of the small group conversations is important. But the proof of that sentiment is demonstrated throughout the day. When participants see an idea from their table conversations identified in the synthesis process and projected back to the group, they will know that someone is looking. And if the presenters respond to that input, the participants will know that it matters. You could say that this response to their ideas fuels the Virtuous Engagement Cycle. If participants begin feeling that no one is looking and it doesn't really matter what they are sending in, then the energy will drain and people will revert to passivity (the old norm).

Participants need to know what the rest of the group is thinking about. Once they have had their own active table conversation, participants are quick to wonder what everyone else was saying. If their conversation has been exciting, and they have come up with the ideas or answers that they feel are best for the organization, they are invested in knowing whether others came up with the same solutions, whether there is some other way to look at it or some other solution to try. This is why it is important to complete the Review stage of the engagement cycle.

Participants need to know how their input will be used and distributed after the meeting. At some point during the meeting, after a few engagement cycles have been completed, the participants begin to wonder what will happen with all of the input from the conversations they've been having. By then they realize how important the answers are from these focused conversations. They are interested not only in what their group came up with, but also in what the other groups put forward. Often, someone will raise their hand and ask, "What's going to happen to all this data after the meeting? Will we be able to have access to it somewhere?" It is best to have a discussion about this during the design phase and be prepared to answer the question. If the group begins feeling that data may be lost to them, this is another way that enthusiasm and energy for subsequent conversations will wane.

In Chapter Six we saw that the roles of Leader and Design Team member are central to giving direction, form, and life to the virtuous meeting. Their initial and pivotal work is done during the two to four months before the meeting. Now we'll look at their roles along with others that allow convergence to unfold.

The Role of Meeting Leader or Convener

The leader sponsors the purpose of the meeting and all efforts toward it. She or he helps envision, articulate, and fulfill it. During the meeting, the leader adds perspective and imperative where necessary to keep everyone focused.

Often, the underlying motivation in choosing a virtuous meeting format is a desire to leverage the synergy that is possible when you bring a large group of people together and focus them. Even more is possible when all participants are from the same organization and focused on the same current realities. The real benefactor of whatever synergy is produced is the meeting leader or convener—whoever it is that takes responsibility for the success of the organization, or for the success of the effort for which the stakeholders have been assembled. However, many leaders experience a reflexive resistance to the openness that is necessary in participant-centered meeting design when they first consider it. The fear of losing control is a common reaction. When that reaction is conscious, it is useful to discuss it and to look at it from all sides. When approached in this way, that fear is usually put to rest and replaced with a sense of opportunity. When it is *unconscious*, it is far more difficult to deal with because those leaders will feel it necessary to move cautiously in the supposedly "open" dialogues designed for the meeting. Senior executives and managers will sense it first. And as participants sense that tentativeness, as they surely will, it will dampen the outcomes of what would otherwise be an open and illuminating discussion of the most important topics facing the leader's organization. In this case, one step forward, and one step back.

In any case, the way in which the participants are engaged must always be designed to provide the leaders of the group with new and valuable insight into the thoughts and feelings of their group. The design and facilitation of the meeting must provide an easy pathway for the leader to understand what the group is saying and then for giving a response to it.

The leader needs to feel safe. While this may be a smaller issue for multi-stakeholder conveners, it is extremely important for organizational leaders. In fact, everyone needs to feel safe in this kind of process, as participants will feel a sense of risk too. But leaders in a hierarchical environment are particularly sensitive to any situation they feel could put them at risk of appearing foolish or unprepared. Their role in the organization is based in part on the respect that they engender. Processes that could put that respect in any kind of jeopardy will be rejected or subverted.

The leader needs to understand how the process works. This is the easiest, best way to make a leader feel safe. The interactive process is not "rocket science," and when explained it will make sense (and feel safe) with any smart person. And for participants too it is essential that the leader understands and publicly endorses the new enlarged (engaged) roles for them in the meeting.

The leader needs to have processes in place to filter the group's input so that the leader is not put "on the spot." The leader must understand the process regarding how input from the table groups is synthesized and how it is presented back to the group. The leader needs to know about this well before the meeting. Of course, how each engagement cycle is designed into the agenda is quite variable. It is best to involve the leader in designing the engagement cycles, so that together you can choose a design that is comfortable for the leader while still providing the maximum opportunity for candor.

The leader needs to understand the participants' experience when they hear responses to what they have been discussing. Once leaders see the input and synthesis coming from their own senior people, they will understand that the input is valuable to the organization. But leaders need to realize that there is a world of difference between just giving input versus giving input and then hearing a response. It is literally the difference between a monologue and a dialogue. Participants are always energized by the small group conversations, and so they are even more interested in what the whole group is saying. As a result of this building interest, the reply from the leadership becomes highly anticipated and valuable for all. In a hierarchical organization, what the top leadership is thinking is very important. Being in a real dialogue with top leaders during the meeting, and in the midst of multiple conversations, allows participants to calibrate the organization's reality with their own and gives them more energy to continue.

The leader needs to sense opportunities for "visible acts of candor" that will lead to greater trust and more openness in the group. These processes are designed so that participants will feel safer being honest with the leaders, even in a hierarchical organization. To seize the moment, and the opportunity, the leader needs to be honest back. It takes only a couple of cycles for a leader to see what can unfold if both sides work with this newfound safety to gradually reveal things that may have been left unsaid. Sometimes what is revealed is simply a vulnerability that is refreshingly human.

It is important that leaders act on these opportunities. They should be coached to watch for the opportunities, and coached in how to exploit them. In practice, this could be a short bit of perspective and encouragement at the moment the group's synthesis is being displayed and the leader is about to return to the stage. If the leader can seize the moment, responding in kind, it moves the whole group forward in trust and openness.

The leader needs to reinforce the value of each contribution and each conversation. This job also lies squarely with the facilitator role, if there is someone in that role other than the leader. But even if the facilitator is reinforcing the value from a process perspective, the leader has the most important voice in reinforcing it from the organization's perspective. The leader drives the purpose of the meeting, and if the design is good, the purpose can only be fulfilled through the robust contributions of the participants. The participants are not having conversations only for their own learning and interest; those conversations are accomplishing the crucial purpose for which everyone was brought together. And it is important to say so, repeatedly.

The leader needs to know the organizational impact of the meeting outcomes going forward, based on the input from the group's conversations. Again this responsibility is shared with the facilitation role. When the first participant raises a hand and asks, "What's going to happen with all of this input?", the first answer is that it fuels the understanding and momentum of the group during the meeting. It may even create the landscape of options into which the group travels as the meeting progresses (depending on the design).

But there is more value in this mirror held up to the group, and the group knows instinctively that it will be useful going forward. So the leader needs to be the champion of leveraging that value after the meeting. That doesn't mean the leader has to be the one who decides and designs how to make the best use of it. But the leader needs to recognize the value and respect and acknowledge the participants for their efforts and goodwill in creating it.

The Role of Participant Engagement Designer

The Participant Engagement Designer brings the vision of high-engagement processes and the know-how for producing them to the Design Team. She or he is entrusted with providing the options and recommendations for the most effective process within each segment of a large meeting's agenda. She or he is authorized by the meeting's leader, driven by the meeting's purpose and desired outcomes, and serves on the Design Team in close partnership with the Design Team leader, facilitator, and technology director.

The Participant Engagement Designer needs to fully understand the purpose of the meeting. Indeed, the Participant Engagement Designer might even lead a process to clarify the meeting purpose. As the meeting purpose is the touchstone for all decision making throughout the design process, making sure it is clear and easily articulated is essential. The Participant Engagement Designer generally knows more than anyone on the team about what is possible as a result of full engagement. She or he is in the best position to push back on poorly conceived purpose statements or on ones that aim far too low. Through repeated descriptions of different interactive processes and their results, this designer can guide the conversations toward the most ambitious and realistically achievable meeting purpose.

The Participant Engagement Designer needs to have direct access to the leader(s). As this member of the Design Team has specialized knowledge of how the engagement processes work—processes at the core of what it means to have a virtuous meeting—she or he needs to be able to discuss them directly with the meeting leaders at various times. While this should seem obvious, there are times when meeting leaders are insulated from the Design Team. Often the Participant Engagement Designer is an outside consultant, and it may be seen as impolitic to connect him or her with a senior executive (leader) directly. But when only the Design Team leader is able to speak directly with the leader, there will be much lost in translation, and opportunities will be lost.

The Participant Engagement Designer needs to have strong influence on decisions about the design of the meeting room. It is surprising how often we have had to spar with a production company about how to lay out the tables in a meeting room, or where to place the Theme Team table. The Participant Engagement Designer can visualize engagement processes unfolding in real time better than anyone on the Design Team. For example, where the key players (roles) are placed in the meeting room is sometimes critically important. So the Participant Engagement Designer must be able to speak up at the appropriate times when room layout decisions are being made.

The Role of Technology Director

The technology director (TD) is responsible for the participant feedback and presentation systems operating as planned in the meeting room. Prior to the meeting, the TD provides the Design Team with options and costs, always with an eye on the feedback systems' capabilities and limits.

The technology director needs to understand the purpose and flow of the meeting. The TD should be engaged as early as possible in the design process and be in close communication with the Design Team leader and Participant Engagement Designer. Once the purpose and desired outcomes of any segment are clear, the TD can offer advice and options for leveraging available technologies to the maximum extent. He or she is in the best position then to suggest other solutions that could solve critical snags in the process design.

The technology director needs to be included in all decisions on changes in the agenda that affect the process. Once the rough outline of the agenda takes shape, the TD should be included in all substantive process decisions. It is surprising how small issues of timing, for example, can impact what the technology can deliver in the meeting room or what might cause a breakdown. In considering a small change, other Design Team members may think "no big deal." But the TD will spot potential problems like this soonest and have options and solutions as soon as possible—often immediately. This allows all who are making design decisions to work with the best information about how to leverage the technical communication capabilities in the meeting room to greatest advantage.

The technology director needs to be the primary contact on the Design Team for all things technical. While not all technical details in the production of a virtuous meeting are important, it is the TD who can and should make that determination. She or he will do it quickly, and also pick up details that may have a big impact on the agenda. The TD should be in contact with all technical providers at the meeting site, any vendors, and any of those internal to the organization holding the meeting. During the planning stage, the TD must know whom to call for technical capabilities and requests or decisions. During the meeting, the TD is the person who can make the quickest assessment if any participant technology goes awry, and who can make the appropriate calls soonest.

The Role of the Facilitator

As we will show in Chapter Ten, the facilitator's role to is support the group to do its best thinking. This effort spans the entire design process from as early as possible to at least through the meeting. The facilitator should be involved in all substantive process design decisions. He or she serves at the pleasure of the Design Team leader and, in particular, the meeting leader.

The facilitator, or whoever is running the process of the meeting from the front of the room, has a key role in making sure the Virtuous Engagement Cycle is used fully and robustly according to the design of the Design Team. Getting it going requires a few important activities, taken in sequence, and the facilitator must be as precise and clear as possible in explaining to the group what the activity is at any moment. Also key, the facilitator must be rigorous in staying on the timeline that the agenda prescribes, so that each part of any engagement cycle can be completed. The facilitator takes responsibility for driving the carefully planned processes to accomplish the desired outcomes.

The facilitator needs to be completely grounded in the design of the meeting. The facilitator in a virtuous meeting is much more than an emcee. There can be an emcee as well, but someone should take the role of facilitating the process—either from the stage or by careful coaching of those on stage. That person may or may not be on the Design Team, but he or she should know the purpose of the meeting, the outcomes desired, the processes to be used, and the detailed flow of the agenda. The facilitator should know not only what the group is doing at any given point, but also why they are doing it and how it relates to what they've done so far and what they will be doing later in the agenda.

The facilitator needs to understand the value and the strengths of this participant engagement capability. Since the participant-centered approach may well be new to many of the participants and presenters alike, the facilitator may need to answer questions or attempt to motivate people by explaining the value of doing things this way and what the benefits will be.

The facilitator needs to understand the engagement cycle and the detail of the sequence of stages. The facilitator has to explain (or coach someone else to explain) how the process works and what the group should do next. So it is important that the person in that role understands when and how the group is moving through the stages of the Virtuous

Engagement Cycle, what needs to happen, and what everyone needs to do to complete each stage.

The facilitator needs to know exactly what the participants' role and activity is at each stage of the cycle and in each segment of the agenda. The facilitator is the guide for the process and so needs to proactively orient the participants at all times to what they should be doing.

The facilitator needs to know the presenters' role and activities. The facilitator needs to be very proactive with presenters, because they may be unfamiliar with not only the process they will be experiencing, but also the value and the design of it. Ideally, the facilitator or others on the Design Team are able to have a briefing with the presenters and bring them all up to speed on the meeting process and design. But in practice it may fall to the facilitator to keep track of each presenter, to make sure that the role is performed correctly.

The facilitator needs to know the timing for each segment. The facilitator is the one who has responsibility for knowing the timing, understanding the reasoning behind the timing, and either making sure everything stays on time or knowing whom to confer with in making timing changes.

The Role of the Presenter

A presenter is one who gives important input to the participants, typically speaking from the stage. He or she may be an executive of the organization or a specialist from inside the organization or outside. In a virtuous large group meeting, most presenters will also be asked to respond to the distilled ideas and questions of the participants after the presentation.

Presenters are mostly unfamiliar with these large group capabilities, and they naturally make assumptions about the process based on their own experience with being in front of many audiences. These assumptions may seem logical, but they are often incorrect. Presenters need to understand what their enhanced role in the process is and be aware of the advantages they gain in following the process as it is designed. Here is an approach a facilitator or Design

Team member can use to prep a presenter thoroughly who is unfamiliar with this "enhanced role" being asked of him or her:

1. Frame the purpose of your coaching as helping the presenter make the best possible presentation in this meeting.
2. Clarify your availability to the presenter before and during the presentation, including when and how.
3. Review the purpose and desired outcomes of the meeting, and especially how the presenter's content is designed to impact each.
4. Review the meeting goal of full engagement as a means for accomplishing the ambitious outcomes.
5. Give an overview of the process that has been designed for the presenter's segment of the agenda, and how it connects with other segments.
6. *Stress the importance of time management* in a meeting focused on convergence and with many participation formats, sometimes in rapid succession. Review what will happen if the presenter runs long in his or her time segment and what support the presenter needs in order to stay within the time allotment.
7. Review the presentation materials (slides, handouts, etc.) and go over the content and process flow of the presentation.
8. Give short scripts the presenter can use for process instructions, transitions, and closing the process.
9. Repeat any and all instructions, as necessary. Probe for uncertainties, anxieties. Choose tips, tricks, crutches, joke lines, as necessary.

Presenters need to understand how the cycle works. Presenters need to know that they are part of a process that has been designed for their segment of the agenda. Often presenters aren't involved very much in the design of the agenda, and they come to the meeting assuming that there is no process beyond the ordinary. They expect to give their presentation and then take some Q&A if there's any time remaining. They need to understand that there is an engagement cycle designed carefully into the agenda and to know what its flow looks like.

Presenters need to understand how to build an effective presentation. Especially in organizational meetings, the time allotted for a presentation may be shortened to allow time for table group discussions and for the presenter to respond to what the table groups come up with. Generally, the time for presentation is not significantly shorter, but it does mean that the presentation may have to be made more concise and focused.

Also, if the presenter understands the Virtuous Engagement Cycle, he or she may want to take the opportunity to cover the most important points and then wait to see what the group wants to hear more about. In other words, rather than trying to touch many points in a longer presentation, the presenter might be able to cover the most useful or critical information in an abbreviated presentation and then go into depth on the issues that the group seems to focus on in their table group conversations.

Presenters need to help determine what question is used to focus the table group discussions. Because presenters are often the content expert in their section of the agenda, it makes sense to get their input on the focusing question. Also, they are the ones who will be responding to the group's input. So they will want to have an influence on what the group is talking about. Knowing the focusing question will help with designing the presentation.

Presenters need to understand the difference between the participant-centered small group discussion method and traditional Q&A. It is fairly common for a Design Team to craft a valuable and productive focusing question for the small group discussions only to have the presenter go off script and say: "Rather than have you do the technology exercise, I'm just going to take questions from the group. Who has a question?"

At that juncture the whole opportunity that was designed is lost and that cycle never gets completed. Part of the reason this happens is that the presenter is not coached beforehand about how the segment is designed. Another reason is that from the perspective of a presenter, the whole engagement cycle is unnecessary. Many times when we have tried to explain the cycle to a presenter, the first reply is: "No, let 'em just ask me; I'm not afraid of what they might ask." Or taking the other tack, "If they have something to say, let them say it to the group. I don't want people hiding behind the computers." We'll address the second remark in Chapter 11 on Leadership, but the first remark is basically sound from the presenters' perspective. They are not thinking about the value to the group; they are simply thinking about their own task. Unless you lead them through thinking about what process would be most advantageous for the group, they won't think of it themselves, because they're thinking of executing their own task. It is not necessarily intuitive that you will get the most important questions by letting everyone talk about what you just said, send in their thoughts, and then see which of those concerns or questions is most widely relevant to the whole group. And often, presenters have never used this sort of capability before, so they haven't given any thought to how it would make their role or their task any different.

Presenters need to understand the sequence and timing of the agenda segment in which they will be presenting and responding. This is basic but very important. The presenters need to know exactly how their segment is designed to unfold in time, just as they would need to know how long they have for their presentation in legacy-style designs. In participant-centered design, they need also to be told how long the table discussions will go and how long they have to respond to the group's input.

Presenters need to understand and help create and finalize the synthesis of small group responses. Again, because this is usually unfamiliar territory for most presenters, letting the presenter know how the synthesis works is important. The presenter can play as big or small a role as he or she wants in helping to craft, or at least oversee, the synthesis of the groups' input.

Presenters need to understand the value of viewing the raw data as it comes in. Generally, while the table groups are in discussion, the presenter is "off duty." The best use of the presenter's time at that moment is to look through the raw data as it comes in from the tables. The group will be shown a synthesized version of this raw data—a sort of picture of the whole. But if the presenter can see some of the actual input coming from the tables, he or she will have a much more detailed and emotional read on what the discussions are really like.

Sometimes speakers like to go out in the room and wander among the tables to hear how the conversations are going. This is a valuable way to get a reading of the activity in the room. Equally as valuable, but less obvious, is seeing the detail that is coming in from a wide cross-section of the small group discussions. It is immediately satisfying for the group when the presenter is able to reference actual input from individual submissions when responding to the synthesis.

Presenters need to understand what will be the most effective way to respond to the group's input. Responding to the group's synthesized "voice" is possibly the most important part of the presenter's role in a participant-centered meeting. There are several different ways to handle this part of the role, depending on how the participants get to review the synthesis and the overall design of that engagement cycle. The presenter needs to be coached on what the design calls for in this response back to the group. It's not necessary for a presenter to know all the possible options for responding back, only the details of the process that the Design Team chose for the presenter's section of the agenda. The response back to the group can be a confusing step in the process for the presenter, especially if she or he is not given good instructions and winds up having to "wing it" on stage.

The Role of Synthesizer

Synthesizers have the crucial task of quickly distilling all of the input that comes in from the group. They are well prepared and coached. Often there are two to three or more synthesizers working in a team (the Theme Team). Synthesizers take responsibility for representing back to the group the essence of what has been said across all of their table group discussions.

This sort of role is often present in small group meetings. The facilitator may play this role, synthesizing the group's ideas on a flip-chart in front of the room in an open discussion format. In a large virtuous meeting, it's not just a matter of recording the comments in a brainstorming activity, but actually aggregating the output from a large number of small group conversations into a series of messages that speak for the whole group.

Synthesizers need to understand the flow of the whole meeting. Synthesizers work very hard in short periods throughout the meeting. It is important for them to understand the flow of the meeting as a whole and to know at which times they will be springing into action.

Synthesizers need to know the exact deliverables and when they are due. The synthesizing task is a real-time task, so timing is very important, and it is necessary to produce results within a tight time frame. At least one person in the synthesizing group has to take responsibility for keeping track of time and keeping the deliverables on time. And it is very important for all the synthesizers to know exactly what they need to produce in the time frame, because time is so limited.

Synthesizers need to know how the presenters and leaders will be interacting with them and with the synthesis. Presenters and leaders may interact with the synthesizers very little or quite a lot. During a meeting, some presenters may be very active with the synthesizers and others may be hands off. It is important for the synthesizers to know who will be interacting with them in what way. As long as they know, they can accommodate the interaction into their working style. It can also be helpful to know what process the presenter will use in responding to the synthesis that is being created. This can help determine more specific deliverables for the synthesizing task.

Synthesizers need to be familiar with the subject matter that the group is discussing in their table conversations. Often a leadership group of an organization will use idiosyncratic terminology and refer to initiatives and past events in articulating the ideas and thoughts that they submit to be synthesized. It is important for those who are synthesizing to be able to quickly understand the nuances and references within the input. Generally, synthesizers are members of the organization— people who are deeply steeped in the issues and situations that are being discussed at the tables.

KEY EXPERIENCES OF THE PARTICIPANT'S NEW ROLE

In normal front-of-the-room meetings, the role of participant is well understood and uncomplicated (if not utterly passive). In virtuous meetings, the participant's experience is the center of attention from the beginning of the design process until the end of the meeting and beyond. The following experiences for the participant bring the new role to life:

1. Listening with directed attention (experienced in the whole group)
2. Discussing a topic, focused by specific questions. This allows participants to a) put their reactions into words along with a few colleagues, and b) hear the reactions of those colleagues. (experienced in the table group)
3. Forming and writing group ideas, with generative, creative, and constructive energy (in table group)
4. Learning what the whole group is thinking and feeling and measuring the whole group's thinking and feelings against one's own thoughts and discussions (in whole group)
5. Hearing the presenter react to the whole group's thinking and feelings (in whole group)

Let's look more closely at these key experiences that define and characterize the participant's new role within the context of small group and large group experiences.

Listening with directed attention. Listening with directed attention creates an active listener. Active listening is different from passive listening. In listening actively a person is (much) more engaged with what is being said. The listener is weighing the content of what she is hearing at each moment. And she is comparing it to what she thought she was going to hear or what she has heard before, or comparing it with her own experiences or belief system. An active listener is listening for what is not being said as well as what is spoken. To be an active listener means actively trying to understand the meaning and the purpose of the person who is speaking.

What do we mean by "directed attention" and how do we create active listeners? To begin with, anyone involved in a conversation is going to be a more active listener than someone who is just hearing a lecture. So the fact that the process is creating a meta-conversation on the large group level means that the participant will already be listening more actively. This is because the participant knows that she is going to be asked to respond to what is being said. In fact, she knows that on the small group level she is going to be required, in some sense, to respond to what is being said and to give her thoughts and opinions about it.

In practice, we often find that it is helpful to let the participant know what question she will be discussing in relation to the *topic* before the presentation begins. This truly directs her attention to what she needs to get out of the presentation in order to provide feedback to the group. Thus "directed" attention is just that: by letting the participants know what they will soon be talking about in their table group discussion, they are able to sharpen their listening to the current presentation.

On the one hand, being involved in a meta-conversation with the presenter in front of the room makes the participants active listeners. But on the other hand, knowing that the next step will be getting into a dynamic conversation at the table about what was said creates a more stimulating environment for listening. Knowing that you are going to get to express yourself about something makes you more focused on what is being presented, as opposed to thinking that you are going to sit through this presentation, then listen to a few questions from the floor, with a few answers from the stage, and then go to a break. That is the definition of "passive."

Discussing a topic, focused by specific questions. The core activity in participant-centered design is the small group discussion, which involves all of the participants. In some ways the presentations are not only the information to talk about, they are the stimulus to provoke thoughts and feelings in the participants. For example: Given what you've heard about our new strategy, what could make it stronger, more achievable? By asking a focused question, the participants' personal and professional experience and knowledge can be harnessed to create something constructive for the organization or stakeholders.

A specific, focusing question (or set of questions) will structure the multiple table conversations across the whole group. Recall that in Case Story 2 of Part One, three focusing questions were used to structure the conversation on quality at the manufacturing plant. This type of question ensures that the conversations are productive, that all of the small conversations synthesize into a quickly digestible whole, and that the results of the conversations will move the group forward.

The value of focused small group discussions is already obvious. As soon as the small group conversation starts, the listener becomes an active participant in the meeting. Rather than sitting still in a chair focused on a single spot in the front of the room, the participant is moving around in the chair looking from one person to another, expressing opinions, maybe enjoying a light moment, but generally listening to others' points of view.

Small groups are ideal for these conversations because it is easy for people to feel comfortable participating, especially when there are people all around the room "buzzing" in their own small groups. An atmosphere of exchange and interest emerges. If the question or topic is well chosen, participants dig into it immediately and are eager to share their reactions, opinions, and ideas. Here is a chance for the participants to "digest" what they just heard. They can hear themselves formulate responses, think through the implications, and entertain the perspectives of their peers, which are most likely different from their own.

Forming and writing group ideas, with generative, creative, constructive energy. The active discussion at the tables is always in response to some kind of focusing question. And the table groups are asked to record their reactions or ideas into a networked laptop or tablet so that they can be synthesized in real time with all of the other small groups' inputs. As the conversation proceeds, each small group begins to formulate responses to the focusing question.

The task of recording the group's ideas in response to the questions guides the group into a constructive and creative mind-set. The group has to use the conversation to reach a goal: some sort of consensus on an answer(s) to the question. Generally, if the question is well designed, the answers to it are things that the participants really want to talk about and want to discover.

So the small discussions are the opposite of idle chatting. They are, more accurately, mini-collaborations. It is fine for participants to disagree with each other and hold different opinions and to believe in different solutions. The key is that they work together to construct, and record, ideas and solutions that reflect what was said around the table. This puts everyone into a focused, contributing mood. And the group members feel ownership of the input sent in from their table.

Learning what the whole group is thinking and feeling. Soon after the table discussion period ends, the group is shown a synthesis of all of the input from the tables—a sort of executive summary of ideas, reactions, and solutions to whatever has been asked. At this stage, each participant gets to see a synopsis of what was discussed in all of the other small group conversations. *This is a fascinating moment.* Each participant can compare the main ideas of the whole group with what was discussed at his table, and also compare it to how he feels about the topic. This is a moment of sudden awareness for the participant. (This is also a moment of self-awareness for the group.) This is the moment when assumptions are tested and either validated or seen to be mistaken. This can also be an "Aha!" moment when alternative ideas appear that the participant had never considered but that now make sense when seen together with the other ideas.

Hearing the presenter react to the whole group's thoughts and feelings. The participant learns what the whole group is thinking and in doing so experiences a sense of awareness that wasn't there before, or at least not confirmed. The participant is very interested to hear how the presenter, often a senior leader, reacts to this new awareness. Because these meetings are often striving to catalyze action and direction for the group, the nature of the presenter's response can help the energy to move in the right direction.

In virtuous meetings, after participants have discussed a topic, created constructive answers, and learned what their group as a whole is thinking and feeling, their enthusiasm and involvement makes them open to support and encouragement and even to constructive criticism. The participant wants to hear back from the leaders and is keen to hear the answers to "Are we headed in the right direction?" The participant wants to know what the view looks like from thirty thousand feet. Sometimes solutions can seem daunting or unattainable, and the participant needs to hear what facts and new developments will lend support to the organization's ability to accomplish what has been envisioned. Or if there are facts that make the group's thinking unrealistic, there is a great thirst to know that as well. Constuctive engagement like this is surely achieved when leaders and participants come together and think together in a virtuous meeting.

As a final word about the expanded role of participants in virtuous meetings, here is a smart model: a meeting communication code from one of our longtime clients—Oxford Leadership Academy (Figure 9.2). It is a fine guide for further enhancing the participants' experience in virtuous large group meetings.

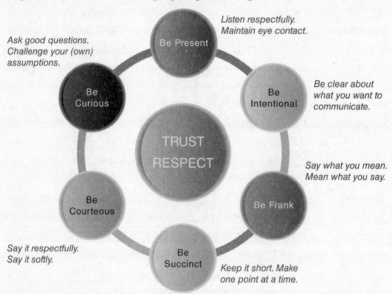

Source: Used by permission of Oxford Leadership Academy

Figure 9.2 High-Performing Team Meeting Communications Code[1]

⟲ CHAPTER NINE • QUICK SUMMARY

- There are eight key roles in producing a virtuous meeting (in order of appearance): leader, agenda designer, Participant Engagement Designer, technology director, facilitator, presenter, synthesizer, and participant.
- Each role has distinct tasks and responsibilities that require specific talents and skills.

- Three of these roles are new for most people and need to be understood and incorporated: the Participant Engagement Designer, the technology director (for high-speed connectivity), and the synthesizer.

- The most important new role is the active participant, who is invited to bring his or her whole self to the meeting—experience, knowledge, ideas, insights, feelings, solutions—and contribute during numerous discussion opportunities.

- There are five new key experiences of participants in their new role: listening with directed attention, discussing a topic focused by specific questions, forming and writing group ideas, learning what the whole group is thinking and feeling, and hearing the presenter react to the whole group's thoughts and feelings.

- It requires more effort to produce a virtuous meeting, but *the gains in shared understanding, alignment, and ownership far outweigh the cost in time and resources.*

CHAPTER TEN

FACILITATION IN VIRTUOUS MEETINGS

Here we look more closely at the role of facilitation—the role that keeps things moving along constructively, keeps eyes on the prize (purpose and outcomes), and balances the incessant pressure of the clock against the much larger pressures and needs of the organization and the group. No small task. *Facilitation* is a term used in many fields and generally means "to make a process easier." Our definition connects facilitation to meetings, and comes from one of the best-selling books on meeting facilitation, the *Facilitator's Guide to Participatory Decision-Making* by Sam Kaner and others.[1] In it, *facilitation* is defined as "the expertise that supports a group to do its best thinking."[2]

The *Facilitator's Guide* was the result of a five-year exploration by a small group of committed organization development consultants into the realities of collaboration, group dynamics, and facilitation. Lead by Sam Kaner, with strong co-thinking from Lenny Lind, Catherine Toldi, Sarah Fisk, and Duane Berger, this team developed some of the clearest language describing the mission and functions of a meeting facilitator and the results toward which she or he should strive. The book states that the facilitator's mission is "to support everyone to do their best thinking" and identifies four key functions of the facilitator that ensure that the mission of the meeting is enacted:[3]

1. Encouraging full participation
2. Promoting mutual understanding

3. Fostering inclusive solutions
4. Cultivating shared responsibility

Kaner and his coauthors emphasize that the performance of these four functions will strengthen the skills, awareness, and confidence of the group members, as well as the structure and capacity of the group as a whole. We recommend the *Facilitator's Guide* particularly for learning the full scope of the role and functions of facilitation. In this chapter, we aim to make facilitator and facilitation more interchangeable, as virtuous meetings don't absolutely require a facilitator—the person—but rather they do require that the *role* of facilitation be handled, and handled well. With one skilled person in the role of facilitator, the process will certainly run more smoothly.

> **Facilitation**—ensuring the design of the process is fulfilled; helping the group to do its best thinking together; guiding the group toward the meeting's desired outcomes through careful attention to group dynamics.

The decision about using a facilitator is a big one. In too many cases, a professional facilitator is not contracted and the task falls to various executives and presenters who must then "fill in" where a professional facilitator would have guided the group's process. We will look at how to handle this situation later in this chapter. For now, we will presume a facilitator has been chosen to support the meeting and we'll describe how he or she would operate from design through delivery and beyond.

In large virtuous meetings, the agenda's design and facilitation work hand in hand to maximize the time available for small group discussions and completed engagement cycles. Consider what a conductor does for an orchestra; facilitation provides similar functions for a virtuous meeting. Both groups need cues on timing and intensity, entrances and exits, in order to function well. In the case of large groups though, the "conducting" can be shared, and it often needs to be.

THE ROLE OF FACILITATION, ON PURPOSE

A meeting's purpose is like the North Star: it gives direction to all outcome and process decisions. For example, "Is ___ going to help us achieve the purpose of this meeting, or not so much? If not, how can we design it better?" These are the essential questions the facilitator helps the team address throughout the design process.

In a large, virtuous meeting, it all begins with purpose—from the original notion about calling the meeting to who is chosen to be on the Design Team, who the presenters are, what topics they will speak on, how the meeting will unfold, and if there will even be a facilitator. When the purpose is strong, and big, and clear . . . big things can happen.

When participants become active contributors, the agenda and process design look more like that of a smaller meeting, where everyone can be in a circle and everyone can speak up. The facilitator preparing for such a large, virtuous meeting should focus on the quality and the value of the table group process first. This puts the facilitator into the participant mind-set. To a participant it doesn't matter whether there are ten tables in the room or fifty or five hundred. If the discussions at each table are well designed and have purpose and value, then each participant will engage with the proceedings no matter the size of the whole group. At the whole group level the facilitator must also consider, and design for, how issues of trust and safety will play out. The way that virtuous meeting cycles are introduced and facilitated makes a big difference in how they are perceived by participants and leaders alike.

FACILITATION: The Mind-set, Principles, and Best Practices

Let's look at these three critical aspects of facilitation. The facilitator has the difficult (and ultimately rewarding) challenge of instilling the virtuous meeting mind-set, principles, and best practices into every-one as the meeting unfolds.

Mind-set

The facilitator must help the group be aware of the meeting's purpose and process. Otherwise, it will be difficult for participants to develop this awareness on their own. Leaders and presenters can help in this task, and their messages should be congruent with the facilitator. Here are some phrases that can help the facilitator instill the virtuous meeting mind-set:

- We're radically increasing interaction among you for our mutual benefit—for you, for our leaders, for our colleagues who are not here, and really for the whole organization.
- We believe this is the way to spend our time together most productively.
- You will be able to express your ideas openly and frequently, and we will work carefully with the collected wisdom of the whole group.
- We have a good plan, we've worked hard on it, and we will adjust it as necessary in order to seize any discovered opportunities.
- We will strive continuously for the greatest mutual results, while focusing on the purpose and desired outcomes of the meeting.

Principles

The facilitator should believe in and facilitate toward certain princi-ples. These principles will motivate everyone on the team, and later participants, to embrace these same principles during the virtuous meeting process:

- Full engagement
- Shared understanding
- Ownership of outcomes
- Increased trust

Best Practices

The facilitator must help the Design Team learn and utilize the best techniques and tools for ensuring success in a participant-centered process and a two-level experience in the virtuous meeting. He or she must ensure that

- Simple, clear instructions are given; repetition is helpful for most people.
- The process is made visible in order to win full engagement; asking participants to trust the process and checking in with them about how it's going will help the facilitator course-correct whenever necessary.
- Trust is discussed openly as a necessary condition for convergence; the facilitator must strive always toward a process that encourages trust and openness.
- Decision rules are made visible.[*]
- Communication is consistently open—from the stage, from each participant, and from the leaders.
- Participants are encouraged to tell their truth, constructively.
- The group's results are always made visible, along with a reiteration of the process that led to them.
- Meeting time is well managed—including time checks, pre-installed "out-of-time" actions, and decision rules for time extensions.

FACILITATING VIRTUOUS ENGAGEMENT CYCLES

With any group that is new to engagement cycles, it is important to introduce the first cycle deliberately and transparently and make the process as visible as possible. The desired outcome of the first cycle is as much about teaching as it is about the fruits it will generate.

---

[*] *The Facilitator's Guide to Participatory Decision-Making* has good guidelines for making decision rules visible on pp. 265–274.

The facilitator should be explicit about the purpose of the segment, the desired outcomes, why this process was chosen, and the roles. Then run the process, reflect on what just happened in the process, reprise the results (especially relative to the desired outcomes), and transition thoughtfully to the next process. After going through this once, the group will get it. Each participant will see his or her role in it and will be awaiting the next one, fully on board. Here is a short list of tips for facilitators. While there are many more, if these are covered the group will be prepared well for success.

1. At the start:
   - Introduce yourself—give a brief account of where you come from and how you came to be here, but a full description of your role and how participants can count on you.
   - Give an overview of the design of the meeting and the design process that put all the pieces together.
   - Give instructions in a clear, succinct, deliberate manner. It is fine to repeat yourself or rephrase once or twice more. Understand that everyone in a large room (or even a small one!) won't hear or completely understand your instructions the first time. Repetition, at least early in a meeting, is good.
   - Frame the current cycle—tie it to the meeting purpose and outcomes.
   - Tell how the cycle will unfold (micro-timing).
   - Give the participants a good description of their role.
   - Give participants a description of the other important roles: leader, synthesizer, agenda designer, Participant Engagement Designer, technology director, facilitator, presenter.
   - Give the time frame for the current segment.
   - Explain that the participants can use a raised hand (or any other signal agreed upon) to indicate that they need help at any time during the process.
   - Say "Start now!"

2. During table group discussions:
   - Walk the room, scanning for process questions or snags.
   - Give one or two time checks and any instructions for moving to a next step.

3. Draw attention to the front and the presenter:
   - Make sounds first, then a few encouraging words, then substantive content about what is next.
   - Reintroduce the leader/presenter with the intention of building momentum by asking a constructive leading question (for example: Where are we headed?) or by reiterating the purpose of the segment and his or her role in it.

4. Close and transition:
   - After the leader/presenter finishes, highlight how the process just unfolded.
   - Make the results visible; repeat if necessary.
   - Tie those results to the segment purpose and to the next step.

As the group moves through the meeting, the structure of the cycles will become familiar and anticipated—as if the group has known it for ages! But it is important to remember that most groups, most people, do not have knowledge of group process and how things unfold in a sequence that has been carefully designed to yield certain desired outcomes. This lack of process awareness is almost a blind spot in our culture. We are so blind, in fact, that following an excellent group process or meeting, it is common for a participant to gush over how good it felt, how fun and productive it was to participate in, and even about the results—but then not have the words to express how the process was designed, what the steps were, or how to do it again in another setting.

Thus, a very important part of facilitation is to give this process awareness to the group whenever possible throughout the meeting. After a long while, it begins to sink in . . . in some people. To be fair, though, the purpose of the meeting isn't to teach good process. Rather, it is to achieve results that only large groups thinking together can accomplish. But the greater value to an organization of this kind of meeting approach is for participants to gain the ability to project this approach into other critical, ongoing situations in the organization. And this can be accomplished through good facilitation in parallel with actually running a virtuous process.

Facilitating from the Side

All that we have described here regarding the facilitator's role and functions implies there is one person doing this role: a professional facilitator. That is the way to ensure the best outcomes. But as we noted earlier, it is often the case for a variety of reasons that a professional facilitator is *not* retained for an organization's most important, large meeting. What then? Is convergence still possible? Surely yes, but a vigorous Plan B is necessary.

Leaders and presenters are critical components of any meeting process that strives for virtuous outcomes, but process leadership is usually not one of their strengths. In Chapter Eleven we focus on the leader's role and how it is most effectively wielded in convergent meetings. Leadership is vital, no doubt, but running a large group interactive process takes other special talents and insights that are vital too. If the decision is made *not* to engage a professional facilitator, it must include a separate decision to begin a thinking process in the Design Team that explicitly spreads the facilitation function across all persons who take the stage during the meeting. For example, in Chapter Six, we looked at the role of the Design Team before and during the meeting. In the situation where there is no person as facilitator, one or more members of the Design Team must step into the critical role of coach to the presenters. Typically, it is the Participant Engagement Designer who is best equipped to step in.

The Participant Engagement Designer is most often an outside consultant who has wide experience with Virtuous Engagement Cycles in large meetings. His or her skills are teachable and transferrable when the situation calls for it. But in any case, that person must become the quarterback of the engagement process—responsible for making sure the essential functions of meeting facilitation get done.

He or she can see how and when and to whom special instructions and coaching must be given.

To make matters more interesting, most presenters and leaders are full of enthusiasm for what they will present to the large group but much less so for anything they might ask the group and then have to respond to their feedback. For most presenters, this is new territory. For some, the image of George C. Scott in the role of General Patton in the movie *Patton* is their vision of leadership and presenting . . . to the troops. Not so much about facilitation!

WORKING WITH PRESENTERS

Presenters are sometimes the last participants to "get on the train" in support of the participant-centered approach that defines a virtuous meeting. They may be last to endorse the convergent purpose and process of the meeting. To be fair, many presenters have presented dozens of times before to the same group or others, maybe even with nearly the same presentation. When they are asked to change the style of it and (worse!) be open to questions that *come from the whole group LIVE*, they are essentially being asked to leave the comfortable confines of known territory to venture into a space that makes them more vulnerable, often for some larger purpose that they don't understand. This is why the initial discussion (and invitation) to the presenter needs to focus on what the purpose of the virtuous meeting is, in concept and design, and why they are being asked to participate.

Clarifying "Why" for Presenters

Some overarching questions that should be brainstormed and answered ahead of an invitation to a presenter could include the following:

- Why are we having this kind of meeting?
- What does the presenter gain by participating?
- What benefits are there to the organization if you have this kind of meeting?

Once presenters are clear about this and are assured that support will be there for them before, during, and after their presentation, it is more likely that they will participate in both the *process* and the *spirit* of the virtuous large group meeting. Then the design process can proceed constructively. Inviting, orienting, and assuring the presenters is critical to everyone's success in a virtuous large group meeting.

It is best when someone on the Design Team takes responsibility for presenter preparation. Whoever takes it on can enlist others in the task who may know certain presenters better. But the goal with each and every presenter is to *enroll* him or her in the purpose, outcomes, and process of the meeting. While each presenter will react slightly differently, all will need to understand the purpose of their part of the process, how it will work, their role in it, and how they will be supported by a team. The first step is to communicate somehow that all of this effort is motivated by the vision of their complete success. When prepared thoroughly, most presenters will do well in the (slightly) expanded role you are asking of them.

And what is it that you are asking? Essentially you are asking presenters not only to give their presentation with their slides as expected, but also to help guide a process of engaging participants and drawing out their feedback. You are asking presenters not only to deliver their best ideas and knowledge (which is familiar and has its own challenges), but also to facilitate the group at certain key points in responding to it (which may be nerve-racking).

Here are a few simple reasons why presenters might be happy to change their presentation style:

1. The content of the main presentation will be more targeted, direct, and outcome-focused (through a closer coordination with the Design Team).
2. Each presenter will look stronger in front of the group, extending his or her expertise with some light, effective facilitation.
3. Each will know within minutes what was heard correctly and what wasn't.

4. Each will have the opportunity to exercise leadership in his or her area of expertise in terms of *ensuring understanding* of the key messages.
5. Each will end the presentation knowing what else needs to be done after the meeting with that group and those messages.

Even with these good reasons for presenters, some will still blanch at the thought of changing their presentation routine. After all, it is human nature to resist change (even for presenters who may be proposing change!). The worst case is when someone agrees to present and goes through all the motions in preparation . . . and then when they're live in front of the group do nothing differently from how they've always done it. They eat up the time that was carefully allotted for a quick round of table group discussion, feedback, theming, and response by the presenter. It has happened. This counter productive outcome is what all the planning and preparation is designed to avoid.

Clarifying "How" for Presenters

Clarifying the purpose and the presenter's role will help avoid this kind of outcome, as will making clear the how-to of the presentation. Each presenter will have different needs in this area, but at a minimum the Design Team member tasked with being the presenter's coach can create a timeline of the presenter's segment and discuss each part in detail. We call this *micro-timing*, as it accounts for every shift in attention or instructions during the presenter's allotted time. The final version of the micro-timing should be on one sheet, with large fonts, and easy to read in a glance. In that form it can sit alongside the presenter's notes on a podium. Further, if you provide actual language that can be used in front of the group regarding those shifts and then customize it to each presenter, comfort will surely increase. Here are some examples:

I'm delighted to share with you the outcomes of our research over the past year, and also to work with you on understanding a few of the critical findings. These findings are profound enough that the Executive Team believes we need to alter our selling process immediately. So I'll present to you and then engage with you around what you heard, your questions, and together we'll make sure there are no misunderstandings.

Okay, let me shift gears now . . . That is a lot of information for you. And I've just reviewed the three critical findings. Now I want you to discuss at your tables this question: What, if anything, is unclear? Or, put another way, What do you need to hear more about? You have ten minutes for this discussion and to input your comments. Then, we will review the comments in a distilled form, and I'll respond to them for fifteen minutes or so. Okay, start your discussions now.

All right, please bring your discussions to a close . . . Enter your last comments . . . Can I have your attention back up here now . . . thanks. The Theme Team has been reading all of your comments while you've been talking. They just briefed me on what they found . . . and I want to put your themes up on the big screen now. Please . . . [reads through them once, quickly]. Very well done. Okay, with respect to the first one . . . [addresses each, in order].

Thank you for your solid reflection on these difficult topics. Your questions pushed even my own understanding of them. Later in the meeting you'll be hearing from the Sales Team, who have also been reviewing your comments here, on what they propose that we do differently, specifically. But for my part, thank you very much.

Once again, time management is critical in virtuous large group meetings. Every presenter must stay within the time bounds given to each segment. It is best to discuss this early and often and to come to an agreement with each presenter about how to advise them, during their presentation, when their time is getting short or has been exceeded. But with careful attention to each presenter's needs and situation, most will find this expanded role easily manageable and more rewarding than business as usual.

In a virtuous large group meeting, accepting an invitation to present to the group carries with it a responsibility, however new and different it may be. But we can't rely on the presenters to intuit this new responsibility. It falls to the Design Team, and specifically to the member who takes responsibility for presenter preparation, to coach and support all the presenters so they can perform their best in delivering their material and guiding the group in their response to it. The design team member will want to use the Virtuous Cycle to orient the presenter to the principles of full engagement, shared understanding, ownership, and trust. In fact, these principles are a good place to start in the process of winning over a presenter and changing a mind-set. Win them over on principles and you will sway them on the advantages of the process as well.

C CHAPTER TEN · QUICK SUMMARY

- Facilitator and facilitation are interchangeable. Virtuous meetings don't *require* a facilitator—the person—but rather they do require that the *facilitation* be handled, and handled well.
- The facilitator of a virtuous meeting should give special attention to the quality and value of the table group discussions and the process that connects them with the plenary.
- Facilitating a virtuous large group process requires instilling the mind-set, principles, and best practices that characterize this new way of meeting.
- When facilitating Virtuous Engagement Cycles, remember that the purpose of the first cycle is as much about teaching as it is about the fruits it will generate.
- Part of facilitation is taking responsibility for the presenters in a virtuous meeting. The goal with each presenter is to *enroll* him or her in the purpose, outcomes, and process of the meeting.

CHAPTER ELEVEN

FACILITATING AS LEADER

V irtuous meetings require leadership. The leader's role is an indispensable one. Without real leadership, this open and generative approach to large meetings that we've been discussing can't even begin. Even before the meeting, the leader sets the tone for the Design Team and the facilitation of the meeting. During the meeting, leaders set the context and desired outcomes for all participants and give the invitation and permission to proceed. They are the ones who can truly "open up the space" by making it safe for real dialogue and disclosure and ideas and contributions to pour forth. As "keepers of the fire"—that is, the spirit of the meeting—they encourage openness in participants, and they reward it early and often with recognition and fresh perspectives. When it is safe to speak up, people always will, as it is in our human nature to do so. But it is also in our nature to shut up tight if there is even the slightest possibility of embarrassment or censure. Leaders move groups quickly past these fears. They guide the proceedings, the dialogue of the whole group, toward action.

To be sure, there is expert coaching and support ready to give strength to leaders whenever it's needed. It is important that all of the leader's actions are seen as congruent and focused on the purpose and outcomes given at the start. The skills to do so can be coached. It is the spirit and willingness to run a virtuous meeting that must genuinely come from within. As the old saying goes: "When the student is ready, the teacher will appear."[1]

There are many dimensions of the leader role, and in leadership, in virtuous meetings. Some have described the role in terms of Quiet

Leadership,[2] while others talk about exhibiting a consistency between the walk and the talk. Still others speak of Authentic Listening[3] as being a key to good leadership (and certainly the best stance for a leader in a virtuous meeting). Leaders treat people with dignity and respect, are fundamentally curious about what others are thinking, and so are naturally open to receiving input. They have a propensity for collaboration and for teaching—virtuous meetings are wonderful opportunities for executive development. In them, top leaders model exactly how to engage a large group of the organization's brightest and best in critical dialogue and problem solving. All of these aspects of leadership are drawn forward in those who choose to lead virtuous meetings.

In order to get a feeling for how this kind of leadership unfolds, in a real setting, consider the following situation . . .

Part One: Participant View from Inside a Meeting

You've arrived thirty minutes early to grab some coffee and chat with friends. This particular meeting sounds like it might be different somehow—at least Cathy Artiste, our CEO, said it would be. She said it had to be, and you wondered what that meant. The invitation email was unusual. She laid out the daunting challenges ahead, the short time we'd have to deal with them, and then said that no leader or leadership team can sort it all out by themselves anymore. This time we would all have to put your heads together and come to a new understanding about what we're going to do. That sounds . . . different. At least, coming from her.

Virtuous, participant-centered meetings require a certain *kind* of leadership, and the consistent promotion of that leadership style as well. Call it virtuous leadership, or as we'll see later from Jim Kouzes and Barry Posner, exemplary leadership.[4] It is leadership *for the whole* and less for the parts. It requires persons who have grown to be comfortable in their own skin and who have a sense of service much more than entitlement. They have personalities more akin to gifted teachers than to coaches of professional sports teams. Virtuous meetings need this kind of leadership. They thrive on it, showcase it, and provide one of the best formats for practicing it.

How one comes to stand in front of a large group is always a unique story; it is the story of a journey. There are paths to the top of organizations that build employees up and empower them to "take off" and other paths where, at worst, people are seen as stepping-stones, and their collective lift never quite exceeds the drag. To be sure, there are forces in the world that can easily push leaders along this other path that pushes toward self-interest, short-term focus, externalized costs, antagonism toward "labor," secrecy, duplicity, or worse. It is all very present in our world. But different situations demand different responses, and different leaders.

The first vignette hints at a different kind of meeting and this different kind of leadership. Let's imagine ourselves back in that meeting, at the moment it begins:

Part Two: Participant View from Inside a Meeting

Doors open. Folks are streaming in. Great music! Energy is high. People are buzzing, looking for their assigned tables. Every table has two iPads on it and six chairs. This is going to be interesting. The room has filled quickly as my colleagues are showing up more on time than usual. A voice comes over the sound system saying the program is about to begin and to take our seats. The lights go all the way down, and an amazing video begins on three screens stretching all across the front of the room. Beautifully produced . . . it's mostly showing our customers. They're not happy. They're complaining rather forcefully, with suggestions all over the place and finally, "XY Systems needs to get its act together, start working together, or forget it from us." With that last customer frozen on the screens, the lights come up, and Cathy Artiste walks on stage and says, "Welcome." And she stands there just looking at us, smiling, for a few extra beats. A few people start clapping . . . for what? Then more. And then we have a good round of applause . . . for Cathy? For the video? Certainly not for the customer

(*continued*)

(continued)

complaints. To me, it feels like we're clapping for . . . maybe hope. For some kind of turning point we know we must reach, somehow. I guess we are clapping in anticipation and giving energy to Cathy. I say to my colleague, "Let the games begin."

Cathy was coming across differently than ever before. She had been hard on people. In fact, when she was brought in to turn things around a year ago, word went around that she was worse than the CEO at GE who did all that firing. And true to form, after giving a rosy picture of our new direction, she announced cut after cut and consolidations and reorganizations. People were hopeful about her at first, but that changed quickly. She was more like the Grim Reaper.

But now, things felt very different, and she was about to lay it all out.

Where does a person need to be "coming from" in order to seize the moment like that? What does a person need to know who has achieved a senior level of responsibility in an organization—maybe even in spite of the path he or she used to get there—in order to help their organization "take off"?

First, to summarize ground we've covered in this book, there is a convergence of realities and capabilities that has allowed the development of participatory thinking and leading over the past couple of decades:

- Urgency—larger, global organizations, bigger challenges, faster cycles
- Unmet needs in organizations and meetings—for speed, agility, alignment
- Technology—Internet, input devices, connectivity, user savvy
- Process design—facilitation, small groups, virtuous cycles, engagement
- Participant-centered design—a large group of small groups, dialogue

The current environment is ripe for leaders to step up their game, for bringing more people into the tent, for breathing life into organizations, for leading in ways they never thought possible. We've been focusing on the part of leading that shows up so visibly in meetings. The virtuous meeting is one of the formats for exercising and building one's leadership skills. So the first key point is knowing that the world has evolved in a direction that invites leaders to take these risks—both for themselves and for the whole.

Second, while many have gone before, each leader's path forward will be unique, challenging, customized, and exciting for all. There is nothing "canned" about this open, participatory approach to leadership. It has to be custom-fitted to both leader and organization in order to work. You have to want it or need it or both. Fortunately, there is a wealth of experience that you can learn from and build upon. Despite how it might appear, this experience can be both challenging and safe.

And third, as we focus on leading throughout a meeting, we will look carefully at the stages of a virtuous meeting in which the leader's involvement is paramount. In each stage, here are the opportunities for virtuous leadership:

- The initial decision: choosing the style of meeting to fit your purposes
- Before the meeting: energizing the Design Team, designing a dynamic agenda
- During the meeting: giving context, completing cycles, making meaning, releasing energy, channeling energy, making smooth transitions, ending with clarity
- After the meeting: giving context, completing longer cycles, making meaning, showing the way forward, connecting the dots

THE INITIAL DECISION

Choosing a two-way, interactive format for an upcoming, important meeting takes leadership of a personal sort. It takes courage, focus, and vision, together with urgency. It takes going out on the limb a little, making a leap of faith, and being somewhat vulnerable. Some leaders have even described that point as stepping into the void. Others have pushed back and asked, "Are you crazy?" or "Why on earth would you do that? It sounds completely counterintuitive and a setup for losing control." After all, they didn't get to their position of leadership by asking those they've been "leading" what they are thinking . . . at least not in a public format. Practically every important, critical meeting they've experienced on their way to the top has consisted of presentations, one after another, by experts or people with positional authority talking to (at) the troops.

These are natural reactions because, in most cases, leaders haven't experienced such an interactive format. They may have heard of using keypads for quick polls and thought that was what was meant by "interactivity." Each time a leader initiates the age-old process of calling for a meeting, it is normal for him or her to hastily outline the meeting purpose and outcomes and then delegate to a small team to begin defining the major topics, issues, presenters, location, dates, and so forth. Later, as the Design Team gets under way and makes its first reports upward, the person-in-charge will begin to think a little more seriously about the upcoming meeting, the high stakes surrounding it, and all the things that could go wrong. They may have unsettled feelings about previous meetings and formats not really working, and then probe for alternatives or for some "out of the box thinking."

This is what leaders have in mind the first time they hear a recommendation by their Design Team that the meeting should take on a new format—a truly interactive one. The team will recommend that the leader fully endorse it—lead it!—in order to get the most value from it. Let's go back to our vignette and hear Cathy in conversation with the meeting designers, whom she's brought in. They have just suggested a participant-centered approach.

Part Three: Leadership View from Inside a Meeting

"Let me get this straight," Cathy says firmly. "You want *me* to introduce this? You want to take precious time away from each presentation and let the audience talk at their tables? That's what we have breakouts for, isn't it? If we do this, we'll lose at least one, maybe two, presentations that we decided were critically important, no? Whose idea is this? Do we have the time? Where has it been done before? Do we have references? Are you able to guarantee that it will work?" It becomes a blistering inquisition once Cathy begins to see what the designers are talking about. There are no easy answers for any of her questions, and the designers begin to feel a little foolish for having suggested this new format in the first place. It sure would've been nice to have one of those sunny "engagement" consultants with them while they got scorched.

It is rarely an easy decision for a leader to choose a participant-centered meeting format the first time. It is more likely that they get coached toward it. It can seem that this approach asks leaders to trust unknown outside people and move seriously outside their own comfort zone during an organizationally critical meeting. Yes, that's exactly what we're describing. This approach changes the game in favor of large rewards for the organization and with very little risk (because the process is so well tested and understood by its practitioners). But it can look scary at first.

Once interactivity is raised as a possibility, a trusted advisor (often a senior human resources or organizational development executive) will try to describe what is involved with the format and its potential rewards. For example: You'll get much closer to knowing what your people are actually thinking, you'll be able to steer the meeting with greater confidence, or you'll have a real shot at good alignment. And they'll address the safety issue by reassuring the leader that there are people who do this professionally, it is a tried-and-true process, and there will be coaching before, during, and after the meeting. The trusted advisor will be measured too—How much do I trust this person, and this new idea? Depending on the trust and the degree to which she or he can make the case for interactivity, the decision to explore holding a participant-centered meeting will hang . . . in . . . the . . . balance. Here's Cathy's response to the consultant:

Part Four: Participant Engagement Specialist's View from Inside a Meeting

Cathy: "Look, this meeting is critically important for us, and for me. I'm anxious. We're running out of time to get focused. We need some fresh ideas and a whole lot of alignment around our next steps together. Why don't you look further into this method before our next meeting. I'd like to talk with one of the consultants about how this thing works. Can you bring one in? Since my a__ will be on the line, I need to understand it really well. Got it? Great. See you next week."

And here's the Participation Engagement Designer's response a week later:

"Cathy, I understand your concerns and the stakes here. And the urgency, the needs, all of it. We're solidly behind you. Here's the essence of what we're proposing about this inter-activity. Let me put it in the form of a question: Which has more value for the organization (and for you) . . . what is presented at the meeting . . . or what the participants actually hear and their ideas about it, and what they'll take home with them? If it's the latter, what I'm suggesting is that without this interactive approach you'll have no way of knowing what your top people are thinking and feeling and whether you have any alignment at all. I'm saying that we can guarantee that you'll have it through this interactive approach, which by the way, we've used thousands of times in meetings like yours over twenty years. It works. It just needs you to endorse it and then to embrace it throughout the meeting. We will support you every step of the way. Once you begin, once you see the first cycle with the group, you will love it. This will be your best meeting ever—I guarantee it."

Finally, invariably, it comes down to the leader's intuition. It is a deeply personal decision—whether and how much to open oneself, on stage no less, to the thoughts and feelings of your brightest and best. A virtuous meeting engages all participants in lively dialogue on one or more critical topics for the results it will produce. The curious leader stands to gain a lot. This is a case of nothing ventured, nothing gained.

BEFORE THE MEETING

When the decision is made to hold a participant-centered meeting, there is often a rush of energy and activity. This is because the leader, the person-in-charge, is typically the last person to buy into the concept of everyone having a voice in the meeting. So the real design phase is jump-started with a series of phone or in-person meetings among the now-energized team of those with a key stake in the outcomes of the meeting. The Design Team can be as small as three people and as large as a dozen. Its mission, as we've seen in Part Three, is to design an interactive agenda and then to produce the meeting.

The leader's role on the Design Team is one of owner, authorizer, and decider-in-chief. It is best to lead the first Design Team meeting in order to discuss the purpose and context of the participant-centered meeting and to help everyone be clear about it. Constraints and possibilities are discussed, areas of challenge are identified, assignments and action plans are set, and the design process is put into the calendar. After the first meeting, it is up to the leader whether to attend all the other meetings or to monitor the progress closely. In any case, it is common practice to hold weekly design meetings in the month or two leading into the main event. The more often the leader can attend the design meetings in person, the better.

Designing a dynamic agenda is challenging the first time (and by the way, not nearly as challenging in later rounds). This is the stage where the support of outside consultants who have been through this process many times can have the most impact. With even the smartest designers, it is easy to fall into familiar (old) patterns of meeting design. The outside consultant can show where, for example, hearing the participants' input can make all the difference in driving toward the purpose of the meeting—and what question or process would elicit that precise input best. And there are issues with timing—in fact, micro-timing—that are difficult for the uninitiated to foresee. But as the agenda goes through its versions, the new patterns become clearer for everyone. The virtuous meeting cycles emerge, timed out and clearly understandable in the agenda. For example, forty minutes for presentation, seven minutes for table discussion and input (and simultaneous theming), and thirteen minutes for responses and reactions to the themes by the presenter. The transitions and their talking points are designed in too.

The talking points are most important for the leader(s). Especially at the beginning of the meeting, it is essential that the leaders tell their version of why a virtuous meeting format was chosen this time—what was the thinking behind it. It is a time to restate the purpose of the meeting in very personal terms, as well as the serious challenges facing the organization. Participants will see clearly and be moved by the leader's willingness to open up for input and discussion on the most difficult issues facing everyone in the room. The leader is essentially modeling the openness that they are asking of the participants in the process to follow. It is an extremely mature way to be in front of the room. But more on that shortly . . .

As the agenda comes together, it is important to consider how participants will be invited to the meeting. They'll already know the dates, and they will have heard rumors that this upcoming meeting will be "different." So what language to use in describing the importance of their new role in this meeting? This message needs to come from the leader and from the heart. It could be an email or a video. But again, outside consultants are invaluable in helping to shape this message, at least the first time. The spirit of the meeting can be conveyed through describing the meeting purpose and context, the urgencies, the new meeting format, interactivity and how we'll use it, and what is being asked of all participants, that is, real participation. The notion is to start the meeting brewing in participants' minds long before they arrive at the actual meeting.

A final important aspect of the design process is that of bringing the presenters up to speed with the new style of meeting in which they'll be presenting. Some presenters will jump at the opportunity, and others will attempt to jump away from it! That is, they may have their routine or their deck of PowerPoints, and they don't want to change anything about it. It is important to provide support for any presenters who need it to help them revisualize their presentations as conversation starters and so much more than information dumps. This requires leadership too! Leveraging positional power, the leader must make it clear to all the presenters that this meeting is so important to the life of the organization that it's being done differently. And in this case, it is more important what the participants are hearing (and thinking) than what you as presenters are presenting. In fact, the presenters are participants too, as is the leader, in the virtuous meeting.

DURING THE MEETING

When participants arrive at the meeting, they'll come with the invitation in mind and a mixture of their own concerns and the rumors they've heard, and they'll see laptops or tablet computers on all the tables. Expectations will be running high, and the spotlight will find the leader as the meeting starts. Here is Cathy *during* the virtuous meeting:

Part Five: Participant View from Inside a Meeting

"Thank you. I want to welcome you again. As I said in the invitation, this is a different kind of meeting. We need to think together, hard, now, to plan the right next steps for us." Cathy talked about the tough situation we're in with the customers, and with our shareholders, and now with the directors. Time was running out. She and the senior team had been trying all the usual methods for saving resources while trying to right the ship, but they couldn't do it alone. "So," she said, "we're going to have a meeting in which we THINK TOGETHER. We are going to lay out for you the full story of where we are, piece by piece, what we're up against, what resources we have, and we want you to have short discussions at your tables as we move through the issues to give your best thinking about what to do about this—from your perspective. We want all the perspectives. We'll see which ones get the most agreement, we'll make some tentative agreements here, and then the senior team will make final decisions next week when we meet.

(continued)

(*continued*)

"This is how process is going to work. You see the iPads on your tables. At various times throughout the meeting, we'll announce from the stage the next thinking exercise. At that point, you'll see the iPad screen change, and there will be a question or two with entry boxes. Please then have your table discussions and enter into the iPads the best ideas you come up with. While you're doing that, over here to my right at this table, we have what we call the Theme Team. Please stand up, I want to introduce you." The four people are well known to all of the participants and come from the R&D, customer service, sales, and marketing departments. "Their job is to read all that you're writing and make quick, joint decisions about the main, big ideas that are coming from the whole room—the themes.

"Let's do a two-minute exercise so you can see how this system works. Take a look at your screens now. You'll see a question there. What is an interesting thought you had on the way to this meeting? There are six of you at each table and two iPads. So get into groups of three. One of you grab the iPad, discuss the question quickly, and enter a response or two. Go ahead and start now. [A minute later] "Okay, it sounds like you all had a few thoughts! Let's see what you've all been thinking."

At this point, the big video screens in front of the room changed to show a long list of comments—I even saw the couple that we put in. Cathy scrolled through the list and picked out a few funny ones and another one that said, "Why does this feel like do or die?" Cathy pointed it out and said, "Amen." That got a little laughter, but people knew it was serious.

"Great, you passed the test! Let's get going. I want to bring up Martin Frost in a minute. He's going to tell you what was behind that opening video that you saw. He has some market research that we've commissioned, as well as some tentative recommendations to share with you. I want you to listen hard to what he's saying, because after thirty minutes or so we're going to use this feedback system again to ask you what you think.

What additions can you make? Or corrections, from your point of view. The Theme Team will distill themes from your input, and Martin will respond to your major points. We will also have open mics on the floor if any of you want to stand up and ask a question. Let's go. Martin, please come up. Thank you."

Ten minutes in and we were already on a new course. Everyone was at full attention, briefed, and ready to contribute.

As the vignette illustrates, the role of the leader includes

- Welcoming—giving context about the meeting and its process
- Briefing—giving context about the business
- Engaging—modeling the new meeting process
- Honoring—completing the engagement cycles
- Reframing—making meaning

In a virtuous meeting, the leader holds the keys for starting up the engine of interactivity. It begins with the welcome, in which the purpose of the meeting and the challenges (threats even) are represented, and then the format introduced, along with a brief explanation for why it was chosen. It concludes with a description of the participants' role—to actively listen to what is presented, think about it, respond to it, and build on it. At various times throughout the meeting, the leader and other presenters will respond to what the group is thinking in their responses to participant input and the themes. In this way, the participants are reinvigorated about their roles and the meeting content.

At some point near the beginning, the leader will switch hats and give a briefing on the state of the organization. Sometimes called "the burning platform" (if the organization is facing a crisis), the purpose of this segment is to get everyone up to the same speed and urgency, focused on the same critical issues, together. This type of segment is normal in a presentation-style meeting too. But in that case, there is no attention paid to what is going on in the minds of the participants—the very people who likely hold the keys to the future of the organization. In the case of the virtuous meeting, the leader is poised to tap and explore the best ideas, concerns, and suggestions of the whole group.

At the beginning of a virtuous meeting, it is important for the leader to carefully model how they want the process to unfold, and how they want the participants to engage. It is beneficial to include a solid round of feedback following this initial briefing. If the feedback does not follow the briefing, then it should follow immediately after the next presentation. In either case, it is best if the leader promptly starts up the participants in the first round of feedback as it sets the norm for the rest of the meeting.

Once the first table discussions are done and the data is collected, it comes time for the themes to be presented. If you are the leader, in the first virtuous cycle you should be front and center in presenting the themes, honoring the work that has gone into generating them (by the participants and then by the Theme Team), and beginning to respond substantively to them. This is where everyone in the room gets their first feeling of "Wow!" about what is happening. Once they've seen the first engagement cycle through to the leader's response to the themes, excitement about the process is instilled. Practically everyone in the room will buy into it and the meeting will be launched in spectacular style (and substance).

As the meeting progresses and various input and engagement cycles are completed, there come many moments for the leader and presenters to reframe what they are hearing from the group. This is where leadership becomes most visible, in the potent combination of the leader's high-level perspective on the organization's current position, his or her willingness to engage the participants' ideas openly, and the ability to synthesize all that is being discussed into new frames of thinking for the whole group. True leadership can be felt by everyone at this point. It is a basic human need to be listened to. And when it happens so visibly, constructively, and sometimes urgently, it is appreciated in the deepest way.

Another important focal point for the leader comes at the end of the meeting—the summary of what was accomplished, the value to the organization and to the leader personally, and what comes next. Here is Cathy ending on a high note:

Part Six: Participant View from Inside a Meeting

Cathy: "I want to say a few more things about what we've accomplished here. I feel personally . . . well, great . . . that we've arrived at these imperatives, and even ranked them. And further, we action-planned them, together. I think the steps are clear for tackling our customers' direst warnings head-on. We'll be clarifying them a step further at the senior team meeting next week and distributing summaries and action items, but if anyone here has questions about them before you gather your own teams next week, email or call me and we'll get the best response back to you, fastest.

"The way we've worked together at this meeting, I would hope excites you as much as it does me. We will get through this current turbulence, and because of this meeting I feel we will do it in style and with grace. Thank you for all your contributions. You were fantastic. *We* were fantastic. Safe travels to all."

In this vignette, Cathy reiterated how the group's messages and imperatives will be used and what the participants can expect to happen next. This simple step, at both the beginning of the meeting and at the end can yield huge gains in terms of participation and honesty. It allows participants to give their best, most constructive input and to properly set their expectations. Leaders want to avoid surprises in decision-making rules and let downs in expectations at all costs. Also important, Cathy gave credit where credit was due and played the role of cheerleader-in-chief. She modeled how she wanted the spirit and substance from the meeting to go on and outward.

AFTER THE MEETING

In some ways, the work of the leader after the meeting is similar to what he or she did during the meeting. If a virtuous meeting is like an organizational inhale, with all kinds of ideas and topics rushing in, the period just after the meeting is like an exhale, where the results of discussions, themes, and reframes are taken back to the workplace and worked. It is the leader and maybe some of the presenters who are primarily responsible for keeping the outcomes of the participant-centered meeting alive, constructive, and "breathing."

And so after the meeting, the leader can give broader context back to the participants now that they all have had their say and new understandings are in place. It is a time to initiate new virtuous cycles, except these cycles may take a week or more to complete, where in the meeting they took an hour. Because they are cycles that must be completed in order to get the value, the time it takes to complete them is less important. With each new cycle comes "response-ability" by the leaders—both a responsibility to respond to the new ideas for the benefit of all and a new found ability to do so. This meaning-making function is central to the role of the active, engaged leader.

KOUZES AND POSNER:
Five Leadership Practices

The view of leadership we have seen through our vignette of Cathy is the result of our facilitation of thousands of meetings. The leadership traits she possesses have all been seen and felt or heard through the anecdotes of partners. In addition, there is another facet of leadership that is about leadership development, on which there has been extensive empirical research. It is valuable to see the leadership that is required by virtuous, participant-centered meetings side by side with leadership qualities determined through research. The gold standard in this area is Jim Kouzes and Barry Posner's Five Practices of Exemplary Leadership model, which is based on research spanning a few decades. In their research, Kouzes and Posner found that, "Leadership is not about personality; it's about behavior—an observable set of skills and abilities."[5]

They asked thousands of people to recall the experiences that represented their "peak leadership." These "personal best" stories revealed five core practices common to all leaders: Model the Way, Inspire a Shared Vision, Challenge the Process, Enable Others to Act, and Encourage the Heart. These same five core practices have held fast since the early 1980s when Kouzes and Posner first distilled them. Let's look at each core practice in the context of leading the way to and through virtuous meetings.

Model the Way

Kouzes and Posner state that leaders must create standards of excellence for others to follow and then set an example for others to follow. The leader who models the way knows that change equals upheaval, and so they set short-term, attainable goals for their team to achieve, knowing that these "small wins" will help them work toward the big goals.

There are few acts bolder than standing in front of the top three hundred managers of the organization you lead and saying, "We're going to dive deep into [critical issue] now, together. It's a tough one, it affects all of us, and I want to crack this with you. I want you to think about this at your tables, and I want to hear your best ideas about it. Then I will respond to your major findings, we'll talk about it, and we'll come to a new understanding about it. Begin your discussions now." After seeing and feeling this moment hundreds of times over twenty years, we can accurately call it "a visible act of leadership." It is powerful for everyone, and it models a way that key stakeholders "should be treated and the way goals should be pursued." It takes leadership and it promotes leadership.

Inspire a Shared Vision

This core practice goes hand in hand with the goals of the virtuous meeting. The leader in Kouzes and Posner's work envisions the future and passionately strives to make it a reality. The leader uses charisma and quiet persuasion to move others to share their dream. They "breathe life into their visions and get people to see exciting possibilities for the future."[6]

In a virtuous meeting, the topics and segments are considered carefully in advance and chosen for maximum value to the organization. When the purpose of the meeting is to inspire a shared vision, leaders can "work" their vision with the group interactively—alternately presenting, then listening and discussing—in a way that can save months or perhaps years in achieving the same degree of "shared." As we've discussed in earlier chapters, advances in technology and process design allow this now. It is up to any leader to step up and take advantage of it. Each authority figure in front of the group will have a different personality and responsibilities, but this behavior or ability to lead the thinking or exploration toward mutually beneficial conclusions is seen by everyone as significant personal leadership.

Challenge the Process

In this core practice, leaders look for creative ways to change the status quo and improve the organization. They experiment and take risks and know that doing so means making mistakes. They accept the disappointments and see failures as learning opportunities.[7]

Leaders who take large groups into participant-centered meetings are clearly "challenging the (normal) process." No one misses it. After the meeting, the innovation in meeting design and productivity is seen as its own reward, and any perceived risks fade as unfounded concerns. It is human to want to be heard, but it is leadership to listen and respond and add value in each cycle. It is a participant-centered meeting format that allows all of this to happen smoothly. The outcomes—learning, understanding, alignment—are seen by most as well worth the effort. Some say "it was the best meeting ever." But the kudos for this type of meeting, and the personal leadership it took to "challenge the process" in this way, accrue to the leader.

Enable Others to Act

Leaders emphasize collaboration and build spirited teams. They actively involve others and create an atmosphere of mutual respect, trust, and human dignity. They know that they must "strengthen others, making each person feel capable and powerful."[8]

Questions or concerns often stop people in their thinking, or in their work. For many leaders in large organizations, questions from employees or team members about direction or resources or priorities, for example, are difficult to engage and answer off the cuff. There is a premium on "getting it right," which often leads to the passage of time and a creeping paralysis. This can take a toll on trust and respect as perceived by employees. By contrast, in a virtuous large meeting the premium is on hearing the big questions as a group and getting the best possible answers from the brain trust in the room. Right now. Owing to the technology and process design, leaders are now able to probe as often as necessary for the question: What are the concerns or best suggestions *now*?

This method is similar to the familiar "5 Whys"—a questioning technique that allows getting quickly to the root cause of a problem. In the case of a virtuous meeting, there are so many participants answering the first round of "Why?" that the theming process will identify the "crowd-sourced" root causes quickly. This process of interactively probing for questions, concerns, and ideas gives leaders a format with which to enable others to act, massively.

The late Michael Doyle, who together with David Straus wrote the seminal *How to Make Meetings Work* in 1976, had a favorite saying that permeated his life's work in meeting facilitation: Go slow to go fast.[9] What he meant was this: involve everyone who will be critical in implementing any large effort . . . in the planning of it. Take a little time (or a lot) at the beginning of a significant project to get the key people "on board" so they can act much more knowledgeably and effectively when the start button is pushed. And what you'll find, Doyle would say, is that the total time of the project to a certain point of completion will be much shorter if you go slow at first, so that you can go fast later. He and Kouzes and Posner are talking about the same thing—putting the spotlight, as leader, on enabling others to act. In a participant-centered meeting, when leaders have this full two-way communication capability in place, it is a relatively simple matter to highlight good ideas and especially "to create an atmosphere of trust and human dignity."

Encourage the Heart

Leaders know that you can't effect extraordinary change without hard work, and that you can't motivate that kind of determination without recognizing people for their efforts. Sharing in the rewards and celebrating as a team are efforts led by a leader who knows how to "make people feel like heroes."[10]

You can see how Enable Others to Act is connected directly to Encourage the Heart. It is a short step from building human dignity to celebrating accomplishments, because people perform best when they are recognized for their contributions. In every virtuous meeting, we know that many feelings do go unarticulated. We've heard many of them because we asked about them, offstage and offline. There are feelings of mutual respect, pride in the organization, and trust in the leaders. These come up often. Participants appreciate being asked what they are thinking, and they respond with enthusiasm. We have found this to be true in cultures spanning the Far East, North America, and Europe. It's true at all levels in organizations, in all types of organizations.

In all stages of the participant-centered meeting experience, from the initial design decisions to the follow-up after a meeting, the good leader meets resistance with heart and a desire to reach out to the whole organization. Leaders who embrace the spirit of shared understanding and shared vision that is at the core of participant-centered virtuous meetings will become more agile in meeting the challenges of an unknown future.

THE VULNERABILITY OF POWER

In 2011, the average tenure of a Fortune 500 CEO was 4.6 years,[11] and for all CEOs just over eight years. While Western culture seems to fawn over CEOs and other senior executives, the data shows their time at the top can be pressurized and short-lived. As a newly appointed CEO enters his or her office for the first time, the urgency to get things done is immediate. Other data[12] show that two-thirds of CEOs are promoted from within after spending an average of thirteen years in management positions in the organization. So in a majority of cases, at least the CEO is intimately familiar with the organization and how it currently runs. But in all cases, the demands of the role, including demands for new skills and performance gains, mostly driven by the constantly changing external landscape, cause many to sputter and fail. Many are forced to revert to old habits and potentially bad ones in order to face the intense challenges that go with the job.

When seen from this perspective, it is easy to understand how it can be hard for many executives to accept the methodical, deliberate design process of a virtuous meeting—and then further, during the meeting, to be open for broad input from eager participants with a kaleidoscope of needs and agendas. But when the going gets tough the choices are few, if any, and executives are wise to consider the best alternative to the status quo—the virtuous meeting. It is a matchup between the power of aligned action, which is developed through open, virtuous communication, against the vulnerability of power.

THE POWER OF VULNERABILITY

Completely on the other hand, consider the insightful work of Dr. Brené Brown, a research scientist and professor at the University of Houston Graduate College of Social Work. Dr. Brown's TED talk, "The Power of Vulnerability,"[13] which she gave in May of 2010, tallied eight million views by early 2013 and thirteen million a year later. It went viral.

Her research, based on thousands of interviews, pointed to a reservoir of power available through facing the vulnerability that is both common and hidden in all of us. Over ten years, she dug deeply into the human condition, beginning with connection—the force that brings us together. Probing further she found the result of the fear of disconnection, which is shame. Underpinning shame, again through thousands of carefully structured interviews, she found what she called *excruciating vulnerability*. By vulnerability she meant that in order for human connection to happen, we must be willing to be seen whole. And underneath it all, she found a sense of worthiness—a strong sense of love and belonging. It was either there, or missing. Those who had this sense of worthiness she called *whole-hearted* people, having (1) a sense of courage, (2) compassion to themselves and others, and (3) strong human connections as a result of authenticity. The other thing in common she found: they fully embraced their vulnerability. They believed that what made them vulnerable made them beautiful. Vulnerability wasn't comfortable, but it was necessary—the willingness to say "I love you" first, or doing something without guarantees. In summarizing ten years of research, she said of the choices we vulnerable ones make, (1) we let ourselves be seen, (2) we love with our whole hearts even without guarantees, (3) we practice gratitude, we lean into joy, and (4) the last and most important, we believe that "I am enough as I am."[14]

Dr. Brown has said, "I've come to believe that leadership has nothing to do with position, salary, or number of direct reports. I believe a leader is anyone who holds her- or himself accountable for finding potential in people and processes." Contrary to the myth of the "all-knowing all-powerful" leader, inspired leadership requires vulnerability: Do we have the courage to show up, be seen, take risks, ask for help, own our mistakes, learn from failure, lean into joy, and can we support the people around us in doing the same?

In considering leadership and leading virtuous meetings, this was sobering research to behold. Dr. Brown names the challenges, the journey, and some of the rewards of an authentic style of leadership that is all somehow necessary within those who lead such meetings. And you can see how many leaders are not able to do it for some of these same reasons. Virtuous meetings are led by those with courage.

This chapter highlights a capability that ties various dimensions of leadership to a newly available large meeting format—the ability now to "listen large" as a leader and to respond, fully informed, to what you're hearing. This ability has never existed. A virtuous meeting is a platform for leadership. It takes leadership to put the platform in place. And it requires ongoing leadership to bring to fruition that which was discussed so whole heartedly during the meeting. This two-way communication capability, whole heartedly led inside the time format of most large organizational meetings, allows for all manner of more effective meeting processes. In fact, it enables the world's most productive meetings.

ℂ CHAPTER ELEVEN • QUICK SUMMARY

- The leader's role is an indispensable one. Leaders are the ones who can truly "open up the space" by making it safe for real dialogue and disclosure, as well as ideas and contributions, to pour forth.

- Virtuous meetings are wonderful opportunities for executive development as top leaders model exactly how to engage a large group of the organization's brightest and best in critical dialogue and problem solving.
- Leading in virtuous meetings requires persons who have grown to be comfortable in their own skin and who have a much greater sense of service than of entitlement.
- The leadership required by virtuous, participant-centered meetings can be examined side by side with leadership qualities determined through research. The gold standard in this area is Jim Kouzes and Barry Posner's Five Practices of Exemplary Leadership model.
- There is a vulnerability of power—CEOs and senior leaders are faced with intense pressures to perform and do it over tenures averaging little more than five years. There is also the power of vulnerability—through a process of self-exploration, courageous leaders can find in themselves a whole hearted way to exercise power.

Case Story 6: A Consulting Firm's Annual Partners Meeting

CASE STORY

It's a good sign when a consulting firm specializing in leadership development uses the same methods they offer to their clients on themselves. Such was the case recently when Covision supported a four-day offsite for a firm with whom we've worked many times over the past decade. The firm has over two hundred partners who deliver their core programs. This annual meeting is especially important as it serves the dual purpose of keeping the partners up-to-date on learnings and new offers, and reinvigorating their engagement and enthusiasm for the values and aspirations of the firm. The challenge with this meeting, however, was that it had become rote, full of presentations, and, by all accounts, just plain boring—exactly the opposite of what the managing director wanted. He brought us in "to spice it up" and make it more engaging, interesting, and productive. He also wanted to showcase the Covision approach to the firm's partners in an effort to spread this way of working together throughout their client group.

We took on the project and immediately saw in the draft agenda too many presentations in a row, with little time for any table discussions and feedback. As repetition is a root cause of boredom, we pushed back a little on the timing. But it appeared as if the two meeting designers weren't following the advice they had given so often to their clients. They seemed to feel that the iPads and the occasional opportunities for feedback from the partners would make the meeting interesting *enough*.

As Day 1 opened, we had the Covision system in place—two iPads on each round table of six participants, a server and backup in the room, a connection to the video projector, and a table for the Theme Team. In this case, one of us and one of the presenters would do the theming (planned as a light task). The design of the first day included mostly presentations, with the iPad system available for participants to send their questions to the presenters. The questions on the iPad screens were

- What do you need to know more about?
- What (if anything) are you concerned about?

There were plenty of data, and clear themes emerged. We could see real honesty in the comments and a constructive tone right from the start. So the presenter was able to energize the Q&A segments with the best questions summarized from the group. All was good enough for the client, although for a virtuous meeting, participation was clearly throttled back.

Midway through the day, on a hunch, the meeting designers decided to switch on the Read button on the iPads. This made the group's input available on each screen, but only to the curious ones because the change wasn't announced. By the end of the day, most had found out the capability and were seen reading the comments, especially during the frequent Q&A segments. But another problem had emerged—each segment was going overtime and the meeting had to be extended a couple of times. There was some grumbling, but dinnertime energy replaced it soon enough, and the day ended well.

Day 2 was featured as Innovation Day in the agenda. The group was using its own methodology for incubating innovation—one of their core offerings to clients. The method uses full-engagement processes to foster innovation thinking more rapidly and substantively than you might expect. There was high energy for the topics in the room, but the discussions, while thoroughly engaging, again grew longer as the day wore on. Those responsible for each segment were not responsible, as it turned out, for the overall agenda, so the session slipped into overtime again.

That evening, in a quick agenda review session, the facilitation problem was identified. Someone needed to step into the facilitator role. The next day would be a long series of reports and discussions based on the work in small groups done earlier in Day 2. And while so many in the firm were world-class facilitators in their client work, no one, including the managing director, wanted to split their focus from the important topics at hand. So one of us volunteered to be at least a time keeper in front of the room. People already knew us and our role at the Theme Team table, so the change would be natural.

The immediate challenge with Day 3 was how to shift the design to make it much more interesting when on paper the agenda read like a day of dull report-outs. We first advised them to make the segments longer in order to run a complete engagement cycle within each segment. Sixty-minute segments were reshaped to ninety minutes—fifteen minutes for the opening report; fifteen minutes for the table discussions and feedback (during which time the presenters read the data too and prepped for how they wanted to respond); the final sixty minutes allotted for open facilitated discussion; and a hard stop at the ninety-minute mark. Each iPad screen had these questions on it:

1. What do you like about what you've heard?
2. What, if anything, is missing?
3. What questions do you have for enriching the next step, for refining our strategies?

Day 3 got under way according to plan and, as hoped, the participants became fully engaged in the flow. Each topic group from the day before presented their findings to the rest of the group. The ensuing whole group discussions were robust by design, as each one was based on everyone's ideas just captured. The process allowed the group to quickly go deeper into a few key areas where all could see it was worth the time. Our coaching advice to each group was not to theme the comments but rather to pull out the most important comments to discuss with the whole group. Each group's findings were tweaked and polished. At the end of each discussion, the whole group was polled: Are these findings moving in the right direction? In all cases the clear majority said yes.

One overarching theme we were able to bring to the group's attention was a keen awareness that they needed to "walk their talk" better. They needed to step up their game and change their own behaviors. There was a gap there between talk and action that was slowly but consistently revealed throughout the day.

This meeting taught us that there is no better way to come to these kinds of results than through the powerful combination of high connectivity, good design, leaders who want more from their meetings, and some basic facilitation. Even the newest partners became secure in putting their ideas out into the room. The Covision system and approach to virtuous meetings—the ability to put your best thoughts quickly and anonymously into the iPad, where everyone can see them—made the subsequent dialogues highly valuable and infinitely more energizing.

Another innovation in the meeting design was an "energy break" between each group's report. For fifteen minutes the whole group was led in a stretching, jumping, bending, and meditating interlude. Like cleansing the palette, the energy breaks made room for fresh thinking and interaction. These breaks made a huge difference in managing the group's positive, constructive ability to focus, so that they could continuously recycle and renew their energy as they worked hard in one room, all day, on difficult issues.

Day 4 was designed for multiple rounds of voting on the action lists, with discussion after each poll. The group quickly arrived at clarity around their Top 10 actions and strategies, and within that list, their Top 3. These were short-term, high-impact actions, with full understanding built around each one. Convergence and alignment was achieved. By keeping the large discussions fact-based, on track, and within the time allotted for them in the agenda, we were able to help the group face the big issues. They really didn't need more than that, and they hadn't bargained for nearly as much. The meeting closed with a capturing of personal commitments, now fully understood, and a general atmosphere of good cheer.

PART FIVE

SCALING VIRTUOUS MEETINGS

TAKING VIRTUOUS MEETINGS BEYOND THE ROOM

The virtuous meeting approach that we have discussed through-out this book is uniquely suited to the challenge of expanding the scale of meetings. In fact, this approach to large meetings was developed to meet the challenges of scale. Our effort over the last twenty years has been to find a way to preserve the individual's voice and contribution within ever-larger groups, so that those groups could come to a shared understanding and generate convergent outcomes. At the heart of this approach is a focus on scale.

Virtuous meetings can scale in two dimensions. First, the number of participants can be scaled as much as needed. We have not yet seen the point at which a convergent meeting has too many participants. We have supported meetings of up to twelve thousand participants that were able to generate convergent outcomes. Certainly larger meetings could be successful. So far, the factors limiting the size of meetings have been the logistics, the difficulties in organization, and the cost for bringing people together, but not the fear that the individual's voice and contribution would be lost.

The second dimension of scale for virtuous meetings is the number of locations that can be simultaneously included in a large meeting. In fact, this dimension of scalability may be the most important one and the one with the most impact on the future of large and very large meetings. Throughout the book we have con-fined our discussion to meetings where all of the participants are in a single plenary room. We wanted to introduce all of the principles of convergent meetings as simply and clearly as possible. We wanted the concepts and examples to be easy to grasp and understand. But once you understand those concepts, you will find that applying them to multi-site meetings is an easy and natural extension of how they are applied in a single meeting room.

IT'S A GREAT BIG WORLD OUT THERE

No matter how large these meetings we've been describing are, even with thousands of participants, everyone meets at the same time, and everyone is together with everyone else in the same venue. But there are an increasing number of meetings that are held where the participants meet together at the same time even though they are in two or more places. What we traditionally think of happening "in the room" is now happening simultaneously across multiple rooms. The terminology used among meeting designers is that if the participants are all together in one location the meeting is same time/same place (ST/SP) or face to face (Figure 12.1), and if the participants are distributed over multiple locations, the meeting is same time/different place (ST/DP).

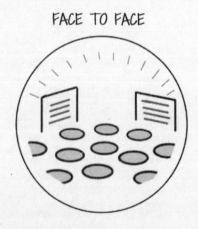

Figure 12.1 Single Location

In the realm of ST/DP meetings, most of us are familiar with teleconferences, usually a handful of people on the phone together having a project meeting or a discussion that typically would have been held face to face twenty years ago. These calls are essential for organizations that are spread out across the country or around the globe. They happen every day, all the time. Also familiar are "virtual" meetings where everyone on a conference call is looking at the same visual image. Sometimes those images are PowerPoint slides, sometimes a shared authoring tool like Google Docs, and sometimes direct video of one or all of the attendees on the call. These kinds of ST/DP events include a lot of project meetings and briefings, but also include webinars, where participants are learners, and "virtual launches," where participants are introduced to a new product or service, and so forth.

ST/DP is a well-known modality from the perspective of conference calls. But what is less common, so far, are large meetings that are held in multiple locations. For convenience here, we will refer to them as *multi-site meetings*. Multi-site meetings can take a few different forms.

If there is a central venue where a meeting is taking place, additional participants can take part in the meeting in one of two modes. Either they can be part of a group at another location, or they can be participating *individually* from wherever they are. In the first case (Figure 12.2), additional participants are seated at tables in a satellite meeting remote from the central meeting venue. They listen

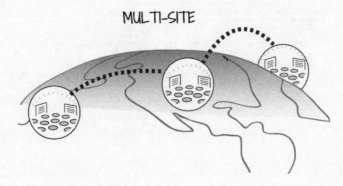

Figure 12.2   A Central Meeting Location and Other Satellite Locations

to presentations and see either video of the presenter or slides that the presenter is talking about. Then during the discussion period they discuss the topic with those at their table and send in their comments and ideas to the synthesizing team via an input device, over the Internet.

In the second case, the additional participants participate individually from their office, home, or other location (Figure 12.3). They use their own computer to listen to the presentations at the main location and to watch streaming video of the presenter and/or the presentation slides. During the discussion period, they are on the phone and are joined into virtual table groups. In these groups, they discuss the topic with a few others, and one person from the group captures and sends the group's best ideas to the synthesizing team over the Internet. Figure 12.3 shows a central location and individuals participating in the meeting from their homes or offices, connected together in these small "virtual table groups."

In the scenarios illustrated by Figure 12.2 and Figure 12.3, the additional participants are involved in small group discussions, and the fruits of their table discussions are synthesized with everything from the other locations. What was discussed at their table group helps to shape the "voice" of the whole group. The synthesizing team uses the software (groupware) to access the input from all of the participants—no matter where they are located. The meeting's size is

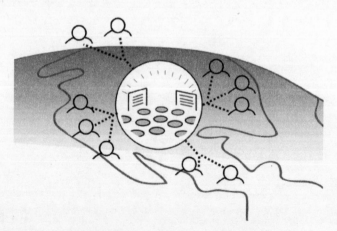

Figure 12.3 A Central Meeting Location with Participants at Home

determined by how many participants are involved in total across all sites, including those participating individually.

A third multi-site configuration merges what we see in Figure 12.2 and Figure 12.3 so that you have both: (1) satellite sites, where participants are sitting together in table groups at different sites, and (2) individuals participating remotely from home or work and having their small group discussion in "virtual table groups." This third multi-site configuration is illustrated in Figure 12.4, where there is a central location, along with satellite locations, and some participants connected individually.

The technical considerations for adding individual participants as active contributors to a multi-site meeting revolve mostly around choosing the right software. Individual participants need to see and hear what is happening at the main location, then join a small teleconference "table group" for the discussion periods. Also, they should be running the same group engagement software as the other remote locations, so that someone from the teleconference "table group" can record the group's ideas and send them over the Internet to the synthesizing team.

Although we have reinforced from the very beginning of this book that a virtuous meeting is not *just* a virtual meeting, another configuration of a virtuous large group meeting *is* a purely virtual one (Figure 12.5). In this case there is no central site where a group of

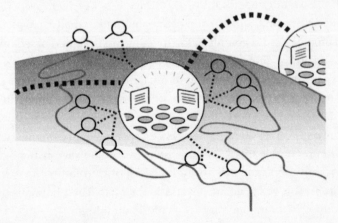

Figure 12.4 A Central Location, Satellite Locations, and Participants Connected Individually

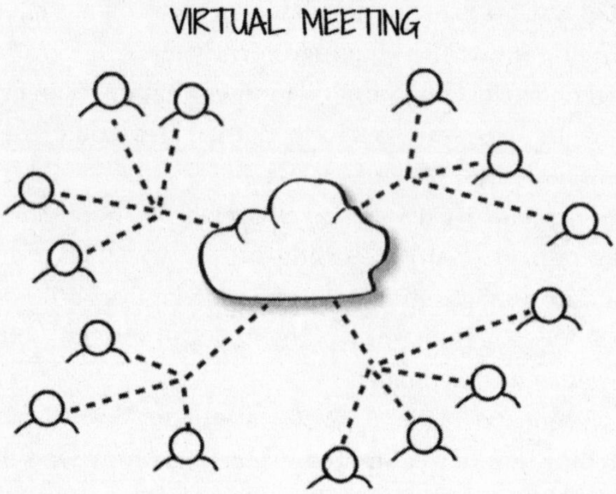

VIRTUAL MEETING

Figure 12.5 Virtual Virtuous Large Group Meeting

people is meeting face to face. Instead, all of the participants are participating individually from home or work. The key difference from other, more commonplace "virtual meetings" is that this virtual meeting is large, the design is participant centered, and the participants are connected to each other in small virtual groups that allow all the participants to be active contributors (even though the meeting is large).

Even though it is a virtual meeting, and no one is gathered face to face, it is still designed as a two-level meeting in which participants spend time in both small group discussions and in the virtual plenary. And the different segments of the meeting are designed based on the Virtuous Engagement Cycle. Participants are able to watch presentations on their computer, then break into small teleconference discussion groups. One member of the small group sends in the group's ideas to a synthesizing team, the input from all of the groups is synthesized into themes, and those themes are presented back to everyone. Participants view and listen to the Review on their computer, and then watch the presenter Respond to the themes of the group. In this way a meta-conversation is established between those convening the meeting and all of those attending.

These elements can be combined in many different configurations. From the point of view of virtuous large group meeting design, any of these configurations are treated essentially the same as a large meeting in a single venue.

However, although multi-site meetings are still relatively rare, there is still the tendency to choose front-of-the-room design when considering a multi-site meeting. We supported one Fortune 100 company for several years with virtuous large meeting design for their "Top 350" leadership meeting. But with the bank crash of 2008 and the resulting scrutiny of how companies spent their money, they decided in 2009 not to hold the annual meeting. Instead, they decided to hold a virtual meeting. Unfortunately, it was very difficult for them to imagine how all of the people, spread across several locations, could actually interact with one another. Delivering information to the group seemed like the only thing they could hope for.

The design they came up with was to have the top officers of the company giving short informational talks. The whole meeting was only two hours long and used only one "participation" format—presentations. The 350 leaders could watch it streaming live, or go back and see the recording of it later.

On the day of the actual virtual "meeting," some of the leaders were gathered at the company's headquarters where the officers were presenting, and some gathered together at other company sites for that two-hour period, but many of them just watched from their office. Attendance, including attendees at the headquarters, at the satellite locations, and individuals watching from their office, was about half of the 350. It was never disclosed how many of the others went back and watched the recording. Afterward, the head of corporate strategy stated that the net value to the organization of the whole exercise was very low. It did not replace most of what the participants got out of the annual leadership meeting. And it did not provide much momentum for the organization.

Of course, their problem was not the multi-site format. Rather, it was the lack of a process designed for engaging the participants. Although they had experienced virtuous meetings in a face-to-face configuration, as soon as they wanted to do a large "virtual meeting" they reverted to front-of-the-room design and processes.

The great opportunity going forward is that multi-site meetings can be convergent. The two keys to convergence that kicked off this book in Part One—the Internet connectivity that bridges locations and the process that makes participants active contributors—can be used to scale up to any size meeting or to any number of locations. Furthermore, the kind of meta-conversation created by the Virtuous Engagement Cycles we introduced in Part Two transcends how many participants are involved or where they are located.

☾ CHAPTER TWELVE • QUICK SUMMARY

- Virtuous meetings scale in two dimensions: number of participants and number of simultaneous locations.
- Virtuous meetings can take several forms in addition to a face-to-face meeting held in a single location.
- Multi-site meetings can be centered in one location but have other satellite locations with large numbers of participants in each place.
- In a second configuration, the multi-site can be centered in one location, but have any number of participants connecting individually from their home or office.
- In a third configuration, the multi-site can also combine multiple satellite locations while also having any number of individual participants in their homes or offices.
- It is also possible to have a completely virtual virtuous meeting, where all of the participants are attending from their own location and there is no central site for the meeting.
- Regardless of the configuration, any multi-site meeting has the possibility of being convergent if you use the virtuous approach.

CHAPTER THIRTEEN

THE ELEMENTS THAT SCALE VIRTUOUS MEETINGS

E verything that we have discussed about virtuous large group meetings applies equally well whether the meeting is taking place in one room or many. In fact, this approach is uniquely adapted for use in large-scale distributed meetings. Every key element of virtuous meeting design scales smoothly and easily to make convergent processes possible over multiple locations.

THE SCALABLE TECHNOLOGY OF CONNECTIVITY

The technology of connectivity is Internet-based; the connectivity that enables convergent processes in large meetings evolved over the last twenty years as the Internet grew. The software that allows instant transmission of the ideas from each of the table groups runs in a web browser. An idea from a table in another country travels as quickly to the team of synthesizers as it would from a table in the plenary hall— at nearly the speed of light!

What this means is that there are no physical barriers to small table groups getting their thoughts to a team of synthesizers. The table group doesn't need to be in the same location as the synthesizing team. We have supported meetings where the table groups are not even on the same continent as the synthesizers. Via the Internet, the software, and the synthesizing team, those table groups can contribute just as fully as the table groups in the central plenary room.

In fact, using the connectivity only in the plenary room is somewhat of an underutilization of the technology. The technology that underlies the connectivity—the Internet and all of the software and hardware that supports it—is specifically built for bridging locations. Of course, it works perfectly to have that network of connectivity in the plenary room of a large meeting. But it works just as perfectly to have the network connecting several different rooms full of table groups or even many small table groups scattered geographically, anywhere in the world.

The considerations around ensuring good connectivity are similar to what they would be for a single-site meeting, but they have to be focused on in each of the locations. Each location needs to have sufficient Internet bandwidth, and the network at each location needs to be able to handle the number of devices that your participants will be using—as we discussed in Chapter Three. The added factor here is that you need to transmit video and audio signals from the central location out to the other locations. The participants at those locations need to see and hear presentations, reviews of the group's input, and responses from the leadership. (With more resources you can also transmit audio and video signals from the other locations back to the central site. In this way, live statements and responses from any of the locations can be shared with the whole group.)

THE SCALABLE ROLE OF ACTIVE CONTRIBUTORS

You change an otherwise passive audience into active contributors when you have a two-level meeting where participants experience being in a small table group and being in the large plenary group. Participants become active as they spend part of the meeting segments in their small table groups immersed in discussion about the topic of the segment. As we've seen, the discussions are focused by specific questions. They come up with ideas in answer to the question, share them around the table, and as they begin to gel, send them to the synthesizing team. Through the synthesis of all of the groups' ideas and sending that synthesis back to the whole group, the participants are able to contribute.

The same process takes place at each table. By being part of a small group discussion, all of the participants are active contributors. This process works the same whether there are ten tables or a hundred tables. But even if there are a thousand tables, it is still just the same for each participant. As long as the meeting has two levels where participants can be in a small group discussion, it really doesn't matter how many people you have in the large group. The two-level design is scalable. The participant's experience of active contribution is not affected by how big the whole group becomes.

Neither is the participant's experience affected by how many locations there are. If there are a hundred tables and a participant is sitting at table thirteen, it won't really matter if table seventy-five is somewhere far across the room, or somewhere far across the world. In groups of this size, several hundred to several thousand, the participant does not expect to meet or greet everyone in the meeting. The concern of the participant is to have a meaningful discussion about the topic and to understand what the whole group is thinking, including the response of the leadership. The participant's role is unaffected by spreading the meeting out over several locations. What the participant does notice is the benefit of not having to travel so far!

A basic principle is this: The more participants you include, the more necessary and meaningful the two-level design becomes. Also, the more distributed the participants are, the more valuable two-level design becomes. If you had sixty-four participants in a room, you might question whether they couldn't all contribute in one big open discussion—keeping the meeting just at the plenary level. But if you have eight groups of eight participants spread over eight different locations, it quickly becomes apparent that you need to use a two-level design. The need for two-level design becomes even more obvious if each of the eight groups has eighty participants.

THE SCALABLE PROCESS OF VIRTUOUS ENGAGEMENT CYCLES

A Virtuous Engagement Cycle is the process that allows active contributors to be in a meta-conversation with those in front of the room. Engagement cycles take place within agenda segments. When they happen frequently throughout the day, they make it possible to achieve convergent outcomes in large and very large meetings.

The Virtuous Engagement Cycle process can be applied to any large group, regardless of size. No matter how many participants are in a meeting, the four steps of the process can be completed. Obviously, the presentation can be delivered to as many people as you want. By having a two-level design to the meeting, it doesn't matter how many participants you have, they can all participate in small group discussions.

The more table groups you have, the more input the synthesizing team will have to synthesize. But the synthesizing activity can also be scaled. We have done meetings with AmericaSpeaks where there were thousands of participants, sometimes spread across several locations. With precise design of the synthesizing team activities and a big enough team, all of the input can still be themed quickly enough to allow the group to create convergence around it.

As an example of what we are talking about here, let's look at what would be different about designing a five-hundred-participant virtuous meeting for three locations, rather than one.

From the process point of view, in terms of the Virtuous Engagement Cycle, everything unfolds the same way that it would if all of the participants were in one room:

1. A presentation is made from the central location.
2. All the participants go into discussion at their tables and start sending in their responses to the focusing question(s). If the participants are seated at tables of six, that means about eighty-four tables spread out across the three locations (e.g., forty tables at the central location and twenty-two tables at each of the other two locations).

3. The synthesizing team reads through all of the input as it comes in. The synthesizing team is usually stationed at one of the locations, generally wherever the presentations are coming from. The team has access to the table groups' ideas from each location through the Internet, and it creates one synthesis from the thoughts coming in from all eighty-four tables.

4. The synthesis is shown to all participants at each of the locations via the audio-video feed.

5. The presenter is able to respond to the synthesis, and everyone at each location is able to see and hear the response.

If you choose to spread the meeting over three locations, the convergent process works as well as it would in a single location, and the design process and considerations (see Part Three) are virtually the same.

The Virtuous Engagement Cycle is a means for large groups to have the kind of convergent meta-conversations that smaller groups have naturally in open discussions. The value of the Virtuous Engagement Cycle process actually increases the more participants you have, because the possibility of worthwhile outcomes through other processes, like a whole group discussion, diminishes. The value increases in the same way as you begin to incorporate multiple locations. Normal group discussion processes, such as raising your hand to get a microphone and making a statement to the whole group, become hopelessly cumbersome when there are large groups in several different locations. By contrast, Virtuous Engagement Cycles provide a way for everyone to be part of a group "voice" and to engage in a dialogue with those in the front of the room.

WHY NOW?

We believe that multi-site meetings are going to become increasingly common in the coming years. The first reason is that with the continued adoption of virtuous meeting design, it will become possible to hold truly effective meetings across multiple locations.

At each location the process will be participant-centered, engaging each participant as a valued contributor. And all of the small group conversations will be rolled up into one synthesized voice that unites the various participants across all of the locations.

The second reason is that the need for large meetings is growing, and costs are a consideration. As collaboration becomes more important and organizations become more complex and interdependent, gathering the right people together becomes a competitive advantage. Lynda Gratton recently told a group of leaders: "It's not the number of great minds that you have working for you that makes the difference. It's how those minds work together that gives you the advantage."[1] Every step of the way, it is a question of bringing the right people together and facilitating an environment in which it is easy for them to collaborate.

The group of people will probably be more diverse and more cross-organizational than in the past. A key component of innovation is cross-pollination and looking outside your traditional areas of focus. But increasingly, it is important to do that as a group, not just as individuals. We recently supported a large extended leadership meeting for the product development division of a Fortune 500 company. Most of the first day of the meeting was spent in small groups with successful entrepreneurs from other industries and small businesses, listening to their stories and hearing about their innovations. The second day was spent with the leaders talking to each other, sharing insights from the first day, and thinking about what was possible to do within their own organizations. The focus of the meeting was innovation, and the biggest innovation was holding the meeting in the first place. The top 240 leaders had never been brought together before! The senior leadership wanted to inspire innovation within the organization, and they realized that they had to bring all of the extended leadership together in order to ignite thinking and connections that would never arise out of business as usual.

The frequency with which you can bring people together is a determining factor in how quickly you can respond to disruptive events and trends in the environment. Even though everyone's plate is too full already, we have consistently seen that if people are able to contribute and can realize real value in the meeting, they want to meet together more often, not less. One organization that we had supported for a few years in their annual leadership meeting had a change of CEO. The new CEO expressed to the group that he wasn't sure whether there was value in continuing to hold the leadership meeting. Interestingly, the new CEO also derided Facebook and Twitter from the stage, saying that he "didn't get it" and implied that it was a bit silly and a waste of time. But, he said, since he was new, he would leave it to the extended leadership team to tell him whether they thought it was worth their time and the money to get together every year: the answer, maybe to his surprise, was a resounding and emphatic "Yes!" That sentiment is transferable to many extended leadership groups today. People feel that they need to gather together more often, not less. In fact, because things can change so much within a year, even an annual meeting cycle begins to feel slow in responding to that change.

Ultimately, if we are to try to take Amy Edmundson's notion of "teaming" to large scale, it will not be enough for the top 150 leaders of an organization to "buy into" and align with the strategy. The means must be found for those 150 leaders to create the strategy too, so that they own it and know how to modify it when the circumstances around them change.

And yet, although the need is becoming greater and greater to gather different groups of people together from different parts of an organization and different geographies, as well as external stake-holders, the logistical and financial barriers are real. Travel, although it has become accepted and completely integrated with the demands of many positions, is nonetheless a great deterrent when it comes to contemplating whether to have a meeting, and if so, who and how many to invite. Travel costs money, takes time, depletes energy, requires recovery time, degrades the environment, makes scheduling more difficult (by adding time to the event itself), and is always subject to random delays and frustrations that make the negative psychological effects more pronounced. Multi-site meetings over-come some of those barriers by incorporating people in the cities, regions, or countries in which they work and reside, so that their travel is greatly reduced or eliminated.

Because you don't have to bring everyone to one location, multi-site virtuous meetings allow you to scale up economically and productively. You can include voices that are necessary but that may have been left out before due to of cost or space considerations. Also, because you can incorporate participants individually, from wherever they happen to be at the time, you can include certain stakeholder groups, particular functions, or field people into specific segments of the meeting. These advantages are especially valuable and natural for organizations that are trying to have an impact or do business in multiple geographies.

In some ways you could see multi-site meetings as a better leveraging of resources. Extra resources are needed to plan the logistics and coordinate between the locations, but those extra resources save time, effort, and energy for all of the participants. A little bit more investment in energy on the planning side saves a lot of energy for everyone who is attending.

The great logistical and cost advantages of multi-site meetings won't amount to much, if all it means is that people will be watching a video feed at the same time or will be able to ask questions of the speaker over their smart phone. If an organization's goal in gathering people together is to foster collaboration, cross-pollinate for innovation, and respond swiftly to disruptive forces, then ensuring that the participants have a voice and can contribute is essential. And multi-site meetings will increase as designers and facilitators begin to adopt the virtuous approach detailed throughout this book.

C CHAPTER THIRTEEN • QUICK SUMMARY

- Virtuous meetings are uniquely adapted for scaling to multiple locations.
- The connectivity of virtuous meetings was built for scaling, and the technology underlying that connectivity—the Internet—was designed and built for bridging locations.
- The role of active contributor in a two-level, virtuous meeting is infinitely scalable. The use of a two-level design means that you

can just keep adding new tables. And the tables don't have to be in the same room, state, or continent.

- The process structure of the Virtuous Engagement Cycle can be used with groups that are very large. And it works just as well across multiple distributed locations as it does in a single ballroom.
- The demand for efficient, large group, multi-site meetings is increasing, because meeting together and collaboration have become so necessary and travel and its costs have become so burdensome.

Case Story 7: Advancing Futures for Adults with Autism National Town Hall

CASE STORY

Over the next two decades, more than one million youths who are diagnosed with autism will move into adulthood. And while there is a history of funding special programs and services for youths with autism, there is almost no funding or services available for those individuals once they become adults. Many of the youths and their families will still need high levels of support once they are adults. So although the needs will remain the same for adults with autism, the services, support, and funding won't be there. This is a situation of enormous impact on our society that will require a nationwide response.

In response to this situation a meeting was called: the Advancing Futures for Adults with Autism National Town Hall in Chicago.[1] We supported AmericaSpeaks in designing a distributed large group virtuous meeting that brought together professionals, family members, and policymakers to have a conversation to generate strategies for providing services. More than a thousand people participated in the meeting, using three different "modes."

Chicago was the central site. By concentrating about 30 percent of the participants there, we were able to provide a focal point. Important leaders in this movement were there, along with dignitaries (including the Mayor and Mrs. Daly) and the press. The live presentations from the stage took place in Chicago. The participants, seated at tables of ten, discussed the issues and sent their thoughts in over networked computers. They voted their priorities with keypad polling devices.

Fifteen satellite sites around the country provided a national scope, ensuring a presence in every region. Each site had a good-sized group of participants. They watched the presentations from Chicago on large screens at their site through a webcast. They also held their discussions at tables of ten, sending in their thoughts to the central site, and voting with keypads, just like in Chicago.

"Virtual tables" allowed equal access for any individuals who wanted to participate from their homes or offices around the country. They participated in small real-time conversations over the Internet that made them equal members of the conversation being held in

Chicago and the satellite sites. They watched the webcast on their own computers, broke into small groups of five or six participants on a special conference call platform to have discussions and send in their thoughts, and voted with keypads on their computers.

Covision's integration of these three participation modes allowed all of the participants to share the same experience and be part of the same conversation and agenda setting.

They all

- Listened to the same information being presented
- Spent time in small group discussions about the issues and sent in their ideas and feedback
- Got to see the rolled-up themes from the whole group's discussions
- Had the opportunity to set priorities by voting on the results of their discussions
- Heard feedback from experts and leaders
- Got to see the real-time priorities of the whole group

By the end of the day, the group had eight prioritized strategies in the areas of funding, staffing, housing, employment, training, and community life. They also had the experience of hundreds of conversations and had captured thousands of practical, in-the-trenches ideas on how to begin implementation of this nationwide agenda. And perhaps what was most significant, they were able to see themselves as a large, whole, action-oriented community. And they had momentum for educating and transforming society to incorporate adults with autism in a more constructive and beneficial way into the future we will all be sharing.

Case Story 8: Tunza International Children and Youth Conference on Climate Change

CASE STORY

Who will suffer the cataclysms of Climate Change? Fifty-two percent of the world's population is under thirty,[1] and they are facing the projections of catastrophe within their lifetimes. And they are children of the Internet. It is easy for them to see that averting disaster will take coordinated global action. No single nation-state has the power to reverse the direction we're headed in—it will take all of us (and them) working together.

But the dilemma for the world's youths is that they have no voice at the table. Although they make up half of the world's population and they will be the ones who experience the full effects of the changes, their age means that they have virtually no representation at crucial Climate Change negotiations.

A few years ago, the TUNZA International Children and Youth Conference decided to create a voice for youths in international negotiations. Their goal at that time was to bring a loud, focused, coordinated voice of world youths into the UN International Climate Change Conference in Copenhagen.[2] The motto of the effort was "Seal the Deal!" (in Copenhagen). Their goal was to create a carefully crafted statement representing the position that the combined youths of the world were taking on the issues of Climate Change. Once that statement was crafted, they hoped to gather one million signatures from youths around the world to present at the Copenhagen conference.

The effort was structured into three stages. First, input was solicited from youths around the world to create the original version of the statement. Second, a large group virtuous meeting was held to generate the final version of the statement. And third, there was a worldwide effort to garner signatures.

The engagement started with a website on which youths could post their thoughts about what the Youth Petition to the Copenhagen conference should contain. All of this input was rolled up into a two-page document that expressed what actions world youths wanted from national governments, from world citizens, and from the world's youths.

For the second stage, we supported a group called Global Voices to pull off a worldwide, distributed, large group virtuous meeting. Many of the people working on the meeting from Global Voices were colleagues of ours from AmericaSpeaks, and the meeting was modeled on the 21st Century Town Hall method. The meeting was centered in Seoul, South Korea. At the central site six hundred youth from around the world, all under twenty-five years old, were brought together to review, strengthen, finalize, and endorse the petition. The six hundred in Seoul were seated in small groups of ten in the plenary, and they were joined by youths around the world participating in small groups from their own countries. These remote participants were able to view a live webcast of the meeting in Seoul and to send in their own thoughts and edits to the group that was editing the petition in real time in the meeting room in Seoul.

The meeting convened at 2:30 P.M. in Seoul, but that meant it began at 10:30 P.M. in Cuernavaca and 6:30 A.M. in Athens. The whole distributed group worked together for three and a half hours, and in the end (2 A.M. in Cuernavaca, 10 A.M. in Athens) they hammered out a final version of the petition that had everyone's endorsement. The process was unprecedented and wonderful to be part of, and it caught wide accolades and coverage in the world press. (In the United States alone, it was covered by the *New York Times*, the *Boston Globe,* the *Washington Post*, and *USA Today*.)

We were in Seoul for the meeting. The Theme Team was set up there, and we were getting input streaming in from all over the world. The process worked the same as if all of the participants had been there in Seoul, but it gave the opportunity for participation to many youths who could not travel to South Korea. One of the remote groups met at the rural homestead of one of the authors in Northern California. Seven young people, mostly in their early twenties, gathered together and ate dinner, then got online with one of their computers at 9:30 P.M. when the meeting began (2:30 P.M. in Seoul). For the next three and a half hours they watched and listened to short presentations in Seoul about the different parts of the state-ment, and then, while the table groups in Seoul were discussing a part of the statement, they had a discussion about it around the table in Northern California and sent in comments about what should be added or changed. They had been sent a copy of the provisional working statement when they registered to attend, so they had that with them to refer to.

Between 9:30 P.M. and 1 A.M., they discussed what actions were needed from national governments, from world citizens, and from the world's youths. Back in Seoul we were synthesizing all of the input together, and dedicated writers were reworking the text of the statement. In this way, even youths across the Pacific Ocean were able to be active contributors in a meeting centered in South Korea. This engagement starts to answer the question: How can you come to meaningful consensus effectively and affordably on a worldwide scale, in order to begin crafting worldwide solutions? The answer lies in good design.

A key factor is effective leveraging of new technologies and possibilities of the Internet. But to make that leveraging effective, the design has to take into account what can be accomplished at each stage of the engagement, and it must pick the tools and the processes that will have the most impact. The design process has to be responsive throughout. (We ended up changing the details of the final deliverable from the Seoul meeting at a highly charged lunch meeting the day before the session.) Effective design makes the costs manageable for even far-reaching engagements, because the Design Team is relatively affordable, and if they can foresee the needs of the participants and put everything necessary into place, the engagement can be executed with technological options that are in reality very affordable.

GLOSSARY

active participant role The participants are processing what they hear and explaining it to others; they are brainstorming and evaluating; they are actively thinking about what they've heard from the stage and how it fits into the context of their own work and role, and they are sharing those thoughts with their peers.

contributing participant role When the content of a participant's active conversations is somehow informing the group.

convergence Integrating the thinking, experience, and passion of a broad range of people to create a mutual way forward.

design levers Design decisions that help us shape the format, tools, timing, roles, and content of the meeting; can include presentation levers, discussion levers, focusing question levers, input levers, and response levers.

Design Team Responsible for what happens in the meeting rooms—the content, process, and room layout.

Design Team leader Reports to the meeting owner, who owns the meeting purpose and has deep knowledge of the culture and relationships with most of the key players; is a relatively fearless and good manager; is a content and process generalist.

exchange   The activity of presenting your own ideas, feelings, and reactions, and listening to others present theirs; the give and take of team discussion and the group digestion that occurs and that in turn produces greater ideation.

facilitation   Ensuring that the design of the process is fulfilled; helping the group do its best thinking together; guiding the group toward the meeting's desired outcomes through careful attention to group dynamics.

generative purpose   A purpose that is not focused on content delivery, but rather on generating outcomes for the group like alignment and ownership; more of a vehicle than a destination, it drives a situation where the participants not only receive information, but also generate new information for themselves and for the organization.

ideation   The individual, creative activity of having an insight or dreaming up an idea; this can happen quite spontaneously, almost from nowhere, or it can happen as a result of stimulation by others in the group.

large (meetings)   The point at which the size of the group discourages or prevents active contribution for many of the participants.

meeting connectivity   A communication technology capability that allows for shifting into small group discussion and back to a large group format in short time frames.

meta-conversation   The exchange of thoughts and ideas between the group and those in the front of the room; an ongoing dialogue process between these two parties, throughout a meeting.

Participant Engagement Designer   A large group process specialist with broad experience in the application of high-speed connectivity to large participant-centered meetings; typically an external consultant; an expert in convergence and a teacher and coach.

participant-centered design   Proceeds from that perspective and, in contrast to a front-of-the-room-centered design, develops opportunities for the participants to be active contributors to the outcomes of the meeting.

participant-centered perspective   Is in contrast to a front-of-the-room-centered perspective, and focuses on what the participants are doing, experiencing, and contributing to the meeting.

passive participant role   Participants are inactive; they can listen, but they can't talk and they have no opportunity to contribute; they do not know what anybody else is thinking about and may not have a clear sense of what they themselves think or feel about what is being said, because they have no opportunity to digest what they're hearing.

shared understanding   When all the participants come to know each other's thoughts, positions, and preferences; all subsequent discussions are then informed by the current discussion, and the team as a whole becomes smarter and more integrated.

Synthesizer   The person who distills quickly all of the input that comes in from the group and represents back to the group the essence of what they have said across all of their table group discussions.

Technology Director   Responsible for the design and operation of the participant feedback and presentation systems in the meeting room(s).

Theme Team   Responsible for reading the data coming in live from all participants at various times during the meeting and creating quick summaries of the main messages—the themes—running through it; summaries are usually shown immediately to the whole group.

Two-level Meeting Design   Participants are in small groups in which they generate their thoughts and exchange their ideas, and at the same time, they are in the plenary group where they find out what everyone else is thinking.

vicious cycle of passive participation   Treating the participants at a large meeting as a passive audience; no one can tell what the participants are thinking, no one knows what anyone else is thinking, and there is no venue for discussion or sense of ownership, which then makes the leaders of the group feel they need to step in and take control, thereby reinforcing the decision to treat the participants as a passive audience.

Virtuous Engagement Cycle Back-and-forth dialogue moving from large group to the small group and back; has four steps that, when complete, create the meta-conversation in the room and repeatable opportunities for engagement and response; each iteration is that much richer and more powerful because of the responses from the last cycle.

virtuous meeting cycle Starts with full engagement; all participant voices are heard, shared understanding is built, the group is able to generate plans and solutions over which they have a sense of ownership; the value of the outcomes, their trust in each other and the process, and their enthusiasm all increase, and the engagement itself becomes more robust.

Introduction

1. "Eli Khamarov quotes," *BrainyQuote*, accessed December 4, 2013, http://www.brainyquote.com/quotes/keywords/virtuous_2.html# xPQMEBSjeZITPkXe.99

Chapter 1

1. Amy Edmondson, *Teaming: How Organizations Learn, Innovate, and Compete in the Knowledge Economy* (San Francisco: Jossey-Bass, 2012), p. 12.
2. Professor Lynda Gratton, March 22, 2013, lecture in Lisbon, Portugal.
3. Amy Edmondson, *Teaming: How Organizations Learn, Innovate, and Compete in the Knowledge Economy* (San Francisco: Jossey-Bass, 2012), p. 22.
4. Professor Lynda Gratton, March 22, 2013, lecture in Lisbon, Portugal.
5. Christopher Elliott, "What Costs Travelers $87 Billion and Is Basically Unavoidable?," *Elliott* (blog), July 21, 2009, http://elliott.org/elliott-blog/what-costs-travelers-87-billion-a-year-and-is-basically-unavoidable/

Chapter 2

1. "Future Search History," Future Search, [n.d.], accessed Dec. 2, 2013, http://www.futuresearch.net/method/whatis/history.cfm
2. "Whole-Scale Change History," Whole-Scale Change, [n.d.], accessed Dec. 2, 2013, http://www.wholescalechange.com/history-and-background
3. "The Conference Model," The Axelrod Group, [n.d.], accessed Dec. 15, 2013, http://www.axelrodgroup.com/conference_model.html
4. "Open Space for Emerging Order," Open Space World, [n.d.], accessed Dec. 15, 2013, http://www.openspaceworld.com/brief_history.htm

5. "America Speaks History," AmericaSpeaks, [n.d.], accessed Dec. 2, 2013, http://americaspeaks.org/about/history/
6. Barbara Benedict Bunker and Billie T. Alban, *The Handbook of Large Group Methods: Creating Systemic Change in Organizations and Communities* (San Francisco: Jossey-Bass, 2006), 19–20.
7. Carolyn Lukensmeyer, telephone interview with author, Jan. 2, 2013.
8. Ibid.
9. Ibid.

Chapter 3

1. Yousri Marzouki and Olivier Oullier, "Revolutionizing Revolutions: Virtual Collective Consciousness and the Arab Spring," *Huffington Post* (blog), posted July 17, 2012, http://www.huffingtonpost.com/yousri-marzouki/revolutionizing-revolutio_b_1679181.html
2. Twitter Engineering, "200 Million Tweets per Day," *Twitter* (blog), posted June 30, 2011, https://blog.twitter.com/2011/200-million-tweets-day
3. Carolyn Lukensmeyer, *Bringing Citizen Voices to the Table* (San Francisco: Jossey-Bass, 2006), 19–20.

Case Story 1

1. "Listening to the City Report of Proceedings," AmericaSpeaks, accessed Jan. 23, 2014, http://americaspeaks.org/wp-content/_data/n_0001/resources/live/final_report_ltc3.pdf (p. 6).
2. Ibid., p. 10.
3. Carter Horsley, "The World Trade Center Redevelopment," *The City Review* (e-zine), accessed Oct. 1, 2013, http://www.thecityreview.com/newwtc.html

Case Story 2

1. Mike Horne, telephone interview with author, May 22, 2011.
2. Ibid.
3. Ibid.

Case Story 5

1. "Clinton Global Initiative," AmericaSpeaks, [n.d.], accessed Jan. 13, 2014, http://americaspeaks.org/clinton-global-initiative/
2. Carolyn Lukensmeyer, email interview with authors.

Chapter 9

1. "High Performing Team Meeting Communication Code," *Oxford Leadership Academy*, found on "Ann Badillo Coaching" page, accessed Jan. 17, 2014, http://www.annbadillo.com/annscan/2007/04/high-performance-team-meeting-communications-code.html

Chapter 10

1. Sam Kaner and others, *Facilitator's Guide to Participatory Decision-Making* (San Francisco: Jossey-Bass, 2007).
2. Ibid., 24.
3. Ibid., 110.

Chapter 11

1. Mabel Collins, *Light on the Path* (Chicago: Rajput Press, 1911; repr.: Whitefish, Mont.: Kessinger, 2010).
2. David Rock, *Quiet Leadership: Six Steps to Transforming Performance at Work* (New York: HarperCollins, 2007).
3. Yaakov Lieder, "Authentic Listening," Chabad, http://www.chabad.org/library/article_cdo/aid/149100/jewish/Authentic-Listening.htm
4. James Kouzes and Barry Posner, *The Leadership Challenge*, 4th ed. (San Francisco: Jossey-Bass, 2008).
5. Ibid., 18.
6. Ibid., 19.
7. Ibid., 19.
8. Ibid., 23.
9. Michael Doyle and David Straus, *How to Make Meetings Work* (Los Angeles: Playboy Press, 1976; repr.: New York: Jove Books, 1982).
10. James Kouzes and Barry Posner, *The Leadership Challenge*, 4th ed. (San Francisco: Jossey-Bass, 2008), p. 32.
11. David Brookmire, "Increase Your Chances of Survival as CEO," *Leadership and Strategy* (blog), *ChiefExecutive.Net.* Dec. 6, 2011, http://chiefexecutive.net/increase-your-chances-of-survival-as-ceo
12. "CEO Statistics," *Statistic Brain*, last modified Dec. 12, 2013, http://www.statisticbrain.com/ceo-statistics/
13. Brené Brown, "The Power of Vulnerability," *TED Talk*, June 2010, posted Dec. 2010, http://www.ted.com/talks/brene_brown_on_vulnerability.html
14. Brené Brown, "Vulnerability and Inspired Leadership," *Leadership Series* (blog), *Impatient Optimists*, http://www.impatientoptimists.org/Posts/2012/11/Leadership-Series-Vulnerability-and-Inspired-Leadership

Chapter 13

1. Professor Lynda Gratton, lecture, March 22, 2013, Lisbon, Portugal.

Case Story 7

1. "Advancing Futures for Adults with Autism National Town Meeting," AmericaSpeaks, [n.d.], accessed Jan. 13, 2014, http://americaspeaks .org/projects/topics/healthcare/advancing-futures-for-adults-with-autism-nationaltown-hall/

Case Story 8

1. Eric Qualman, "Over 50% of the World's Population Is Under 30: Social Media on the Rise," *SocialEconomics*, posted April 13, 2010, http:// www.socialnomics.net/2010/04/13/over-50-of-theworlds-population-is-under-30-social-media-on-the-rise/
2. "Biggest-Ever Youth Gathering on Climate Change to Call for Real Action in Copenhagen," United National Environment Programme, July 2009, http://www.unep.org/Documents.Multilingual/Default.asp? DocumentID=593&ArticleID=6253&l=en

Since the early 1990s, **Karl Danskin** has focused on developing the means for participants in large meetings to transition from passive audience to active contributors. He has worked on the design of hundreds of large organizational meetings throughout Europe and the United States. He has worked with the top leadership teams of many Fortune 500 companies such as Texas Instruments and Genentech. He has worked across every sector, primarily in leadership meetings focused on developing and sharing business strategy.

Concurrently, Danskin has been part of the core team of Covision. He has taken a leading role in the "project" of developing the Virtuous Meeting method and promoting its usage. His thinking has been shaped by his close association with Todd Erickson, Josh Kaufman, and Lenny Lind. He was a contributor, with Lind and Erickson, to the second edition of *The Handbook of Large Group Methods* (Jossey-Bass, 2006). He is currently head of Strategy and Thought Leadership at Covision.

Working in partnership with AmericaSpeaks, Danskin has been a principal designer and facilitator of the theming function in some of the largest civic meetings ever to be held as virtuous meetings—including a 4,500-person meeting in New York and a 10,000-person meeting held simultaneously in three cities—as well as in high-profile meetings such as the World Economic Forum, Clinton Global Initiative, and the European Biodiversity Summit.

Danskin approaches organization development and meeting design from a holistic worldview that stems from a long study of classical Chinese arts. His view is informed by Taoist philosophy as well as practical experience with meditation, Chi Kung, Chinese medicine, and the calendar arts. He was the director of the original Healing Tao Video Library. He has been a student of Fong Ha and Jeffrey Yuen, and has taught throughout the San Francisco Bay Area, including being on staff at the Acupressure Institute in Berkeley and the Shiatsu Institute in San Francisco.

Danksin's education was at UC Berkeley in theater, philosophy, and literature. After university, he founded and was the artistic director of a theater company in San Francisco. As an international hotbed for new theater at that time, Danskin's company was critically acclaimed and eventually garnered financial support from both West German television and the NEA. The company won a Critics Circle award for one of the original plays written by Mr. Danskin's wife. The theater broke new ground in large-scale outdoor performance and did work in Canada and Eastern Europe as well as in the United States.

Danskin is passionate about healthy environmental design and sustainability. He and his acupuncturist wife, Melinda, live on a forty-two-acre homestead in the redwoods in Northern California. They produce their own solar electricity and practice biodynamic permaculture. They also keep dairy goats and chickens and cultivate a wide range of both Western and Chinese medicinal herbs.

*   *   *

Lenny Lind is founder and chairman of Covision and a senior consultant. Lind has been involved with organizational communications—media and processes—particularly in large meetings, since 1975. Then, he covered them as a freelance corporate photographer. In 1985, he cofounded Covision as a video production company, specializing in videos with organization development purposes and designed to make people think. These videos were often shown at large meetings.

In 1991, through a fortuitous video project, Lind discovered early attempts at software for *facilitating* better meetings. Soon after, Lind partnered with Jim Ewing of Executive Arts and began developing software that enabled real whole group dialogue and understanding in meetings. Within a year, Covision shifted out of video production altogether and into supporting interactive meetings.

During the period from 1992 to 1996, Lind coauthored with Sam Kaner, Cathy Toldi, Sarah Fisk, and Duane Berger, the best-selling *Facilitator's Guide to Participatory Decision Making* (Jossey-Bass, 2014).

Over two decades, Covision pioneered the use of interactive technology in increasingly larger meetings, especially ones that sought convergence and alignment. He and his team have since served over four thousand meetings of fifty to ten thousand participants each around the world, in a wide variety of senior leadership meetings and multi-stakeholder summits. In each, meeting owners determined it was important to *think together*.

Notable Covision projects include "Listening to the City," two community summits in New York immediately after 9/11, the opening general session of the World Economic Forum in 2005, four annual meetings of the Clinton Global Initiative from 2005 to 2009, and the New York Forum–Africa, in Libreville, Gabon, in 2012.

In 2011, Lind passed the presidency of Covision to Josh Kaufman and has focused on client projects, promoting real participant engagement as a key to realizing the most effective outcomes in large organizational meetings.

INDEX

307

Discuss stage
  Clinton Global Initiative and,
    198–202
  design levers and, 162–166
  implementation of, 104–106
  in Virtuous Engagement
    Cycles, 100–103
discussion
  levers for. *See* discussion levers
  polling vs., 57–58
  of topics, focused by
    questions, 223–224
  in Virtuous Engagement
    Cycles. *See* Discuss stage
discussion levers
  facilitator selection in, 179
  format in, 178–179
  seating arrangements in,
    176–177
  small group size in, 178–179
  timing/duration in, 177–178
diversity, 133
Doyle, Michael, 261
DTs (Design Teams). *See* Design
  Teams (DTs)
duration. *See* time management

E
Edmondson, Amy, 6, 7, 287
enabling others, 260–261
encouraging the heart, 261–262
energized participation, 93–94
engagement
  cycles of. *See* Virtuous
    Engagement Cycles
  high level of, 81–82
  of participants. *See* Participant
    Engagement Designers
  small groups within larger
    meetings for, 92–93
  as stage in meetings, 255
enrolling presenters, 238
every participant speaking, 90

excruciating vulnerability, 263
executive summaries, 103
exemplary leadership. *See also*
  Five Practices of Exemplary
  Leadership, 244, 258

F
Facebook, 287
face-to-face meetings
  designing, 122
  software for, 47
  virtual meetings vs., 279
facilitation
  best practices for, 231–233
  clarifying "how" in, 239–241
  clarifying "why" in, 237–239
  in discussion levers, 179
  introduction of, 229–230
  by leaders. *See* facilitation by
    leadership
  mind-set of, 231–232
  presenters and, 237–241
  principles of, 231–232
  purpose in, 231
  role of, 214–216, 231
  from the side, 236
  of Virtuous Engagement
    Cycles, 233–237
facilitation by leadership
  after meetings, 257–258
  case story about, 266–269
  challenging the process in,
    260
  enabling others to act in,
    260–261
  encouraging the heart in,
    261–262
  Five Practices of Exemplary
    Leadership for, 258–262
  initial decisions in, 247–251
  inspiring shared vision in,
    259–260
  introduction to, 243–247